THE GOSPELS
IN MODERN ENGLISH

*For a description of this book
and some Press opinions of it,
see back cover.*

Religious Books in the Fontana Series

The Gospels

in Modern English

Translated by

J. B. PHILLIPS

COLLINS

fontana books

First published in 1952 by Geoffrey Bles
First issued in Fontana Books Sept. 1957
Second Impression in Fontana Books Oct. 1957
Third Impression in Fontana Books Dec. 1957
Fourth Impression in Fontana Books June 1958

PRINTED IN GREAT BRITAIN
COLLINS CLEAR-TYPE PRESS: LONDON AND GLASGOW

CONTENTS

Books Recommended
for New Testament Study

INTRODUCING THE NEW TESTAMENT
A. M. Hunter (S.C.M. Press)

A FRESH APPROACH TO THE NEW TESTAMENT
H. G. G. Herklots (S.C.M. Press)

THE GOSPELS—A SHORT INTRODUCTION
Vincent Taylor (Epworth Press)

TRANSLATOR'S PREFACE

THERE is a peculiar difficulty in translating the Gospels of the New Testament into modern English. In the first place, the task is generally undertaken by Christians, who are necessarily acquainted with the unsurpassable cadences and rhythms of the Authorised Version, and consequently find it almost impossible to relinquish forms of expression which are mostly archaic and often obscure. One is therefore tempted to suppose that the best translation into modern English would be made by someone quite unfamiliar with the Authorised Version, but with a good knowledge of the Greek *koine* (the colloquial language of that time) and a proper command of the ordinary English of to-day. Such a person, being completely uninfluenced by traditional reverence, would be able to give us as nearly as possible a modern English equivalent of the simple unpolished Greek of the first three Gospels (and, as some would say, of John's Gospel[1] as well).

Further, although most people, however great their reverence for the New Testament may be, do not hold a word-by-word theory of inspiration, yet when they approach the four Gospels, and what may be the *ipsissima verba* of Christ, they unconsciously seek this kind of translation. (Such reverence for the actual words of Holy Writ was shown in those older editions of the Bible which printed in italics words which were necessary for the sense, but which were not actually present in the Greek and Hebrew!) But in reading a modern work translated from a foreign language into

[1] There is a significant example of the disagreement of scholars over the Greek of John's Gospel, quoted in Professor C. C. Torrey's *The Origin of the Gospels*: "The late J. H. Moulton, a most accomplished grammarian, speaks of Jn.'s 'uneasy movement in the region of unfamiliar idiom,' and concludes that 'the linguistic evidence all goes to show that the author of the Fourth Gospel was a man who, while cultured to the last degree, wrote Greek after the fashion of men of quite elementary attainment.' Side by side with this may be put the verdict of Schmiedel, that this evangelist 'abounds in subtle variations' in his

English, we are not in the least concerned with a word-for-word version: all we want is to know accurately the thought of the author and, if possible, to recapture something of the style of the original work. We do not care if a sentence be inverted or expanded or re-arranged, so long as we are confident that a conscientious translator is faithfully conveying the meaning of his author to our minds and hearts.

Unfortunately this kind of translation, which is real translation, becomes almost impossible when we approach the four Gospels. Most people refuse to believe that the majesty and dignified simplicity of the Authorised Version, however lovely in themselves, are no more a part of the original message than the scarlet and blue and gold illumination on a medieval manuscript. Yet, though we may not like it, there is in fact very little sublime simplicity or simple grandeur in the original Greek of the four Gospels. We face a queer paradox—that the earliest and most reliable accounts of the life of the very Son of God Himself were written in a debased language which had lost its classical beauty.

There is a further difficulty. Throughout the centuries these four documents have been subjected to a closer and more meticulous examination of the texts and their variations than any other historical records whatsoever. Subtle meanings are extracted where almost certainly no subtlety was intended, and single Greek words are sometimes made to bear an undue significance. Worse still, it is only too easy to " read back " into comparatively simple language the results of centuries of acute doctrinal conflict.

Since, then, there is considerable disagreement among scholars over many points of translation, and since no one has written *koine* for many centuries, the best method to adopt in translating the Gospel records would appear to be:

(1) To " forget " completely the majesty and beauty of the Authorised Version.

(2) To translate the Greek text as one would translate any other document from a foreign language, with the same conscientiousness but also with the same freedom

vocabulary and in his use of tenses ; and that these distincitons are natural to one ' so long habituated to Greek as to be able to play on its words and utilise to the utmost its minute differences of grammatical expression.' "

in conveying, as far as possible, the meaning and style of the original writer.

The following version is a modest attempt to translate the Gospels on these lines.

I should like to acknowledge useful comments and criticisms from many friends, and especially to thank the Rev. R. Selby Wright, the Rev. J. P. H. Hobson, the Rev. G. H. G. Hewitt, the Rev. Professor C. F. D. Moule, H. Caiger, Esq., F.R.C.S.; and H. V. Gosling, Esq., Ph.D., who, though living in Canada, has been a most useful critic, supplying me with books at present unobtainable in this country. I must make it clear, however, that none of the above must be taken as responsible for the decisions I have had to make in translation.

Finally, I would like to thank most warmly Margery Hopkins and Joan Carter, who have given me invaluable secretarial help.

I append a short list of recommended books which may be of service to those who want to make a further study of the New Testament.

J. B. PHILLIPS

Redhill, 1962

PREFACE TO THE FONTANA EDITION

A THOROUGH revision of my translation of the four Gospels has now been made. I should like to thank many correspondents in various parts of the world for pointing out minor errors, and for helpful suggestions. The work of revision has taken several months and I confess myself astonished at the large number of small corrections I have felt bound to make. The only excuse I have to offer is that the original work was done amid the busyness and pressure of parochial duties, and that until recently there has not been time for a word-by-word revision.

J. B. PHILLIPS

Swanage, 1957

THE GOSPEL OF
MATTHEW

Early tradition ascribed this Gospel to the apostle Matthew, but scholars nowadays almost all reject this view.

The author, whom we still can conveniently call Matthew, has plainly drawn on the mysterious " Q," which may have been a collection of oral traditions. He has used Mark's Gospel freely, though he has rearranged the order of events and has in several instances used different words for what is plainly the same story. The style is lucid, calm and " tidy." Matthew writes with a certain judiciousness as though he himself had carefully digested his material and is convinced not only of its truth but of the divine pattern that lies behind the historic facts.

Matthew is quite plainly a Jew who has been convinced of Jesus' messianic claim. It is probable that he is writing primarily for fellow Jews. The frequent references to the Old Testament, the sense that Jesus' primary mission is to the " lost sheep" of the house of Israel and the implication that the Church, founded on the rock of Peter's faith, is the new Israel all bear the marks of a converted Jew writing for fellow Jews. He attempts to convey a logical conviction that the new teaching was not only prophesied in the old but does in fact supersede it in the divine plan.

If Matthew wrote, as is now generally supposed, somewhere between 85 and 90, this Gospel's value as a Christian document is enormous. It is, so to speak, a second generation view of Jesus Christ the Son of God and the Son of Man. It is being written at that distance in time from the great Event where sober reflection and sturdy conviction can perhaps give a better balanced portrait of God's unique revelation of Himself than could be given by those who were so close to the Light that they were partly dazzled by it.

The ancestry of Jesus Christ

THIS is the record of the ancestry of Jesus Christ who was the descendant of both David and Abraham:

Abraham was the father of Isaac, who was the father of Jacob, who was the father of Judah and his brothers, who

was the father of Perez and Zerah (whose mother was Tamar).
Perez was the father of Hezron, who was the father of Ram,
who was the father of Amminadab, who was the father of
Nahshon, who was the father of Salmon, who was the father
of Boaz (whose mother was Rahab). Boaz was the father of
Obed (whose mother was Ruth), and Obed was the father of
Jesse, who was the father of King David, who was the father
of Solomon (whose mother was Uriah's wife). Solomon was
the father of Rehoboam, who was the father of Abijah, who
was the father of Asa, who was the father of Jehoshaphat,
who was the father of Joram, who was the father of Uzziah,
who was the father of Jotham, who was the father of Ahaz,
who was the father of Hezekiah, who was the father of
Manasseh, who was the father of Amon, who was the father
of Josiah, who was the father of Jechoniah and his brothers,
at the time of the Deportation to Babylon. After the Baby-
lonian Exile Jechoniah was the father of Shealtiel, who was
the father of Zerubbabel, who was the father of Abiud, who
was the father of Eliakim, who was the father of Azor, who
was the father of Sadoc, who was the father of Achim, who
was the father of Eliud, who was the father of Eleazar, who
was the father of Matthan, who was the father of Jacob,
who was the father of Joseph, who was the husband of
Mary, the mother of Jesus Christ.

The genealogy of Jesus Christ may thus be traced for
fourteen generations from Abraham to David, fourteen from
David to the Deportation to Babylon, and fourteen more
from the Deportation to Christ Himself.

His birth in human history   1 : 18

The birth of Jesus Christ happened like this. When Mary
was engaged to Joseph, just before their marriage, she was
discovered to be pregnant—by the Holy Spirit. Whereupon
Joseph, her future husband, who was a good man and did not
want to see her disgraced, planned to break off the engage-
ment quietly. But while he was turning the matter over in
his mind an angel of the Lord appeared to him in a dream
and said, " Joseph, son of David, do not be afraid to take
Mary as your wife ! What she has conceived is conceived

through the Holy Spirit, and she will give birth to a son, whom you will call Jesus ('the Saviour') for it is he who will save his people from their sins."

All this happened to fulfil what the Lord had said through the prophet:

Behold, the virgin shall be with child, and shall bring forth a son, and they shall call his name Immanuel ("Immanuel" means "God with us").

When Joseph woke up he did what the angel had told him.   He married Mary, but had no intercourse with her until she had given birth to a son.   Then he gave him the name Jesus.

Herod, suspicious of the new-born king, takes vindictive precautions   2 : 1

Jesus was born in Bethlehem, in Judaea, in the days when Herod was king of the province.   Not long after his birth there arived from the east a party of astrologers making for Jerusalem and enquiring as they went, "Where is the child born to be King of the Jews? For we saw his star in the east and we have come here to pay homage to him."

When King Herod heard about this he was deeply perturbed, as indeed were all the other people living in Jerusalem. So he summoned all the Jewish Scribes[1] and Chief Priests together and asked them where "Christ" should be born. Their reply was: " In Bethlehem, in Judaea, for this is what the prophet wrote about the matter:

And thou Bethlehem, land of Judah,
Art in no wise least among the princes of Judah:
For out of thee shall come forth a governor,
Which shall be shepherd of my people Israel."

Then Herod invited the wise men to meet him privately and found out from them the exact time when the star

[1] See Appendix, Note 1.

appeared. Then he sent them off to Bethlehem saying,
"When you get there, search for this little child with the
utmost care. And when you have found him come back and
tell me—so that I may go and worship him too."

The wise men listened to the King and then went on their
way to Bethlehem. And now the star, which they had seen
in the east, went in front of them as they travelled until at
last it shone immediately above the place where the little
child lay. The sight of the star filled them with indescribable
joy.

So they went into the house and saw the little child with
his mother Mary. And they fell on their knees and worshipped him. Then they opened their treasures and presented
him with gifts—gold, incense and myrrh.

Then, since they were warned in a dream not to return to
Herod, they went back to their own country by a different
route.

But after they had gone the angel of the Lord appeared to
Joseph in a dream and said, " Get up now, take the little
child and his mother and escape to Egypt. Stay there until
I tell you. For Herod means to seek out the child and kill
him."

So Joseph got up, and taking the child and his mother
with him, in the middle of the night, set off for Egypt, where
he remained until Herod's death.

This again is a fulfilment of the Lord's word spoken
through the prophet :

Out of Egypt did I call my son.

When Herod saw that he had been fooled by the wise men
he was furiously angry. He issued orders, and killed all the
male children of two years and under in Bethlehem and the
surrounding district—basing his calculation on his careful
questioning of the wise men.

Then Jeremiah's prophecy was fulfilled :

A voice was heard in Ramah,
Weeping and great mourning,
Rachel weeping for her children ;
And she would not be comforted, because they are not.

Jesus is brought to Nazareth   2 : 19

But after Herod's death an angel of the Lord again appeared to Joseph in a dream and said, " Now get up and take the infant and his mother with you and go into the land of Israel. For those who sought the child's life are dead."

So Joseph got up and took the little child and his mother with him and journeyed towards the land of Israel. But when he heard that Archelaus was now reigning as King of Judaea in the place of his father Herod, he was afraid to enter the country. Then he received warning in a dream to turn aside into the district of Galilee and came to live in a small town called Nazareth—thus fulfilling the old prophecy, that he should be called a Nazarene.

The prophesied " Elijah " : John the Baptist   3 : 1

In due course John the Baptist arrived, preaching in the Judaean desert : " You must change your hearts—for the Kingdom of Heaven has arrived ! "

This was the man whom the prophet Isaiah spoke about in the words :

The voice of one crying in the wilderness,
Make ye ready the way of the Lord,
Make his paths straight.

John wore clothes of camel-hair with a leather belt round his waist, and lived on locusts and wild honey. The people of Jerusalem and of all Judaea and the Jordan district flocked to him, and were baptized by him in the river Jordan, publicly confessing their sins.

But when he saw many Pharisees and Sadducees[1] coming for baptism he said, " Who warned you, you serpent's brood, to escape from the wrath to come ? Go and do something to show that your hearts are really changed. Don't suppose that you can say to yourselves, ' We are Abraham's children,' for I tell you that God could produce children of Abraham out of these stones !

" The axe already lies at the root of the tree, and the tree

[1] See Appendix, Note 1.

that fails to produce good fruit will be cut down and thrown into the fire. It is true that I baptize you with water as a sign of your repentance, but the One Who follows me is far stronger than I am—indeed I am not fit to carry his shoes. He will baptize you with the fire of the Holy Spirit. He comes all ready to separate the wheat from the chaff and very thoroughly will he clear his threshing-floor—the wheat he will collect into the granary and the chaff he will burn with a fire that can never be put out."

John baptizes Jesus   3 : 13

Then Jesus came from Galilee to the Jordan to be baptized by John. But John tried to prevent him. "I need you to baptize *me*," he said. "Surely *you* do not come to me?" But Jesus replied, "It is right for us to meet all the Law's demands—let it be so now."

Then John agreed to his baptism. Jesus came straight out of the water afterwards, and suddenly the heavens opened and he saw the Spirit of God coming down like a dove and resting upon him. And a Voice came out of Heaven saying, "This is my dearly-loved Son, in Whom I am well pleased."

Jesus faces temptation alone in the desert   4 : 1

Then Jesus was led by the Spirit up into the desert, to be tempted by the devil. After a fast of forty days and nights he was very hungry.

"If you really are the Son of God," said the tempter, coming to him, "tell these stones to turn into loaves."

Jesus answered, "The Scripture says '*Man shall not live by bread alone, but by every word that proceedeth out of the mouth of God*.'"

Then the devil took him to the Holy City, and set him on the highest ledge of the Temple. "If you really are the Son of God," he said, "throw yourself down. For the Scripture says :

He shall give his angels charge concerning thee :
And on their hands they shall bear thee up,
Lest haply thou dash thy foot against a stone."

"Yes," retorted Jesus, "and the Scripture also says ' *Thou shalt not tempt the Lord thy God*.'"

Once again the devil took him to a very high mountain, and from there showed him all the kingdoms of the world and their magnificence. "Everything there I will give you," he said to him, "if you will fall down and worship me."

"Away with you, Satan!" replied Jesus, "the Scripture says,

> *Thou shalt worship the Lord thy God, and him only shalt thou serve.*"

Then the devil let him alone, and angels came to him and took care of him.

Jesus begins his ministry, in Galilee, and calls his first   4 : 12
disciples

Now when Jesus heard that John had been arrested he went back to Galilee. He left Nazareth and came to live in Capernaum, a lake-side town in the Zebulun-Naphtali territory. In this way Isaiah's prophecy came true:

> The land of Zebulun and the land of Naphtali,
> Toward the sea, beyond Jordan,
> Galilee of the Gentiles,
> The people which sat in darkness
> Saw a great light,
> And to them which sat in the region and shadow of death,
> To them did light spring up.

From that time Jesus began to preach and to say, "You must change your hearts—for the Kingdom of Heaven has arrived."

While he was walking by the lake of Galilee he saw two brothers, Simon (Peter) and Andrew casting their large net into the water. They were fishermen, so Jesus said to them, "Follow me and I will teach you to catch men!"

At once they left their nets and followed him.

Then he went farther on and saw two more men, also brothers, James and John. They were aboard the boat with their father Zebedee repairing their nets, and he called them.

At once they left the boat, and their father, and followed
him.

Jesus teaches, preaches and heals   4 : 23

Jesus now moved about through the whole of Galilee,
teaching in their synagogues and preaching the good news
about the Kingdom, and healing every disease and disability
among the people. His reputation spread throughout Syria,
and people brought to him all those who were ill, suffering
from all kinds of diseases and pains—including the devil-
possessed, the insane and the paralysed. He healed them,
and was followed by enormous crowds from Galilee, the
Ten Towns, Jerusalem, Judaea and from beyond the river
Jordan.

Jesus proclaims the new values of the Kingdom   5 : 1

When Jesus saw the vast crowds he went up the hill-side
and after he had sat down his disciples came to him.

Then he began his teaching by saying to them,

" How happy are the humble-minded, for the Kingdom of
Heaven is theirs !

" How happy are those who know what sorrow means,
for they will be given courage and comfort !

" Happy are those who claim nothing, for the whole earth
will belong to them !

" Happy are those who are hungry and thirsty for goodness, for they will be fully satisfied !

" Happy are the merciful, for they will have mercy shown
to them !

" Happy are the utterly sincere, for they will see God !

" Happy are those who make peace, for they will be
known as sons of God !

" Happy are those who have suffered persecution for the
cause of goodness, for the Kingdom of Heaven is theirs !

" And what happiness will be yours when people blame
you and ill-treat you and say all kinds of slanderous things
against you for my sake ! Be glad then, yes, be tremendously
glad—for your reward in Heaven is magnificent. They
persecuted the prophets before your time in exactly the same
way.

" You are the earth's salt. But if the salt should become

tasteless, what can make it salt again? It is completely use-less and can only be thrown out of doors and stamped under foot.

"You are the world's light—it is impossible to hide a town built on the top of a hill. Men do not light a lamp and put it under a bucket. They put it on a lamp-stand and it gives light for everybody in the house.

"Let your light shine like that in the sight of men. Let them see the good things you do and praise your Father in Heaven.

Christ's authority surpasses that of the Law   5 : 17

"You must not think that I have come to abolish the Law or the prophets; I have not come to abolish them but to complete them. Indeed, I assure you that, while Heaven and earth last, the Law will not lose a single dot or comma until its purpose is complete. This means that whoever now relaxes one of the least of these commandments and teaches men to do the same will himself be called least in the Kingdom of Heaven. But whoever teaches and practises them will be called great in the Kingdom of Heaven. For I tell you that your goodness must be a far better thing than the goodness of the Scribes and Pharisees before you can set foot in the Kingdom of Heaven at all!

"You have heard that it was said to the people in the old days, '*Thou shalt not murder*,' and anyone who does so must stand his trial. But I say to you that anyone who is angry with his brother must stand his trial; anyone who con-temptuously calls his brother a fool[1] must face the Supreme Court; and anyone who looks down on his brother as a lost soul is himself heading straight for the fire of destruction.

"So that if, while you are offering your gift at the altar, you should remember that your brother has something against you, you must leave your gift there before the altar and go away. Make your peace with your brother first, then come and offer your gift. Come to terms quickly with your opponent while you have the chance, or else he may hand you over to the judge and the judge in turn hand you over to the officer of the court and you will be thrown into

[1] See Appendix, Note 2.

prison. Believe me, you will never get out again till you have paid your last farthing!

"You have heard that it was said to the people in the old days, '*Thou shalt not commit adultery.*' But I say to you that every man who looks at a woman lustfully has already committed adultery with her—in his heart.

"Yes, if your right eye leads you astray pluck it out and throw it away; it is better for you to lose one of your members than that your whole body should be thrown on to the rubbish-heap.

"Yes, if your right hand leads you astray cut it off and throw it away; it is better for you to lose one of your members than that your whole body should go to the rubbish-heap.

"It also used to be said that whoever divorces his wife must give her a proper certificate of divorce. But I say to you that whoever divorces his wife except on the ground of unfaithfulness is making her an adulteress. And whoever marries the woman who has been divorced also commits adultery.

"Again, you have heard that the people in the old days were told—'*Thou shalt not forswear thyself, but shalt perform unto the Lord thine oaths,*' but I say to you, Don't use an oath at all. Don't swear by Heaven, for it is God's throne, nor by the earth for it is His footstool, nor by Jerusalem for it is the city of the Great King. No, and don't swear by your own head, for you cannot make a single hair—white or black! Whatever you have to say let your 'yes' be a plain 'yes' and your 'no' be a plain 'no'—anything more than this has a taint of evil.

"You have heard that it used to be said '*An eye for an eye and a tooth for a tooth,*' but I tell you, Don't resist the man who wants to harm you. If a man hits your right cheek, turn the other one to him as well. If a man wants to sue you for your coat, let him have it and your overcoat as well. If anybody forces you to go a mile with him, do more—go two miles with him. Give to the man who asks anything from you, and don't turn away from the man who wants to borrow.

"You have heard that it used to be said '*Thou shalt love thy neighbour and hate thine enemy,*' but I tell you, Love your enemies, and pray for those who persecute you, so that you may be sons of your Heavenly Father. For He makes His sun rise upon evil men as well as good, and He sends His rain upon honest and dishonest men alike.

" For if you love only those who love you, what credit is that to you ? Even tax-collectors do that ! And if you exchange greetings only with your own circle, are you doing anything exceptional ? Even the pagans do that much. No, you are to be perfect, like your Heavenly Father.

The new life is not a matter of outward show   6 : 1
" Beware of doing your good deeds conspicuously to catch men's eyes or you will miss the reward of your Heavenly Father.

" So, when you do good to other people, don't hire a trumpeter to go in front of you—like those play-actors in the synagogues and streets who make sure that men admire them. Believe me, they have had all the reward they are going to get ! No, when you give to charity, don't even let your left hand know what your right hand is doing, so that your giving may be secret. Your Father Who knows all secrets will reward you.

" And then, when you pray, don't be like the play-actors. They love to stand and pray in the synagogues and at street-corners so that people may see them at it. Believe me, they have had all the reward they are going to get. But when you pray, go into your own room, shut your door and pray to your Father privately. Your Father who sees all private things will reward you. And when you pray don't rattle off long prayers like the pagans who think they will be heard because they use so many words. Don't be like them. After all God, Who is your Father, knows your needs before you ask Him. Pray then like this :

Our Heavenly Father, may your Name be honoured ;
May your Kingdom come, and your Will be done on earth
    as it is in Heaven.
Give us this day the bread we need,
Forgive us what we owe to you, as we have also forgiven
    those who owe anything to us.
Keep us clear of temptation, and save us from Evil.

Forgiveness of fellow-man is essential   6 : 14

"For if you forgive other people their failures, your Heavenly Father will also forgive you. But if you will not forgive other people, neither will your Heavenly Father forgive you your failures.

"Then, when you fast, don't look like those miserable play-actors! For they deliberately disfigure their faces so that people may see that they are fasting. Believe me, they have had all their reward. No, when you fast, brush your hair and wash your face so that nobody knows that you are fasting—let it be a secret between you and your Father. And your Father who knows all secrets will reward you.

Put your trust in God alone   6 : 19

"Don't pile up treasures on earth, where moth and rust can spoil them and thieves can break in and steal. But keep your treasure in Heaven where there is neither moth nor rust to spoil it and nobody can break in and steal. For wherever your treasure is, you may be certain that your heart will be there too!

"The lamp of the body is the eye. If your eye is sound, your whole body will be full of light. But if your eye is evil, your whole body will be full of darkness. If all the light you have is darkness, it is dark indeed!

"No one can be loyal to two masters. He is bound to hate one and love the other, or support one and despise the other. You cannot serve God and the power of money at the same time. That is why I say, Don't worry about living —wondering what you are going to eat or drink, or what you are going to wear. Surely life is more important than food, and the body more important than the clothes you wear. Look at the birds in the sky. They never sow nor reap nor store away in barns, and yet your Heavenly Father feeds them. Aren't you much more valuable to Him than they are? Can any of you, however much he worries, make himself an inch taller? And why do you worry about clothes? Consider how the wild flowers grow. They neither work nor weave, but I tell you that even Solomon in all his glory was never arrayed like one of these! Now if God so clothes the flowers of the field, which are alive to-day and

burnt in the stove to-morrow, is He not much more likely
to clothe you, you ' little-faiths ' ?

" So don't worry and don't keep saying, ' What shall we
eat, what shall we drink or what shall we wear ? ' ! That is
what pagans are always looking for ; your Heavenly Father
knows that you need them all. Set your heart on His Kingdom and His Goodness, and all these things will come to you
as a matter of course.

" Don't worry at all then about to-morrow. To-morrow
can take care of itself ! One day's trouble is enough for
one day.

The common sense behind right behaviour   7 : 1
" Don't criticise people, and you will not be criticised.
For you will be judged by the way you criticise others, and
the measure you give will be the measure you receive.

" Why do you look at the speck of sawdust in your
brother's eye and fail to notice the plank in your own? How
can you say to your brother, ' Let me get the speck out of
your eye,' when there is a plank in your own? You fraud !
Take the plank out of your own eye first, and then you can
see clearly enough to remove your brother's speck of dust.

" You must not give holy things to dogs, nor must you
throw your pearls before pigs—or they may trample them
underfoot and turn and attack you.

" Ask and it will be given to you. Search and you will
find. Knock and the door will be opened for you. The one
who asks will always receive ; the one who is searching will
always find, and the door is opened to the man who knocks.

" If any of you were asked by his son for bread would
you be likely to give him a stone, or if he asks for a fish
would you give him a snake ? If you then, for all your evil,
quite naturally give good things to your children, how much
more likely is it that your Heavenly Father will give good
things to those who ask Him ?

" Treat other people exactly as you would like to be
treated by them—this is the essence of all true religion.

" Go in by the narrow gate. For the wide gate has a broad
road which leads to disaster and there are many people going
that way. The narrow gate and the hard road lead out into
life and only a few are finding it.

Living, not professing, is what matters   7 : 15

"Be on your guard against false religious teachers, who come to you dressed up as sheep but are really greedy wolves. You can tell them by their fruit. Do you pick a bunch of grapes from a thorn-bush or figs from a clump of thistles? Every good tree produces good fruit, but a bad tree produces bad fruit. A good tree is incapable of producing bad fruit, and a bad tree cannot produce good fruit. The tree that fails to produce good fruit is cut down and burnt. So you may know men by their fruit.

"It is not everyone who keeps saying to me 'Lord, Lord' who will enter the Kingdom of Heaven, but the man who actually does my Heavenly Father's Will.

"In 'that Day' many will say to me, 'Lord, Lord, didn't we preach in your name, didn't we cast out devils in your name, and do many great things in your name?' Then I shall tell them plainly, 'I have never known you. Go away from me, you have worked on the side of evil!'

To follow Christ's teaching means the only real security   7 : 24

"Everyone then who hears these words of mine and puts them into practice is like a sensible man who built his house on the rock. Down came the rain and up came the floods, while the winds blew and roared upon that house—and it did not fall because its foundations were on the rock.

"And everyone who hears these words of mine and does not follow them can be compared with a foolish man who built his house on the sand. Down came the rain and up came the floods, while the winds blew and battered that house till it collapsed, and fell with a great crash."

When Jesus had finished these words the crowd were astonished at the power behind his teaching. For his words had the ring of authority, quite unlike those of their Scribes.

Jesus cures leprosy, and heals many other people   8 : 1

Large crowds followed him when he came down from the hill-side. There was a leper who came and knelt in front of him. "Sir," he said, "if you want to, you can make me clean." Jesus stretched out his hand and placed it on the leper saying, "Of course I want to. Be clean!" And at once he was clear of the leprosy.

"Mind you say nothing to anybody," Jesus told him. "Go straight off and show yourself to the priest and make the offering for your recovery that Moses prescribed, as evidence to the authorities."

Then as he was coming into Capernaum a centurion approached. "Sir," he implored him, "my servant is in bed at home paralysed and in dreadful pain."

"I will come and heal him," said Jesus to him.

"Sir," replied the centurion, "I'm not important enough for you to come under my roof. Just give the order, please, and my servant will recover. I'm a man under authority myself, and I have soldiers under me. I can say to one man 'Go' and I know he'll go, or I can say 'Come here' to another and I know he'll come—or I can say to my servant 'Do this' and he'll always do it."

When Jesus heard this, he was astonished. "Believe me," he said to those who were following him, "I have never found faith like this, even in Israel! I tell you that many people will come from east and west and sit at my table with Abraham, Isaac and Jacob in the Kingdom of Heaven. But those who should have belonged to the Kingdom will be banished to the darkness outside, where there will be tears and bitter regret."

Then he said to the centurion, "Go home now, and everything will happen as you have believed it will."

And his servant was healed at that actual moment.

Then, on coming into Peter's house Jesus saw that Peter's mother-in-law had been put to bed with a high fever. He touched her hand and the fever left her. And then she got up and began to see to their needs.

When evening came they brought to him many who were possessed by evil spirits, which he expelled with a word. Indeed he healed all who were ill. Thus was fulfilled Isaiah's prophecy :

Himself took our infirmities and bare our diseases.

When Jesus had seen the great crowds around him he gave orders for departure to the other side of the lake. But before they started, one of the Scribes came up to Jesus and said to him, "Master, I will follow you wherever you go."

"Foxes have earths, birds in the sky have nests, but the Son of Man has nowhere that he can call his own," replied Jesus.

Another of his disciples said, "Lord, let me first go and bury my father."

But Jesus said to him, "Follow me, and leave the dead to bury their own dead."

Jesus shows his mastery over the forces of nature   8 : 23

Then he went aboard the boat, and his disciples followed him. Before long a terrific storm sprang up and the boat was awash with the waves. Jesus was sleeping soundly and the disciples went forward and woke him up.

"Lord, save us!" they cried. "We are drowning!"

"What are you so frightened about, you little-faiths?" he replied.

Then he got to his feet and rebuked the wind and the waters and there was a great calm. The men were filled with astonishment and kept saying, "Whatever sort of man is this—why, even the wind and the waves do what he tells them!"

When he arrived on the other side (which is the Gadarenes' country) he was met by two devil-possessed men who came out from among the tombs. They were so violent that nobody dared to use that road.

"What have you got to do with us, Jesus, you Son of God?" they screamed at him. "Have you come to torture us before the proper time?"

It happened that in the distance there was a large herd of pigs feeding. So the devils implored him, "If you throw us out, send us into the herd of pigs!"

"Then go!" said Jesus to them.

And the devils came out of the two men and went into the pigs. Then quite suddenly the whole herd rushed madly down a steep cliff into the lake and were drowned.

The swineherds took to their heels, and ran to the town. There they poured out the whole story, not forgetting what had happened to the two men who had been devil-possessed. Whereupon the whole town came out to meet Jesus, and as soon as they saw him implored him to leave their territory.

Jesus heals in his own town   9 : 1

So Jesus re-embarked on the boat, crossed the lake, and came to his own town. Immediately some people arrived bringing him a paralytic lying flat on his bed. When Jesus saw the faith of those who brought him he said to the paralytic, "Cheer up, my son! Your sins are forgiven."

At once some of the Scribes thought to themselves, "This man is blaspheming," but Jesus realised what they were thinking, and said to them, "Why must you have such evil thoughts in your minds? Do you think it is easier to say to this man 'Your sins are forgiven' or 'Get up and walk'? But to make it quite plain that the Son of Man has full authority on earth to forgive sins"—and here he spoke to the paralytic—"Get up, pick up your bed and go home." And the man got to his feet and went home. When the crowds saw what had happened they were filled with awe and praised God for giving such power to men.

Jesus calls a "sinner" to be his disciple   9 : 9

Jesus left there and as he passed on he saw a man called Matthew sitting at his desk in the tax-collector's office.

"Follow me!" he said to him—and the man got to his feet and followed him.

Later, as Jesus was in the house sitting at the dinner-table, a good many tax-collectors and other disreputable people came on the scene and joined him and his disciples. The Pharisees noticed this and said to the disciples, "Why does your Master have his meals with tax-collectors and sinners?" But Jesus heard this and replied:

"It is not the fit and flourishing who need the doctor, but those who are ill! Suppose you go away and learn what this means: 'I desire mercy and not sacrifice.' In any case I did not come to invite the 'righteous' but the 'sinners.'"

He explains the joy and strength of the new order   9 : 14

Then John's disciples approached him with the question, "Why is it that we and the Pharisees observe the fasts, but your disciples do nothing of the kind?"

"Can you expect wedding-guests to mourn while they have the bridegroom with them?" replied Jesus. "The day will come when the bridegroom will be taken away from them—they will certainly fast then !

"Nobody sews a patch of unshrunken cloth on to an old coat, for the patch will pull away from the coat and the hole will be worse than ever. Nor do people put new wine into old wineskins—otherwise the skins burst, the wine is spilt and the skins are ruined. But they put new wine into new skins and both are preserved."

Jesus heals a young girl, and several others in need   9 : 18

While he was saying these things to them an official came up to him and, bowing low before him, said :

"My daughter has just this moment died. Please come and lay your hand on her and she will come back to life ! "

At this Jesus got to his feet and followed him, accompanied by his disciples. And on the way a woman who had had a hæmorrhage for twelve years approached him from behind and touched the edge of his cloak.

"If I can only touch his cloak," she kept saying to herself, "I shall be all right."

But Jesus turned right round and saw her.

"Cheer up, my daughter," he said, "your faith has made you well ! " And the woman was completely cured from that moment.

Then when Jesus came into the official's house and noticed the flute-players and the noisy crowd he said, "You must all go outside ; the little girl is not dead, she is fast asleep."

This was met with scornful laughter. But when Jesus had forced the crowd to leave, he came right into the room, took hold of her hand, and the girl got up. And this became the talk of the whole district.

As Jesus passed on his way two blind men followed him with the cry, "Have pity on us, Son of David ! " And when he had gone inside the house these two men came up to him.

"Do you believe I can do it ? " he said to them.

"Yes, Lord," they replied.

Then he touched their eyes, saying, "You have believed and you will not be disappointed."

Then their sight returned, but Jesus sternly warned them, "Don't let anyone know about this." Yet they went outside and spread the story throughout the whole district.

Later, when Jesus and his party were coming out, they brought to him a dumb man who was possessed by a devil. As soon as the devil had been ejected the dumb man began to talk. The crowds were simply amazed and said, " Nothing like this has ever been seen in Israel." But the Pharisees' comment was, " He throws out these devils because he is in league with the Devil himself."

Jesus is touched by the people's need   9 : 35
Jesus now travelled through all the towns and villages, teaching in their synagogues, proclaiming the gospel of the Kingdom, and healing all kinds of illness and disability. As he looked at the vast crowds he was deeply moved with pity for them, for they were as bewildered and miserable as a flock of sheep with no shepherd.

" The harvest is great enough," he remarked to his disciples, " but the reapers are few. So you must pray to the Lord of the Harvest to send men out to reap it."

Jesus sends out the Twelve with divine power   10 : 1
Jesus called his twelve disciples to him and gave them authority to expel evil spirits and heal all kinds of disease and infirmity. The names of the Twelve Apostles were:

First, Simon, called Peter, with his brother, Andrew ;
James and his brother John, sons of Zebedee ;
Philip and Bartholomew,
Thomas, and Matthew the tax-collector,
James, the son of Alphaeus, and Thaddaeus,
Simon the Patriot, and Judas Iscariot, who later turned traitor.

These were the twelve whom Jesus sent out, with the instructions : " Don't turn off into any of the heathen roads, and don't go into any Samaritan town. Concentrate on the lost sheep of the house of Israel. As you go proclaim that the Kingdom of Heaven has arrived. Heal the sick, raise the dead, cure the lepers, drive out devils—give, as you have received, without any charge whatever.

" Don't take any gold or silver or even coppers to put in your purse ; nor a knapsack for the journey, nor even a change of clothes, or sandals or a staff—the workman is worth his keep!

"Wherever you go, whether it is into a town or a village, find out someone who is respected, and stay with him until you leave. As you enter his house give it your blessing. If the house deserves it, the peace of your blessing will come to it. But if it doesn't, your peace will return to you.

"And if no one will welcome you or even listen to what you have to say, leave that house or town and once outside it shake off the dust of that place from your feet. Believe me, Sodom and Gomorrah will fare better in the Day of Judgment than that town.

He warns them of troubles that lie ahead   10 : 16

"Here am I sending you out like sheep with wolves all round you; so be as wise as serpents and yet as harmless as doves. But be on your guard against men. For they will take you to the courts and flog you in their synagogues. You will be brought into the presence of governors and kings because of me—to give your witness to them and to the heathen.

"But when they do arrest you, never worry about how you are to speak or what you are to say. You will be told at the time what you are to say. For it will not be really you who are speaking but the Spirit of your Father speaking through you.

"Brothers are going to betray their brothers to death, and fathers their children. Children are going to betray their parents and have them executed. You yourselves will be universally hated because of my name. But the man who endures to the very end will be safe and sound.

"But when they persecute you in one town make your escape to the next. Believe me, you will not have covered the towns of Israel before the Son of Man arrives. The disciple is not superior to his teacher any more than the servant is superior to his master, for what is good enough for the teacher is good enough for the disciple as well, and the servant will not fare better than his master. If men call the Master of the Household the 'Prince of Evil,' what sort of names will they give to his servants? But never let them frighten you, for there is nothing covered up which is not going to be exposed nor anything private which will not be made public. The things I tell you in the dark you must say in the day-light, and the things you hear in your private ear you must proclaim from the house-tops.

They should reverence God but have no fear of man   10 : 28
" Never be afraid of those who can kill the body but are powerless to kill the soul ! Far better to stand in awe of the One Who has the power to destroy body and soul in the fires of destruction !

" Two sparrows sell for a farthing, don't they ? Yet not a single sparrow falls to the ground without your Father's knowledge. The very hairs of your head are all numbered. Never be afraid, then—you are far more valuable than sparrows.

" Every man who publicly acknowledges me I shall acknowledge in the presence of my Father in Heaven, but the man who disowns me before men I shall disown before my Father in Heaven.

The prince of peace comes to bring division   10 : 34
" Never think I have come to bring peace upon the earth. No, I have not come to bring peace but a sword ! For I have come to set a man against his own father, a daughter against her own mother, and a daughter-in-law against her mother-in-law. A man's enemies will be those who live in his own house.

" Anyone who puts his love for father or mother above his love for me does not deserve to be mine, and he who loves son or daughter more than me is not worthy of me, and neither is the man who refuses to take up his cross and follow my way. The man who has found his own life will lose it, but the man who has lost it for my sake will find it.

" Whoever welcomes you, welcomes me ; and whoever welcomes me is welcoming the One Who sent me.

" Whoever welcomes a prophet just because he is a prophet will get a prophet's reward. And whoever welcomes a good man just because he is a good man will get a good man's reward. Believe me, anyone who gives even a drink of water to one of these little ones, just because he is my disciple, will by no means lose his reward."

When Jesus had finished giving his twelve disciples these instructions he went on from there to teach and preach in the towns in which they lived.

John enquires about Christ : Christ speaks about John   11 : 2

John the Baptist was in prison when he heard what Christ was doing, and he sent a message through his own disciples asking the question, " Are you the One Who was to come or are we to look for somebody else ? "

Jesus gave them this reply, " Go and tell John what you see and hear—that blind men are recovering their sight, cripples are walking, lepers being healed, the deaf hearing, the dead being brought to life and the Good News is being given to those in need. *And happy is the man who never loses his faith in me.*"

As John's disciples were going away Jesus began talking to the crowd about John :

" What did you go out into the desert to look at ? A reed waving in the breeze ? No ? Then *what* was it you went out to see ?—a man dressed in fine clothes ? But the men who wear fine clothes live in the courts of kings ! But what did you really go to see—a prophet ? Yes, I tell you, a prophet and far more than a prophet ! This is the man of whom the Scripture says :

Behold, I send my messenger before thy face,
Who shall prepare thy way before thee.

" Believe me, no one greater than John the Baptist has ever been born of all mankind, and yet a humble member of the Kingdom of Heaven is greater than he.

" From the days of John the Baptist until now the Kingdom of Heaven has been taken by storm and eager men are forcing their way into it. For the Law and all the Prophets foretold it till the time of John and—if you can believe it—John himself is the ' Elijah ' who must come before the Kingdom. The man who has ears to hear must use them !

" But how can I show what the people of this generation are like ? They are like children sitting in the market-place calling out to their friends, ' We played at weddings for you but you wouldn't dance, and we played at funerals and you wouldn't cry!' For John came in the strictest austerity and people say, 'He's crazy!' Then the Son of Man came, enjoying life, and people say, 'Look, a drunkard and a glutton—the bosom-friend of the tax-collector and the sinner.' Ah well, Wisdom stands or falls by her own actions."

Jesus denounces apathy—and thanks God that simple   11 : 20
men understand his message

Then Jesus began reproaching the towns where most of his miracles had taken place because their hearts were unchanged.

"Alas for you, Chorazin! Alas for you, Bethsaida! For if Tyre and Sidon had seen the demonstrations of God's power which you have seen they would have repented long ago in sackcloth and ashes. Yet I tell you this, that it will be more bearable for Tyre and Sidon in the Day of Judgment than for you.

"And as for you, Capernaum, are you on your way up to heaven? I tell you you will go hurtling down among the dead! If Sodom had seen the miracles that you have seen, Sodom would be standing to-day. Yet I tell you now that it will be more bearable for the land of Sodom in the Day of Judgment than for you."

At this same time Jesus said, "Oh Father, Lord of Heaven and earth, I thank you for hiding these things from the clever and intelligent and for showing them to mere children. Yes, I thank You, Father, that this was Your Will."

Then he said: "Everything has been put in my hands by my Father, and nobody knows the Son except the Father. Nor does anyone know the Father except the Son—and the man to whom the Son chooses to reveal Him.

"Come to me, all of you who are weary and over-burdened and I will give you rest! Put on my yoke and learn from me. For I am gentle and humble in heart and you will find rest for your souls. For my yoke is easy and my burden is light."

Jesus rebukes the Sabbatarians   12 : 1

It happened then that Jesus passed through the cornfields on the Sabbath day. His disciples were hungry and began picking the ears of wheat and eating them. But the Pharisees saw them do it.

"There, you see," they remarked to Jesus, "your disciples are doing what the Law forbids them to do on the Sabbath."

"Haven't any of you read what David did when he and his companions were hungry?" replied Jesus, "—how he went into the House of God and ate the Presentation Loaves, which he and his followers were not allowed to eat since only priests can do so?

"Haven't any of you read in the Law that every Sabbath day priests in the Temple can break the Sabbath and yet remain blameless? I tell you that there is something more important than the Temple here. If you had grasped the meaning of the Scripture '*I desire mercy and not sacrifice*,' you would not have been so quick to condemn the innocent! For the Son of Man is master even of the Sabbath."

Leaving there he went into their synagogue, where there happened to be a man with a shrivelled hand.

"Is it right to heal anyone on the Sabbath day?" they asked him—hoping to bring a charge against him.

"If any of you had a sheep which fell into a ditch on the Sabbath day, would he not take hold of it and pull it out?" replied Jesus. "How much more valuable is a man than a sheep? You see, it is right to do good on the Sabbath day."

Then Jesus said to the man, "Stretch out your hand!" He did stretch it out, and it was restored as sound as the other.

But the Pharisees went out and held a meeting against Jesus and discussed how they could get rid of him altogether.

Jesus retires to continue his work   12 : 15

But Jesus knew of this and he left the place.

Large crowds followed him and he healed them all, with the strict injunction that they should not make him conspicuous by their talk, thus fulfilling Isaiah's prophecy:

Behold, my servant whom I have chosen;
My beloved in whom my soul is well pleased:
I will put my Spirit upon him,
And he shall declare judgment to the Gentiles.
He shall not strive, nor cry aloud;
Neither shall any one hear his voice in the streets.

A bruised reed shall he not break,
And smoking flax shall he not quench,
Till he send forth judgment unto victory.
And in his name shall the Gentiles hope.

Then a devil-possessed man who could neither see nor
speak was brought to Jesus. He healed him, so that the
dumb man could both speak and see. At this the whole
crowd went wild with excitement, and people kept saying,
" Can this be the Son of David ? "

The Pharisees draw an evil conclusion, and Jesus rebukes   12 : 24
them

But the Pharisees on hearing this remark said to each
other, " This man is only expelling devils because he is in
league with Beelzebub, the prince of devils."

Jesus knew what they were thinking and said to them,
" Any kingdom divided against itself is bound to collapse,
and no town or household divided against itself can last for
long. If it is Satan who is expelling Satan, then he is divided
against himself—so how do you suppose that his kingdom
can continue ? And if I expel devils because I am an ally
of Beelzebub, what alliance do your sons make when they
do the same thing ? They can settle that question for you !
But if I am expelling devils by the Spirit of God, *then the
Kingdom of God has swept over you unawares !* How do you
suppose anyone could get into a strong man's house and
steal his property unless he first tied up the strong man ?
But if he did that, he could ransack his whole house.

" The man who is not on my side is against me, and the
man who does not gather with me is really scattering. That
is why I tell you that men may be forgiven for every sin
and blasphemy, but blasphemy against the Spirit cannot be
forgiven. A man may say a word against the Son of Man
and be forgiven, but whoever speaks against the Holy Spirit
cannot be forgiven either in this world or in the world to
come !

" You must choose between having a good tree with good
fruit or a rotten tree with rotten fruit. For you can tell a
tree at once by its fruit.

" You serpent's brood, how can you say anything good

out of your evil hearts ? For a man's words depend on what fills his heart. A good man gives out good—from the goodness stored in his heart ; a bad man gives out evil—from his store of evil. I tell you that men will have to answer at the Day of Judgment for every careless word they utter—for it is your words that will acquit you, and your words that will condemn you ! "

Jesus refuses to give a sign   12 : 38

Then some of the Scribes and Pharisees said, " Master, we want to see a sign from you." But Jesus told them :

" It is an evil and unfaithful generation that craves for a sign, and no sign will be given to it—except the sign of the prophet Jonah. For just as Jonah was in the belly of that great sea-monster for three days and nights, so will the Son of Man be in the heart of the earth for three days and nights. The men of Nineveh will stand up with this generation in the Judgment and will condemn it. For they did repent when Jonah preached to them, and you have more than Jonah's preaching with you now ! The Queen of the South will stand up in the Judgment with this generation and will condemn it. For she came from the ends of the earth to listen to the wisdom of Solomon, and you have more than the wisdom of Solomon with you now !

The danger of spiritual emptiness   12 : 43

" When the evil spirit goes out of a man it wanders through waterless places looking for rest and never finding it. Then it says, ' I will go back to my house from which I came.' When it arrives it finds it unoccupied, but cleaned and all in order. Then it goes and collects seven other spirits more evil than itself to keep it company, and they all go in and make themselves at home. The last state of that man is worse than the first—and that is just what will happen to this evil generation."

Jesus and his relations   12 : 46

While he was still talking to the crowds, his mother and his brothers happened to be standing outside wanting to speak to him. Somebody said to him, " Look, your mother and your brothers are outside wanting to speak to you."

But Jesus replied to the one who told him, "Who is my mother, and who are my brothers?"; then with a gesture of his hand towards his disciples he went on, "There are my mother and brothers! For whoever does the will of my Heavenly Father is brother and sister and mother to me."

Jesus tells the parable of the seed   13 : 1

It was on the same day that Jesus went out of the house and sat down by the lake-side. Such great crowds collected round him that he went aboard a small boat and sat down while all the people stood on the beach. He told them a great deal in parables, and began :

"There was once a man who went out to sow. In his sowing some of the seeds fell by the road-side and the birds swooped down and gobbled them up. Some fell on stony patches where they had very little soil. They sprang up quickly in the shallow soil, but when the sun came up they were scorched by the heat and withered away because they had no roots. Some seeds fell among thorn-bushes and the thorns grew up and choked the life out of them. But some fell on good soil and produced a crop—some a hundred times what had been sown, some sixty and some thirty times. The man who has ears to hear should use them!"

At this the disciples approached him and asked, "Why do you talk to them in parables?"

"Because you have been given the chance to understand the secrets of the Kingdom of Heaven," replied Jesus, "but they have not. For when a man has something, more is given to him till he has plenty. But if he has nothing even his nothing will be taken away from him. This is why I speak to them in these parables; because they go through life with their eyes open, but see nothing, and with their ears open, but understand nothing of what they hear. They are the living fulfilment of Isaiah's prophecy which says :

By hearing ye shall hear, and shall in no wise understand;
And seeing ye shall see, and shall in no wise perceive :
For this people's heart is waxed gross,
And their ears are dull of hearing,
And their eyes they have closed ;

Lest haply they should perceive with their eyes,
And hear with their ears,
And understand with their heart,
And should turn again,
And I should heal them.

"But how fortunate you are to have eyes that see and ears that hear! Believe me, a great many prophets and good men have longed to see what you are seeing and they never saw it. Yes, and they longed to hear what you are hearing and they never heard it.

"Now listen to the parable of the sower. When a man hears the message of the Kingdom and does not grasp it, the evil one comes and snatches away what was sown in his heart. This is like the seed sown by the road-side. The seed sown on the stony patches represents the man who hears the message and eagerly accepts it. But it has not taken root in him and does not last long—the moment trouble or persecution arises through the message he gives up his faith at once. The seed sown among the thorns represents the man who hears the message, and then the worries of this life and the illusions of wealth choke it to death and so it produces no 'crop' in his life. But the seed sown on good soil is the man who both hears and understands the message. His life shows a good crop, a hundred, sixty or thirty times what was sown."

Good and evil grow side by side in this present world   13 : 24

Then he put another parable before them. "The Kingdom of Heaven," he said, "is like a man who sowed good seed in his field. But while his men were asleep his enemy came and sowed weeds among the wheat, and went away. When the crop came up and ripened, the weeds appeared as well. Then the owner's servants came up to him and said, 'Sir, didn't you sow good seed in your field? Where did all these weeds come from?' 'Some blackguard has done this to spite me,' he replied. 'Do you want us then to go out and pull them all up?' said the servants. 'No,' he returned, 'if you pull up the weeds now, you would pull up the wheat with them. Let them both grow together till the harvest. And at harvest-time I shall tell the reapers, 'Collect all the weeds first and tie them up in bundles ready to burn, but collect the wheat and store it in my barn.'"

The Kingdom's power of growth, and widespread influence   13 : 31

Then he put another parable before them : "The Kingdom of Heaven is like a tiny grain of mustard seed which a man took and sowed in his field. As a seed it is the smallest of them all, but it grows to be the biggest of all plants. It becomes a tree, big enough for birds to come and nest in its branches."

This is another of the parables he told them : "The Kingdom of Heaven is like yeast, taken by a woman and put into three measures of flour until the whole lot had risen."

All these things Jesus spoke to the crowd in parables, and he did not speak to them at all without using parables—to fulfil the prophecy :

I will open my mouth in parables ;
I will utter things hidden from the foundation of the world.

Jesus again explains a parable to his disciples   13 : 36

Later, he left the crowds and went indoors, where his disciples came and said, "Please explain to us the parable of the weeds in the field."

"The one who sows the good seed is the Son of Man," replied Jesus. "The field is the whole world. The good seed ? That is the sons of the Kingdom, while the weeds are the sons of the evil one. The blackguard who sowed them is the Devil. The harvest is the end of this world. The reapers are angels.

"Just as weeds are gathered up and burned in the fire so will it happen at the end of this world. The Son of Man will send out his angels and they will uproot from the Kingdom everything that is spoiling it, and all those who live in defiance of its laws, and will throw them into the blazing furnace, where there will be tears and bitter regret. Then the good will shine out like the sun in their Father's Kingdom. The man who has ears should use them !

More pictures of the Kingdom of Heaven   13 : 44

"Again, the Kingdom of Heaven is like some treasure
which has been buried in a field. A man finds it and buries
it again, and goes off overjoyed to sell all his possessions to
buy himself that field.

"Or again, the Kingdom of Heaven is like a merchant
searching for fine pearls. When he has found a single pearl
of great value, he goes and sells all his possessions and
buys it.

"Or the Kingdom of Heaven is like a big net thrown into
the sea collecting all kinds of fish. When it is full, the fishermen haul it ashore and sit down and pick out the good ones
for the barrels, but they throw away the bad. That is how
it will be at the end of this world. The angels will go out
and pick out the wicked from among the good and throw
them into the blazing furnace, where there will be tears and
bitter regret.

"Have you grasped all this?"

"Yes," they replied.

"You can see then," returned Jesus, "how every one
who knows the Law and becomes a disciple of the Kingdom
of Heaven is like a householder who can produce from his
store both the new and the old."

Jesus is not appreciated in his native town   13 : 53

When Jesus had finished these parables he left the place,
and came into his own country. Here he taught the people
in their own synagogue, till in their amazement they said,
"Where does this man get this wisdom and these powers?
He's only the carpenter's son. Isn't Mary his mother, and
aren't James, Joseph, Simon and Judas his brothers? And
aren't all his sisters living here with us? Where did he get
all this?" And they were deeply offended with him.

But Jesus said to them, "No prophet goes unhonoured
except in his own country and in his own home!"

And he performed very few miracles there because of their
lack of faith.

Herod's guilty conscience   14 : 1

About this time Herod, governor of the province, heard
the reports about Jesus and said to his men, "This must be

John the Baptist : he has risen from the dead. That is why miraculous powers are at work in him."

For previously Herod had arrested John and had him bound and put in prison, all on account of Herodias, the wife of his brother Philip. For John had said to him, " It is not right for you to have this woman." Herod wanted to kill him for this, but he was afraid of the people, since they all thought John was a prophet. But during Herod's birthday celebrations Herodias' daughter delighted him by dancing before his guests, so much so that he swore to give her anything she liked to ask. And she, prompted by her mother, said, " I want you to give me, here and now, on a dish, the head of John the Baptist ! " Herod was aghast at this, but because he had sworn in front of his guests, he gave orders that she should be given what she had asked. So he sent men and had John beheaded in the prison. Then his head was carried in on a dish and presented to the young girl who handed it to her mother. Later John's disciples came, took his body and buried it. Then they went and told the news to Jesus. When he heard it he went away by boat to a deserted place, quite alone.

Jesus feeds a tired and hungry crowd   14 : 13*b*

Then the crowds heard of his departure and followed him out of the towns on foot. When Jesus emerged from his retreat he saw a vast crowd and was very deeply moved and cured the sick among them. As evening fell his disciples came to him and said, " We are right in the wilds here and it is very late. Send away these crowds now, so that they can go into the villages and buy themselves food."

" There's no need for them to go away," returned Jesus. " You give them something to eat ! "

" But we haven't anything here," they told him, " except five loaves and two fish." To which Jesus replied, " Bring them here to me."

He told the crowd to sit down on the grass. Then he took the five loaves and the two fish in his hands, and, looking up to Heaven, he thanked God, broke the loaves and passed them to his disciples who handed them to the crowd. Everybody ate and was satisfied. Afterwards they collected twelve baskets full of the pieces which were left over. Those who ate numbered about five thousand men, apart from the women and children.

Jesus again shows his power over the forces of nature   14 : 22

Directly after this Jesus insisted on his disciples' getting aboard their boat and going on ahead to the other side, while he himself sent the crowds home. And when he had sent them away he went up the hill-side quite alone, to pray. When it grew late he was there by himself while the boat was by now a long way from the shore at the mercy of the waves, for the wind was dead against them. In the small hours Jesus went out to them, walking on the water of the lake. When the disciples caught sight of him walking on the water they were terrified. " It's a ghost ! " they said, and screamed with fear. But at once Jesus spoke to them. " It's all right ! It's I myself, don't be afraid ! "

" Lord, if it's really you," said Peter, " tell me to come to you on the water."

" Come on then," replied Jesus.

Peter stepped down from the boat and did walk on the water, making for Jesus. But when he saw the fury of the wind he panicked and began to sink, calling out, " Lord, save me ! " At once Jesus reached out his hand and caught him, saying, " You little-faith ! What made you lose your nerve like that ? " Then, when they were both aboard the boat, the wind dropped. The whole crew came and knelt down before Jesus crying, " You are indeed the Son of God ! "

When they had crossed over to the other side of the lake, they landed at Gennesaret, and when the men of that place had recognised him, they sent word to the whole surrounding country and brought all the diseased to him. They implored him to let them " touch just the edge of his cloak," and all those who did so were cured.

The dangers of tradition   15 : 1

Then some of the Scribes and Pharisees from Jerusalem came and asked Jesus, " Why do your disciples break our ancient tradition and eat their food without washing their hands properly first ? "

" Tell me," replied Jesus, " why do you break God's

commandment through your tradition? For God said, 'Honour thy father and thy mother,' and 'He that speaketh evil of father or mother, let him die the death.' But you say that if a man tells his parents, 'Whatever use I might have been to you is now given to God,' then he owes no further duty to his parents. And so your tradition empties the commandment of God of all its meaning. You hypocrites! Isaiah described you beautifully when he said:

This people honoureth me with their lips;
But their heart is far from me.
But in vain do they worship me,
Teaching as their doctrines the precepts of men."

Superficial and true cleanliness   15 : 10

Then he called the crowd to him and said, "Listen, and understand this thoroughly! It is not what goes *into* a man's mouth that makes him common or unclean. It is what comes *out* of a man's mouth that makes him unclean."

Later his disciples came to him and said, "Do you know that the Pharisees are deeply offended by what you said?"

"Every plant which my Heavenly Father did not plant will be pulled up by the roots," returned Jesus. "Let them alone. They are blind guides, and when one blind man leads another blind man they will both end up in the ditch!"

"Explain this parable to us," broke in Peter.

"Are you still unable to grasp things like this?" replied Jesus. "Don't you see that whatever goes *into* the mouth passes into the stomach and then out of the body altogether? But the things that come *out* of a man's mouth come from his heart and mind, and it is they that really make a man unclean. For it is from a man's mind that evil thoughts arise—murder, adultery, lust, theft, perjury and blasphemy. These are the things which make a man unclean, not eating without washing his hands properly!"

A Gentile's faith in Jesus   15 : 21

Jesus then left that place and retired into the Tyre and Sidon district. There a Canaanite woman from those parts came to him crying at the top of her voice:

"Lord, have pity on me! My daughter is in a terrible state—a devil has got into her!"

Jesus made no answer, and the disciples came up to him and said, "Do send her away—she's still following us and calling out."

"I was only sent," replied Jesus, "to the lost sheep of the house of Israel."

Then the woman came and knelt at his feet. "Lord, help me," she said.

"It is not right you know," Jesus replied, "to take the children's food and throw it to the dogs."

"Yes, Lord, I know, but even the dogs live on the scraps that fall from their master's table!"

"You certainly don't lack faith," returned Jesus, "it shall be as you wish."

And at that moment her daughter was cured.

Jesus heals and feeds vast crowds of people   15 : 29

Jesus left there, walked along the shore of the lake of Galilee, then climbed the hill and sat down. And great crowds came to him, bringing with them people who were lame, crippled, blind, dumb and many others. They simply put them down at his feet and he healed them. The result was that the people were astonished at seeing dumb men speak, men healed, lame men walking about and blind men having recovered their sight. And they praised the God of Israel.

But Jesus quietly called his disciples to him. "My heart goes out to this crowd," he said. "They've stayed with me three days now and have no more food. I don't want to send them home without anything or they will collapse on the way."

"Where could we find enough food to feed such a crowd in this deserted spot?" said the disciples.

"How many loaves have you?" asked Jesus.

"Seven, and a few small fish," they replied.

Then Jesus told the crowd to sit down comfortably on the ground. And when he had taken the seven loaves and the fish into his hands, he broke them with a prayer of thanksgiving and gave them to the disciples to pass on to the people. Everybody ate and was satisfied, and they picked up seven baskets full of the pieces left over. Those who ate numbered four thousand men apart from women and children. Then Jesus sent the crowds home, boarded the boat and arrived at the district of Magadan.

Jesus again refuses to give a sign   16 : 1

Once the Pharisees and the Sadducees arrived together to test him, and asked him to give them a sign from Heaven. But he replied, " When the evening comes you say, ' Ah, fine weather—the sky is red.' In the morning you say, ' There will be a storm to-day, the sky is red and threatening.' Yes, you know how to interpret the look of the sky but you have no idea how to interpret the signs of the times ! A wicked and unfaithful age insists on a sign ; and it will not be given any sign at all but that of the prophet Jonah." And he turned on his heel and left them.

He is misunderstood by the disciples   16 : 5

Then his disciples came to him on the other side of the lake, forgetting to bring any bread with them. " Keep your eyes open," said Jesus to them, " and be on your guard against the ' yeast ' of the Pharisees and Sadducees ! " But they were arguing with each other, and saying, " We forgot to bring the bread." When Jesus saw this he said to them, " Why all this argument among yourselves about not bringing any bread, you little-faiths ? Don't you understand yet, or have you forgotten the five loaves and the five thousand, and how many baskets you took up afterwards ; or the seven loaves and the four thousand and how many baskets you took up then ? I wonder why you don't yet understand that I wasn't talking about bread at all—when I told you to beware of the yeast of the Pharisees and Sadducees." Then they grasped the fact that he had not told them to beware of yeast in the ordinary sense but of the teaching of the Pharisees and Sadducees.

Peter's bold affirmation   16 : 13

When Jesus reached the Caesarea-Philippi district he asked his disciples a question. " Who do people say the Son of Man is ? "

" Well, some say John the Baptist," they told him.

" Some say Elijah, others Jeremiah or one of the prophets."

" But what about you ? " he said to them. " Who do you say that I am ? "

Simon Peter answered, " You ? You are Christ, the Son of the Living God ! "

" Simon, son of Jonah, you are a fortunate man indeed ! " said Jesus, " for it was not your own nature but my Heavenly Father Who has revealed this truth to you ! Now I tell you that you are Peter the rock, and it is on this rock that I am going to found my Church, and the powers of Death will never prevail against it. I will give you the keys of the Kingdom of Heaven ; whatever you forbid on earth will be what is forbidden in Heaven and whatever you permit on earth will be what is permitted in Heaven ! "[1] Then he impressed on his disciples that they should not tell anyone that he was Christ.

Jesus speaks about his passion, and the cost of following him 16 : 21

From that time onwards Jesus began to explain to his disciples that he would have to go to Jerusalem, and endure much suffering from the Elders, Chief Priests and Scribes, and finally be killed ; and be raised to life again on the third day.

Then Peter took him on one side and started to remonstrate with him over this, " God bless you, Master ! Nothing like this must happen to you ! " Then Jesus turned round and said to Peter, " Out of my way, Satan ! . . . you stand right in my path, Peter, when you look at things from man's point of view and not from God's."

Then Jesus said to his disciples, " If anyone wants to follow in my footsteps he must give up all right to himself, take up his cross and follow me. For the man who wants to save his life will lose it ; but the man who loses his life for my sake will find it. For what good is it for a man to gain the whole world at the price of his own soul ? What could a man offer to buy back his soul once he had lost it ?

" For the Son of Man will come in the glory of his Father and in the company of His angels and then he will repay every man for what he has done. Believe me, there are some

[1] See Appendix, Note 3.

standing here to-day who will know nothing of death till they have seen the Son of Man coming as King."

Three disciples glimpse the glory of Christ   17 : 1

Six days later Jesus chose Peter, James and his brother John, to accompany him high up on the hill-side where they were quite alone. There his whole appearance changed before their eyes, his face shining like the sun and his clothes as white as light. Then Moses and Elijah were seen talking to Jesus.

"Lord," exclaimed Peter, "it is wonderful for us to be here! If you like I could put up three shelters, one each for you and Moses and Elijah——"

But while he was still talking a bright cloud overshadowed them and a Voice came out of the cloud:

"This is My dearly-loved Son in Whom I am well pleased. Listen to Him!"

When they heard this Voice the disciples fell on their faces, overcome with fear. Then Jesus came up to them and touched them.

"Get up and don't be frightened," he said. And as they raised their eyes there was no one to be seen but Jesus himself.

On their way down the hill-side Jesus warned them not to tell anyone about what they had seen until after the Son of Man had risen from the dead. Then the disciples demanded, "Why is it, then, that the Scribes always say Elijah must come first?"

"Yes, Elijah does come first," replied Jesus, "and begins the world's reformation. But I tell you that Elijah has come already and men did not recognise him. They did what they liked with him, and they will do the same to the Son of Man."

Then they realised that he had been referring to John the Baptist.

Jesus heals an epileptic boy   17 : 14

When they returned to the crowds again a man came and knelt in front of Jesus. "Lord, do have pity on my son," he said, "for he is a lunatic and is in a terrible state. He is always falling into the fire or into the water. I did bring him to your disciples but they couldn't cure him."

"You really are an unbelieving and difficult people," Jesus returned. "How long must I be with you, and how long must I put up with you? Bring him here to me!"

Then Jesus reprimanded the evil spirit and it went out of the boy, who was cured from that moment.

Afterwards the disciples approached Jesus privately and asked, "Why weren't we able to get rid of it?"

"Because you have so little faith," replied Jesus. "I assure you that if you have as much faith as a grain of mustard-seed you can say to this hill, 'Up you get and move over there!' and it will move—you will find nothing is impossible."

As they went about together in Galilee, Jesus told them, "The Son of Man is going to be handed over to the power of men, and they will kill him. And on the third day he will be raised to life again." This greatly distressed the disciples.

Jesus pays the Temple-tax—in an unusual way!   17 : 24

Then when they arrived at Capernaum the Temple tax-collectors came up and said to Peter, "Your master doesn't pay Temple-tax, we presume?"

"Oh yes, he does!" replied Peter. Later when he went into the house Jesus anticipated what he was going to say. "What do *you* think, Simon?" he said. "Who do the kings of this world get their rates and taxes from—their own people or from others?"

"From others," replied Peter.

"Then the family is exempt," Jesus told him. "Yet we don't want to give offence to these people, so go down to the lake and throw in your hook. Take the first fish that bites, open his mouth and you'll find a coin. Take that and give it to them, for both of us."

Jesus commends the simplicity of children   18 : 1

It was at this time that the disciples came to Jesus with the question, "Who is really greatest in the Kingdom of Heaven?" Jesus called a little child to his side and set him on his feet in the middle of them all. "Believe me," he said, "unless you change your whole outlook and become like little children you will never enter the Kingdom of Heaven. It is the man who can be as humble as this little child who is 'greatest' in the Kingdom of Heaven.

"Anyone who welcomes one child like this for my sake is welcoming me. But if anyone leads astray one of these little children who believe in me he would be better off thrown into the depths of the sea with a mill-stone hung round his neck! Alas for the world with its pitfalls! In the nature of things there must be pitfalls, yet alas for the man who is responsible for them!

The right way may mean costly sacrifice   18 : 8

"If your hand or your foot is a hindrance to your faith, cut it off and throw it away. It is a good thing to go into Life maimed or crippled—rather than to have both hands and feet and be thrown on to the everlasting fire. Yes, and if your eye leads you astray, tear it out and throw it away. It is a good thing to go one-eyed into Life—rather than to have both your eyes and be thrown on the fire of the rubbish-heap.

"Be careful that you never despise a single one of these little ones—for I tell you that they have angels who see my Father's face continually in Heaven.

"What do you think? If a man has a hundred sheep and one wanders away from the rest, won't he leave the ninety-nine on the hill-side and set out to look for the one who has wandered away? Yes, and if he should chance to find it I assure you he is more delighted over that one than he is over the ninety-nine who never wandered away. You can understand then that it is never the Will of your Father in Heaven that a single one of these little ones should be lost.

Reconciliation must always be attempted   18 : 15

"But if your brother wrongs you, go and have it out with him at once—just between the two of you. If he will listen to you, you have won him back as your brother. But if he will not listen to you, take one or two others with you so that everything that is said may have the support of two or three witnesses. And if he still won't pay any attention, tell the matter to the church. And if he won't even listen to the church then he must be to you just like a pagan—or a tax-collector!

The connection between earthly conduct and spiritual   18 : 18
reality

" Believe me, whatever you forbid upon earth will be
what is forbidden in Heaven, and whatever you permit on
earth will be what is permitted in Heaven.[1]

" And I tell you once more that if two of you on earth
agree in asking for anything it will be granted to you by my
Heavenly Father. For wherever two or three people come
together in my name, I am there, right among them ! "

The necessity for forgiveness   18 : 21

Then Peter approached him with the question, " Master,
how many times can my brother wrong me and I must
forgive him ? Would seven times be enough ? "

" No," replied Jesus, " not seven times, but seventy times
seven ! For the Kingdom of Heaven is like a king who
decided to settle his accounts with his servants. When he
had started calling in his accounts, a man was brought to
him who owed him millions of pounds. And when it was
plain that he had no means of repaying the debt, his master
gave orders for him to be sold as a slave, and his wife and
children and all his possessions as well, and the money to be
paid over. At this the servant fell on his knees before his
master, ' Oh, be patient with me ! ' he cried, ' and I will
pay you back every penny ! ' Then his master was moved
with pity for him, set him free and cancelled the debt.

" But when this same servant had left his master's presence,
he found one of his fellow-servants who owed him a few
shillings. He grabbed him and seized him by the throat,
crying, ' Pay up what you owe me ! ' At this his fellow-servant
fell down at his feet, and implored him, ' Oh, be patient with
me, and I will pay you back ! ' But he refused and went out
and had him put in prison until he should repay the debt.

" When the other fellow-servants saw what had happened,
they were horrified and went and told their master the whole
incident. Then his master called him in.

" ' You wicked servant ! ' he said. ' Didn't I cancel all
that debt when you begged me to do so ? Oughtn't you to
have taken pity on your fellow-servant as I, your master,

[1] See Appendix, Note 3.

took pity on you?' And his master in anger handed him over to the gaolers till he should repay the whole debt. This is how my Heavenly Father will treat you unless you each forgive your brother from your heart."

The divine principle of marriage   19 : 1

When Jesus had finished talking on these matters, he left Galilee and went on to the district of Judaea on the far side of the Jordan. Vast crowds followed him, and he cured them there.

Then the Pharisees arrived with a test-question.

" Is it right," they asked, " for a man to divorce his wife on any grounds whatever ? "

" Haven't you read," he answered, " that the One Who created them from the beginning made them male and female and said : ' *For this cause shall a man leave his father and mother, and shall cleave to his wife ; and the twain shall become one flesh* ' ? So they are no longer two separate people but one. No man therefore must separate what God has joined together."

" Then why," they retorted, " did Moses command us to give a written divorce-notice and dismiss the woman ? "

" It was because you knew so little of the meaning of love that Moses allowed you to divorce your wives ! But that was not the original principle. I tell you that anyone who divorces his wife on any grounds except her unfaithfulness and marries some other woman commits adultery."

His disciples said to him, " If that is a man's position with his wife, it is not worth getting married ! "

" It is not everybody who can live up to this," replied Jesus, "—only those who have a special gift. For some are incapable of marriage from birth, some are made incapable by the action of men, and some have made themselves so for the sake of the Kingdom of Heaven. Let the man who can accept what I have said accept it."

Jesus welcomes children   19 : 13

Then some little children were brought to him, so that he could put his hands on them and pray for them. The disciples frowned on the parents' action but Jesus said :

" You must let little children come to me, and you must never stop them. The Kingdom of Heaven belongs to little children like these!" Then he laid his hands on them and went on his way.

Jesus shows that keeping the Commandments is not enough 19 : 16

Then it happened that a man came up to him and said, "Master, what good thing must I do to secure eternal life?"

"I wonder why you ask me about what is good?" Jesus answered him. "Only One is good. But if you want to enter that life you must keep the commandments."

"Which ones?" he asked.

"*Thou shalt do no murder, Thou shalt not commit adultery, Thou shalt not steal, Thou shalt not bear false witness, Honour thy father and thy mother: and Thou shalt love thy neighbour as thyself,*" replied Jesus.

"I have carefully kept all these," returned the young man. "What is still missing in my life?"

Then Jesus told him, "If you want to be perfect, go now and sell your property and give the money away to the poor —you will have riches in Heaven. Then come and follow me!"

When the young man heard that he turned away crestfallen, for he was very wealthy.

Then Jesus remarked to his disciples, "Believe me, a rich man will find it very difficult to enter the Kingdom of Heaven. Yes, I repeat, a camel could more easily squeeze through the eye of a needle than a rich man get into the Kingdom of God!"

The disciples were simply amazed to hear this, and said, "Then who can possibly be saved?"

Jesus looked steadily at them and replied, "Humanly speaking it is impossible; but with God anything is possible!"

Jesus declares that sacrifice for the Kingdom will be repaid 19 : 27

At this Peter exclaimed, "Look, we have left everything and followed you. What is that going to be worth to us?"

"Believe me," said Jesus, "when I tell you that in the next world, when the Son of Man shall sit down on his glorious throne, you who have followed me will also sit on twelve thrones and become judges of the twelve tribes of Israel. Every man who has left houses or brothers or sisters or father or mother or children or land for my sake will receive it all back many times over, and will inherit eternal life. But many who are first now will be last then—and the last first!

But God's generosity may appear unfair   20 : 1

"For the Kingdom of Heaven is like a farmer going out early in the morning to hire labourers for his vineyard. He agreed with them on a wage of a silver coin a day and sent them to work. About nine o'clock he went out and saw some others standing about in the market-place with nothing to do. 'You go to the vineyard too,' he said to them, 'and I will pay you a fair wage.' And off they went. At about midday and again at about three o'clock in the afternoon he went out and did the same thing. Then about five o'clock he went out and found some others standing about. 'Why are you standing about here all day doing nothing?' he asked them. 'Because no one has employed us,' they replied. 'You go off into the vineyard as well, then,' he said.

"When evening came the owner of the vineyard said to his foreman, 'Call the labourers and pay them their wages, beginning with the last and ending with the first.' So those who were engaged at five o'clock came up and each man received a silver coin. But when the first to be employed came they reckoned they would get more, but they also received a silver coin a man. As they took their money they grumbled at the farmer and said, 'These last fellows have only put in one hour's work and you've treated them exactly the same as us who have gone through all the hard work and heat of the day!'

"But he replied to one of them, 'My friend, I'm not being unjust to you. Wasn't our agreement for a silver coin a day? Take your money and go home. It is my wish to give the late-comer as much as I give you. May I not do what I like with what belongs to me? Must you be jealous because I am generous?'

"So, many who are the last now will be first then and the first last."

Jesus' final journey to Jerusalem   20 : 17
Then, as he was about to go up to Jerusalem, Jesus took

the twelve disciples aside and spoke to them as they walked along. " Listen, we are now going up to Jerusalem and the Son of Man will be handed over to the Chief Priests and the Scribes—and they will condemn him to death. They will hand him over to the heathen to ridicule and flog and crucify. And on the third day he will rise again ! "

At this point the mother of the sons of Zebedee arrived with her sons and knelt in front of Jesus to ask him a favour.

" What is it you want ? " he asked her.

" Please say that these two sons of mine may sit one on each side of you when you are King ! " she said.

" You don't know what it is you are asking," replied Jesus. " Can you two drink what I have to drink ? "

" Yes, we can," they answered.

" Ah, you will indeed ' drink my drink,' " Jesus told them, " but as for sitting on either side of me, that is not for me to grant—that belongs to those for whom my Father has planned it."

When the other ten heard of this incident they were highly indignant with the two brothers.

But Jesus called them to him and said :

" You know that the rulers of the heathen lord it over them and that their great ones have absolute power ? But it must not be so among you. No, whoever among you wants to be great must become the servant of you all, and if he wants to be first among you he must be your slave—just as the Son of Man has not come to be served but to serve, and to give his life to set many others free."

He restores sight to two blind men   20 : 29

A great crowd followed them as they were leaving Jericho, and two blind men who were sitting by the roadside, hearing that it was Jesus who was passing by, cried out, " Have pity on us, Lord, you Son of David ! " The crowd tried to hush them up, but this only made them cry out more loudly still, " Have pity on us, Lord, you Son of David ! "

Jesus stood quite still and called out to them, " What do you want me to do for you ? "

" Lord, let us see again ! "

And Jesus, deeply moved with pity, touched their eyes. At once their sight was restored, and they followed him.

Jesus' final entry into Jerusalem   21 : 1

As they approached Jerusalem and came to Bethphage and the Mount of Olives, Jesus sent two disciples ahead telling them, " Go into the village in front of you and you will at once find there an ass tethered, and a colt with her. Untie them and bring them to me. Should anyone say anything to you, you are to say, ' The Lord needs them,' and he will send them immediately."

All this happened to fulfil the prophet's saying :

Tell ye the daughter of Zion,
Behold, thy King cometh unto thee,
Meek and riding upon an ass,
And upon a colt the foal of an ass.

So the disciples went off and followed Jesus' instructions. They brought the ass and the colt, and put their cloaks on them, and Jesus took his seat. Then most of the crowd spread their own cloaks on the road, while others cut down branches from the trees and spread them in his path. The crowds who went in front of him and the crowds who followed behind him all shouted, " God save the Son of David ! Blessed is the man who comes in the Name of the Lord ! God save him from on high ! "

And as he entered Jerusalem a shock ran through the whole City. " Who *is* this ? " men cried. " This is Jesus the prophet," replied the crowd, " the man from Nazareth in Galilee ! "

Then Jesus went into the Temple and drove out all the buyers and sellers there. He overturned the tables of the money-changers and the benches of those who sold doves, crying :

" It is written, ' *My house shall be called a house of prayer.*' But you have turned it into a thieves' kitchen ! "

And there in the Temple the blind and the lame came to him, and he healed them. But when the Chief Priests and the Scribes saw the wonderful things he had done, and that children were shouting in the Temple the words, " God save the Son of David," they were highly indignant. " Can't you hear what these children are saying ? " they asked Jesus.

"Yes," he replied, "and haven't you ever read the words, 'Out of the mouth of babes and sucklings thou hast perfected praise'?" And he turned on his heel and went out of the city to Bethany, where he spent the night.

His strange words to the fig-tree   21 : 18

In the morning he came back early to the city and felt hungry. He saw a fig-tree growing by the side of the road, but when he got to it he discovered there was nothing on it but leaves.

"No more fruit shall ever grow on you!" he said to it, and all at once the fig-tree withered away. When the disciples saw this happen they were simply amazed. "How on earth did the fig-tree wither away quite suddenly like that?" they asked.

"Believe me," replied Jesus, "if you have faith and have no doubts in your heart, you will not only do this to a fig-tree but even if you should say to this hill, 'Get up and throw yourself into the sea,' it will happen! Everything you ask for in prayer, if you have faith, you will receive."

Jesus meets a question with a counter-question   21 : 23

Then when he had entered the Temple and was in the act of teaching, the Chief Priests and Jewish Elders came up to him and said, "What authority have you for what you're doing, and who gave you that authority?"

"I am also going to ask you one question," Jesus replied to them, "and if you answer it I will tell you what authority I have for what I do. John's baptism, now, did it come from Heaven or was it purely human?"

At this they began arguing among themselves, "If we say, 'It came from Heaven,' he will say to us, 'Then why didn't you believe in him?' If on the other hand we should say, 'It was purely human'—well, frankly, we are afraid of the people—for all of them consider John was a prophet."

So they answered Jesus, "We do not know."

"Then I will not tell you by what authority I do these things!" returned Jesus. "But what is your opinion about this? There was a man with two sons. He went to the first and said, 'Go and work in my vineyard to-day, my son.' He said, 'All right, sir'—but he never went near it.

Then the father approached the second son with the same request. He said, 'I won't.' But afterwards he changed his mind and went. Which of these two did what their father wanted?"

"The second one," they replied.

"Yes, and I tell you that tax-collectors and prostitutes are going into the Kingdom of God in front of you!" retorted Jesus. "For John came to you as a saint, and you did not believe him—yet the tax-collectors and the prostitutes did! And, even after seeing that, you would not change your minds and believe him.

Jesus tells a pointed story   21 : 33

"Now listen to another story. There was once a man, a land-owner, who planted a vineyard, fenced it round, dug out a hole for the wine-press and built a watch-tower. Then he let it out to farm-workers and went abroad. When the vintage-time approached he sent his servants to the farm-workers to receive his share of the proceeds. But they took the servants, beat up one, killed another, and drove off a third with stones. Then he sent some more servants, a larger party than the first, but they treated them in just the same way. Finally he sent his own son, thinking, 'They will respect my son.' Yet when the farm-workers saw the son they said to each other, 'This fellow is the future owner. Come on, let's kill him and we shall get everything that he would have had!' So they took him, threw him out of the vineyard and killed him. Now when the owner of the vineyard returns, what will he do to those farm-workers?"

"He will kill those scoundrels without mercy," they replied, "and will let the vineyard out to other tenants, who will give him the produce at the right season."

"And have you never read these words of Scripture," said Jesus to them:

The stone which the builders rejected,
The same was made the head of the corner:
This was from the Lord,
And it is marvellous in our eyes?

"Here, I tell you, lies the reason why the Kingdom of God is going to be taken away from you and given to a people who will produce its proper fruit."

When the Chief Priests and the Pharisees heard his parables they realised that he was speaking about them. They longed to get their hands on him, but they were afraid of the crowds, who regarded him as a prophet.

The Kingdom is not to be lightly disregarded   22 : 1

Then Jesus began to talk to them again in parables.

"The Kingdom of Heaven," he said, "is like a king who arranged a wedding for his son. He sent his servants to summon those who had been invited to the festivities, but they refused to come. Then he tried again; he sent some more servants, saying to them, 'Tell those who have been invited, "Here is my wedding-breakfast all ready, my bullocks and fat cattle have been slaughtered and everything is prepared. Come along to the festivities."' But they took no notice of this and went off, one to his farm, and another to his business. As for the rest, they got hold of the servants, treated them disgracefully, and finally killed them. At this the king was very angry and sent his troops and killed those murderers and burned down their city. Then he said to his servants, 'The wedding feast is quite ready, but those who were invited were not good enough for it. So go off now to all the street corners and invite everyone you find there to the feast.' So the servants went out on to the streets and collected together all those whom they found, bad and good alike. And the hall became filled with guests. But when the king came in to inspect the guests, he noticed among them a man not dressed for a wedding. 'How did you come in here, my friend,' he said to him, 'without being properly dressed for the wedding?' And the man had nothing to say. Then the king said to the ushers, 'Tie him up and throw him into the darkness outside. There he can weep and regret his folly!' For many are invited but few are chosen."

A clever trap—and a penetrating answer   22 : 15

Then the Pharisees went off and discussed how they could trap him in argument. Eventually they sent their disciples with some of the Herod-party to say this, " Master, we know that you are an honest man who teaches the way of God faithfully and that you are not swayed by men's opinion of you.   Obviously you don't care for human approval. Now tell us—*Is it right to pay taxes to Caesar or not ?* "

But Jesus knowing their evil intention said, " Why try this trick on me, you frauds ! Show me the money you pay the tax with."   They handed him a coin, and he said to them, " Whose face is this and whose name is in the inscription ? "

" Caesar's," they said.

" Then give to Caesar," he replied, " what belongs to Caesar and to God what belongs to God ! "

This reply staggered them and they let him alone.

Jesus exposes the ignorance of the Sadducees   22 : 23
On the same day some Sadducees (who deny that there is any resurrection) approached Jesus with this question : " Master, Moses said if a man should die without any children, his brother should marry his widow and raise up a family for him. Now, we have a case of seven brothers. The first one married and died, and since he had no family he left his wife to his brother. The same thing happened with the second and the third, right up to the seventh. Last of all the woman herself died. Now in this ' resurrection,' whose wife will she be of these seven men—for she belonged to all of them ? "

" You are very wide of the mark," replied Jesus to them, " for you are ignorant of both the Scriptures and the power of God.   For in the Resurrection there is no such thing as marrying or being given in marriage—men live like the angels in Heaven. And as for the matter of the resurrection of the dead, haven't you ever read what was once said to you by God Himself, ' I am the God of Abraham, the God of Isaac and the God of Jacob ' ? God is not God of the dead but of living men ! " When the crowds heard this they were astounded at his teaching.

The greatest commandments in the Law   22 : 36
When the Pharisees heard that he had silenced the Sadducees they came up to him in a body, and one of them, an

expert in the Law, put this test-question : " Master, what are we to consider the Law's greatest commandment ? "

Jesus answered him, " ' Thou shalt love the Lord thy God, with all thy heart, and with all thy soul and with all thy mind.' This is the first and great commandment. And there is a second like it : ' Thou shalt love thy neighbour as thyself.' The whole of the Law and the Prophets depends on these two commandments."

Jesus puts an unanswerable question   22 : 41

Then Jesus asked the assembled Pharisees this question : " What is your opinion about Christ ? Whose son is he ? "

" The Son of David," they answered.

" How then," returned Jesus, " does David when inspired by the Spirit call him Lord ? He says :

The Lord said unto my *Lord,*
Sit thou on my right hand,
Till I put thine enemies underneath thy feet ?

If David then calls him Lord, how can he be his son ? "

Nobody was able to answer this and from that day on no one dared to ask him any further questions.

He publicly warns people against their religious leaders   23 : 1

Then Jesus addressed the crowds and his disciples. " The Scribes and the Pharisees speak with the authority of Moses," he told them, " so you must do what they tell you and follow their instructions. But you must not imitate their lives ! For they preach but do not practise. They pile up back-breaking burdens and lay them on other men's shoulders—yet they themselves will not raise a finger to move them. Their whole lives are planned with an eye to effect. They increase the size of their phylacteries[1] and lengthen the tassels of their robes ; they love seats of honour at dinner parties and front places in the synagogues. They love to be greeted with respect in public places and to have men call them ' Rabbi ! ' Don't you ever be called ' Rabbi ' —you have only one Teacher, and all of you are brothers.

[1] Phylacteries : strips of parchment inscribed with texts from the Law, worn on the arm and forehead.

And don't call any human being ' father '—for you have one
Father and He is in Heaven. And you must not let people
call you ' leaders '—you have only one Leader, Christ ! The
only ' superior ' among you is the one who serves the others.
For every man who promotes himself will be humbled, and
every man who learns to be humble will find promotion.

"But alas for you, you Scribes and Pharisees, play-actors
that you are ! You lock the doors of the Kingdom of Heaven
in men's faces ; you will not go in yourselves neither will you
allow those at the door to go inside.

"Alas for you, you Scribes and Pharisees, play-actors !
You scour sea and land to make a single convert, and then
you make him twice as ripe for destruction as you are yourselves.

"Alas for you, you blind leaders ! You say, ' If anyone
swears by the Temple it amounts to nothing, but if he swears
by the gold of the Temple he is bound by his oath.' You
blind fools, which is the more important, the gold or the
Temple which sanctifies the gold ? And you say, ' If anyone
swears by the altar it doesn't matter, but if he swears by the
gift placed on the altar he is bound by his oath.' Have you
no eyes—which is more important, the gift, or the altar which
sanctifies the gift ? Any man who swears by the altar is
swearing by the altar and by whatever is offered upon it ; and
anyone who swears by the Temple is swearing by the
Temple and by Him Who dwells in it; and anyone who
swears by Heaven is swearing by the Throne of God and by
the One Who sits upon that Throne.

"Alas for you, Scribes and Pharisees, you utter frauds !
For you pay your tithe on mint and aniseed and cummin,
and neglect the things which carry far more weight in the
Law—justice, mercy and good faith. These are the things
you should have observed—without neglecting the others.
You call yourselves leaders, and yet you can't see an inch
before your noses, for you filter out the mosquito and
swallow the camel.

"What miserable frauds you are, you Scribes and Pharisees ! You clean the outside of the cup and the dish, while
the inside is full of greed and self-indulgence. Can't you see,
Pharisee ? First wash the inside of a cup, and then you can
clean the outside.

" Alas for you, you hypocritical Scribes and Pharisees !
You are like white-washed tombs, which look fine on the
outside but inside are full of dead men's bones and all
kinds of rottenness. For you appear like good men on the
outside—but inside you are a mass of pretence and
wickedness.

" What miserable frauds you are, you Scribes and Pharisees ! You build tombs for the prophets, and decorate
monuments for good men of the past, and then say, ' If we
had lived in the times of our ancestors we should never have
joined in the killing of the prophets.' Yes, ' your ancestors '
—*that* shows you to be sons indeed of those who murdered
the prophets. Go ahead then, and finish off what your
ancestors tried to do ! You serpents, you viper's brood, how
do you think you are going to avoid being condemned to
the rubbish-heap ? Listen to this : ' I am sending you
prophets and wise and learned men ; and some of these you
will kill and crucify, others you will flog in your synagogues
and hunt from town to town. So that on your hands is all
the innocent blood spilt on this earth, from the blood of
Abel the good to the blood of Zachariah, Barachiah's son,
whom you murdered between the sanctuary and the altar.
Yes, I tell you that all this will be laid at the doors of this
generation.

Jesus mourns over Jerusalem, and foretells its destruction   23 : 37
" Oh, Jerusalem, Jerusalem ! You murder the prophets
and stone the messengers that are sent to you. How often
have I longed to gather your children round me like a bird
gathering her brood together under her wings—and you
would never have it. Now all you have left is your house.
I tell you that you will never see me again till the day when
you cry, ' Blessed is He Who comes in the Name of the
Lord ! ' "

Then Jesus went out of the Temple and was walking away
when his disciples came up and drew his attention to its
buildings. " You see all these ? " replied Jesus. " I tell you
every stone will be thrown down till there is not a single
one left standing upon another."

And as he was sitting on the slope of the Mount of Olives
his disciples came to him privately and said, " Tell us, when

will this happen? What will be the signal for your coming and the end of this world?"

"Be careful that no one misleads you," returned Jesus, "for many men will come in my name saying 'I am Christ,' and they will mislead many. You will hear of wars and rumours of wars—but don't be alarmed. Such things must indeed happen, but that is not the end. For one nation will rise in arms against another, and one kingdom against another, and there will be famines and earthquakes in different parts of the world. But all that is only the beginning of the birth-pangs. For then comes the time when men will hand you over to persecution, and kill you. And all nations will hate you because you bear my name. Then comes the time when many will lose their faith and will betray and hate each other. Yes, and many false prophets will arise, and will mislead many people. Because of the spread of wickedness the love of most men will grow cold, though the man who holds out to the end will be saved. This good news of the Kingdom will be proclaimed to men all over the world as a witness to all the nations, and then the end will come.

Jesus prophesises a future of suffering 24 : 15

"When the time comes, then, that you see the 'abomination' of desolation' prophesied by Daniel 'standing in the sacred place'—the reader should note this—then is the time for those in Judaea to escape to the hills. A man on his house-top must not waste time going into his house to collect any-thing; a man at work in the fields must not go back home to fetch his clothes. Alas for the pregnant, alas for those with tiny babies at that time! Pray God that you may not have to make your escape in the winter or on the Sabbath day, for then there will be great misery, such as has never happened from the beginning of the world until now, and will never happen again! Yes, if those days had not been cut short no human being would survive. But for the sake of God's people those days are to be shortened.

"If anyone says to you then, 'Look, here is Christ!' or 'There He is!' don't believe it. False Christs and false prophets are going to appear and will produce great signs and wonders to mislead, if it were possible, even God's own people. Listen, I am warning you. So that if people say to

you, 'There He is, in the desert!' you are not to go out
there. If they say, 'Here He is, in this inner room!' don't
believe it. For as lightning flashes across from east to west
so will the Son of Man's coming be. 'Wherever there is a
dead body, there the vultures will flock.'

At the end of time the Son of Man will return   24 : 29
   " Immediately after the misery of those days the sun will
be darkened, the moon will fail to give her light, the stars
will fall from the sky, and the powers of heaven will be
shaken. Then the Sign of the Son of Man will appear in the
sky, and all the nations of the earth will wring their hands
as they see the Son of Man coming on the clouds of the sky
in power and great splendour. And He will send out His
angels with a loud trumpet-call and they will gather together
His chosen from the four winds—from one end of the
heavens to the other.
   " Learn what the fig-tree can teach you. As soon as its
branches grow full of sap and produce leaves you know that
summer is near. So when you see all these things happening
you may know that He is near, at your very door! Believe
me, this generation will not disappear till all this has taken
place. Earth and sky will pass away, but my words will
never pass away! But about that actual day and time no one
knows—not even the angels of Heaven, nor the Son, only
the Father. For just as life went on in the days of Noah
so will it be at the coming of the Son of Man. In those days
before the Flood people were eating, drinking, marrying
and being given in marriage until the very day that Noah
went into the Ark, and knew nothing about the Flood until
it came and destroyed them all. So will it be at the coming
of the Son of Man. Two men will be in the field; one is
taken and one is left behind. Two women will be grinding
at the hand-mill; one is taken and one is left behind. You
must be on the alert, then, for you do not know when your
Master is coming. You can be sure of this, however, that if
the householder had known what time of night the burglar
would arrive, he would have been ready for him and would
not have allowed his house to be broken into. That is why
you must always be ready, for you do not know what time
the Son of Man will arrive.

Vigilance is essential   24 : 45

"Who then is the faithful and sensible servant, whom his master put in charge of his household to give the others their food at the proper time? Well, he is fortunate if his master finds him doing that duty on his return! Believe me, he will promote him to look after all his property. But if he should be a bad servant who says to himself, 'My master takes his time about returning,' and should begin to beat his fellow-servants and eat and drink with drunkards, that servant's master will return suddenly and unexpectedly, and will punish him severely and send him to share the penalty of the unfaithful—to his bitter sorrow and regret!

"In those days the Kingdom of Heaven will be like ten bridesmaids who took their lamps and went out to meet the bridegroom. Five of them were sensible and five were foolish. The foolish ones took their lamps but did not take any oil with them. But the sensible ones brought their lamps and oil in their flasks as well. Then, as the bridegroom was a very long time, they all grew drowsy and fell asleep. But in the middle of the night there came a shout, 'Wake up, here comes the bridegroom! Out you go to meet him!' Then up got all the bridesmaids and attended to their lamps. The foolish ones said to the sensible ones, 'Please give us some of your oil—our lamps are going out!' 'Oh no,' returned the sensible ones, 'there might not be enough for all of us. Better go to the oil-shop and buy some for yourselves.' But while they had gone off to buy the oil the bridegroom arrived, and those bridesmaids who were ready went in with him for the festivities and the door was shut behind them. Later on the rest of the bridesmaids came and said, 'Oh please, sir, open the door for us!' But he replied, 'I tell you I don't know you!' So be on the alert—for you do not know the day or the time.

Life is hard for the faint-hearted   25 : 14

"It is just like a man going abroad who called his household servants together before he went and handed his property over to them to manage. He gave one five thousand pounds, another two thousand and another one thousand—according to their respective abilities. Then he went away.

"The man who had received five thousand pounds went

out at once and by doing business with this sum he made another five thousand. Similarly the man with two thousand pounds made another two thousand. But the man who had received one thousand pounds went off and dug a hole in the ground and hid his master's money.

"Some years later the master of these servants arrived and went into the accounts with them. The one who had the five thousand pounds came in and brought him an additional five thousand with the words, 'You gave me five thousand pounds, sir; look, I've increased it by another five thousand.' 'Well done!' said his master, 'you're a sound, reliable servant. You've been trustworthy over a few things, now I'm going to put you in charge of much more. Come in and share your master's rejoicing." Then the servant who had received two thousand pounds came in and said, 'You gave me two thousand pounds, sir; look, here's two thousand more that I've managed to make by it.' 'Well done!' said his master, 'you're a sound, reliable servant. You've been trustworthy over a few things, now I'm going to put you in charge of many. Come in and share your master's pleasure.'

"Then the man who had received the one thousand pounds came in and said, 'Sir, I always knew you were a hard man, reaping where you never sowed and collecting where you never laid out—so I was scared and I went off and hid your thousand pounds in the ground. Here is your money, intact.'

"'You're a wicked lazy servant!' his master told him. 'You say you knew that I reap where I never sowed and collect where I never laid out? Then you ought to have put my money in the bank, and when I came I should at any rate have received what belongs to me with interest. Take his thousand pounds away from him and give it to the man who now has the ten thousand!' (For the man who has something will have more given to him and will have plenty. But as for the man who has nothing, even his 'nothing' will be taken away.) 'And throw this useless servant into the darkness outside, where he can weep and wail over his stupidity.'

The final Judgment   25 : 31

"But when the Son of Man comes in his splendour with all his angels with him, then he will take his seat on his glorious throne. All the nations will be assembled before him and he will separate men from each other like a shepherd separating sheep from goats. He will place the sheep on his right hand and the goats on his left.

"Then the King will say to those on his right: 'Come, you who have won my Father's blessing! Take your inheritance—the Kingdom reserved for you since the foundation of the world! For I was hungry and you gave me food. I was thirsty and you gave me a drink. I was lonely and you made me welcome. I was naked and you clothed me. I was ill and you came and looked after me. I was in prison and you came to see me there.'

"Then the true men will answer him, 'Lord, when did we see *you* hungry and give you food? When did we see *you* thirsty and give you something to drink? When did we see *you* lonely and make you welcome, or see *you* naked and clothe you, or see *you* ill or in prison and go to see you?'

"And the King will reply, 'I assure you that whatever you did for the humblest of my brothers you did for me.'

"Then he will say to those on his left, 'Out of my presence, cursed as you are, into the eternal fire prepared for the devil and his angels! For I was hungry and you gave me nothing to eat. I was thirsty and you gave me nothing to drink. I was lonely and you never made me welcome. When I was naked you did nothing to clothe me; when I was sick and in prison you never cared about me.'

"Then they too will answer him, 'Lord, when did we ever see *you* hungry, or thirsty, or lonely, or naked, or sick, or in prison, and fail to look after you?'

"Then the King will answer them with these words, 'I assure you that whatever you failed to do to the humblest of my brothers you failed to do to me.'

"And these will go off to eternal punishment, but the true men to eternal life."

Jesus announces his coming death   26 : 1

When Jesus had finished all this teaching he spoke to his disciples, "Do you realise that the Passover will begin in two days' time; and the Son of Man is going to be betrayed and crucified?"

An evil plot—and an act of love 26 : 3

At that very time the Chief Priests and Elders of the people had assembled in the court of Caiaphas, the High Priest, and were discussing together how they might get hold of Jesus by some trick and kill him. But they kept saying, "It must not be during the Festival or there might be a riot."

Back in Bethany, while Jesus was in the house of Simon the leper, a woman came to him with an alabaster flask of most expensive perfume, and poured it on his head as he was at table. The disciples were indignant when they saw this, and said, "What is the point of such wicked waste? Couldn't this perfume have been sold for a lot of money which could be given to the poor?" Jesus knew what they were saying and spoke to them, "Why must you make this woman feel uncomfortable? She has done a beautiful thing for me. You have the poor with you always, but you will not always have me. When she poured this perfume on my body, she was preparing it for my burial. I assure you that wherever the gospel is preached throughout the whole world, this deed of hers will also be recounted, as her memorial to me."

The betrayal is arranged 26 : 14

After this, one of the Twelve, Judas Iscariot by name, approached the Chief Priests. "What will you give me," he said to them, "if I hand him over to you?" They settled with him for thirty silver coins, and from then on he looked for a convenient opportunity to betray Jesus.

The last supper 26 : 17

On the first day of Unleavened Bread the disciples came to Jesus with the question, "Where do you want us to make our preparations for you to eat the Passover?"

"Go into the city," Jesus replied, "to a certain man there and say to him, 'The Master says, "My time is near. I am going to keep the Passover with my disciples at your house."'" The disciples did as Jesus had instructed them and prepared the Passover. Then late in the evening he took his place at table with the Twelve and during the meal he said, " I tell you plainly that one of you is going to betray me." They were deeply distressed at this and each began to say to him in turn, " Surely, Lord, I am not the one ? " And his answer was, " The man who has dipped his hand into the dish with me is the man who will betray me. It is true that the Son of Man will follow the road foretold by the Scriptures, but alas for the man through whom he is betrayed ! It would be better for that man if he had never been born." And Judas, who actually betrayed him, said, " Master, am I the one ? "

" As you say ! " replied Jesus.

In the middle of the meal Jesus took a loaf and after blessing it he broke it into pieces and gave it to the disciples. " Take and eat this," he said, " it is my body." Then he took a cup and, after thanking God, he gave it to them with the words, " Drink this, all of you, for it is my blood, the blood of the New Agreement shed to set many free from their sins. I tell you I will drink no more wine until I drink it fresh with you in my Father's Kingdom." Then they sang a hymn together and went out to the Mount of Olives. There Jesus said to them, " To-night every one of you will lose his faith in me. For the Scripture says, ' *I will smite the shepherd, and the sheep of the flock shall be scattered abroad.*' But after I have risen I shall go before you into Galilee ! "

At this Peter exclaimed, " Even if everyone should lose his faith in you, I never will ! "

" I tell you, Peter," replied Jesus, " that to-night, before the cock crows, you will disown me three times."

" Even if it means dying with you I will never disown you," said Peter. And all the disciples made the same protest.

The prayer in Gethsemane   26 : 36

Then Jesus came with the disciples to a place called Gethsemane and said to them, " Sit down here while I go over there and pray." Then he took with him Peter and the two sons of Zebedee and began to be in terrible distress and misery. " My heart is nearly breaking," he told them, " stay here and keep watch with me." Then he walked on a little way and fell on his face and prayed, " My Father, if it is possible let this cup pass from me—yet it must not be what I want, but what You want."

Then he came back to the disciples and found them fast asleep. He spoke to Peter, " Couldn't you three keep awake with me for a single hour ? Watch and pray, all of you, that you may not have to face temptation. Your spirit is willing, but human nature is weak."

Then he went away a second time and prayed, " My Father, if it is not possible for this cup to pass from me without my drinking it, then Your Will must be done."

And he came and found them asleep again, for they could not keep their eyes open. So he left them and went away again and prayed for the third time using the same words as before. Then he came back to his disciples and spoke to them, " Are you still going to sleep and take your ease ? In a moment you will see the Son of Man betrayed into the hands of evil men. Wake up, let us be going ! Look, here comes my betrayer ! "

The betrayal   26 : 47

And while the words were still on his lips Judas, one of the Twelve, appeared with a great crowd armed with swords and staves, sent by the Chief Priests and Jewish Elders. (The traitor himself had given them a sign, " The one I kiss will be the man. Get him ! ")

Without any hesitation he walked up to Jesus. " Greetings, Master ! " he cried and kissed him affectionately. " Judas, my friend," replied Jesus, " *why are you here ?* "

Then the others came up, seized hold of Jesus and held him. Suddenly one of Jesus' disciples drew his sword, slashed at the High Priest's servant and cut off his ear. At this Jesus said to him, " Put your sword back into its proper place. All those who take the sword die by the sword. Do you imagine that I could not appeal to my Father, and He would at once send more than twelve legions of angels to defend me ? But then, how would the Scriptures be fulfilled which say that all this must take place ? "

And then Jesus spoke to the crowds around him : " So you've come out with your swords and staves to capture me like a bandit, have you ? Day after day I sat teaching in the Temple and you never laid a finger on me. But all this is happening as the prophets said it would." And at this point all the disciples deserted him and made their escape.

Jesus before the High Priest 26 : 57

The men who had seized Jesus took him off to Caiaphas the High Priest in whose house the Scribes and Elders were assembled. Peter followed him at a safe distance right up to the High Priest's courtyard. Then he went inside and sat down with the servants and waited to see the end.

Meanwhile the Chief Priests and the whole Council did all they could to find false evidence against Jesus to get him condemned to death. They failed completely. Even after a number of perjurers came forward they still failed. In the end two of these stood up and said, " This man said, ' I can pull down the Temple of God and rebuild it in three days.' " Then the High Priest rose to his feet and addressed Jesus, " Have you no answer ? What about the evidence of these men against you ? " But Jesus was silent. Then the High Priest said to him, " I command you by the living God, to tell us on your oath if you are Christ, the Son of God." Jesus said to him, " I am. Yes, and I tell you that in the future you will see the Son of Man sitting at the right hand of Power and coming on the clouds of Heaven."

At this the High Priest tore his robes and cried, " That was blasphemy ! Where is the need for further witnesses ? Look, you've heard the blasphemy—what's your verdict now ? " And they replied, " He deserves to die."

Then they spat in his face and knocked him about, and some slapped him, crying, " Prophesy, you Christ, who was that who hit you ? "

Peter disowns his master 26 : 69

All this time Peter was sitting outside in the courtyard, and a maidservant came up to him and said, " Weren't you with Jesus, the man from Galilee ? " But he denied it before them all, saying, " I don't know what you're talking about." Then when he had gone out into the porch, another maid caught sight of him and said to those who were there, " This man was with Jesus of Nazareth." And again he denied it with an oath—" I don't know the man ! " A few minutes later those who were standing about came up to

Peter and said to him, " You certainly are one of them, you know ; it's obvious from your accent." At that he began to curse and swear—" I tell you I don't know the man ! " Immediately the cock crew, and the words of Jesus came back into Peter's mind—" Before the cock crows you will disown me three times." And he went outside and wept bitterly.

When the morning came, all the Chief Priests and Elders of the people met in council to decide how they could get Jesus executed. Then they marched him off with his hands tied, and handed him over to Pilate the Governor.

The remorse of Judas   27 : 3

Then Judas, who had betrayed him, saw that he was condemned and in his remorse returned the thirty silver coins to the Chief Priests and Elders, with the words, " I was wrong—I have betrayed an innocent man to death."

" And what has that got to do with us ? " they replied. " That's your affair."

And Judas flung down the silver in the Temple and went outside and hanged himself. But the Chief Priests picked up the money and said, " It is not legal to put this into the Temple treasury. It is, after all, blood-money." So, after a further consultation, they purchased with it the Potter's Field to be a burial-ground for foreigners, which is why it is called " the Field of Blood " to this day. And so the words of Jeremiah the prophet came true :

> And they took the thirty pieces of silver, the price of him that was priced, whom certain of the children of Israel did price ; and they gave them for the potter's field, as the Lord appointed me.

Jesus before Pilate   27 : 11

Meanwhile Jesus stood in front of the Governor, who asked him, " Well, you—*are* you the King of the Jews ? " " Yes, I am," replied Jesus.

But while the Chief Priests and Elders were making their accusations, he made no reply at all. So Pilate said to him, " Can you not hear the evidence they're bringing against you?" And to the Governor's amazement, Jesus did not answer a single one of their accusations.

Now it was the custom at festival-time for the Governor to release any prisoner whom the people chose. And it happened that at this time they had a notorious prisoner called Barabbas. So when they assembled to make their usual request, Pilate said to them, "Which one do you want me to see free, Barabbas or Jesus called Christ?" For he knew very well that the latter had been handed over to him through sheer malice. And indeed while he was actually sitting on the Bench his wife sent a message to him—"Don't have anything to do with that good man! I went through agonies dreaming about him last night!" But the Chief Priests and Elders persuaded the mob to ask for Barabbas and demand Jesus' execution. Then the Governor spoke to them, "Which of these two are you asking me to release?"

"Barabbas!" they cried.

"Then what am I to do with Jesus who is called Christ?" asked Pilate.

"Have him crucified!" they all cried. At this Pilate said, "Why, what is his crime?" But their voices rose to a roar, "Have him crucified!" When Pilate realised that nothing more could be done but that there would soon be a riot, he took a bowl of water and washed his hands before the crowd, saying, "I take no responsibility for the death of this man. You must see to that yourselves." To this the whole crowd replied, "Let his blood be on us and on our children!" Whereupon Pilate released Barabbas for them, but he had Jesus flogged and handed over for crucifixion.

Then the Governor's soldiers took Jesus into the Governor's palace and collected the whole guard around him. There they stripped him and put a scarlet cloak upon him. They twisted some thorn-twigs into a crown and put it on his head and put a stick into his right hand. They bowed low before him and jeered at him with the words, "Hail, Your Majesty, King of the Jews!" Then they spat on him, took the stick and hit him on the head with it. And when they had finished their fun, they stripped the cloak off again, put his own clothes upon him and led him off for crucifixion. On their way out of the city they met a man called Simon, a native of Cyrene in Africa, and they compelled him to carry Jesus' cross.

The Crucifixion   27 : 33

Then when they came to a place called Golgotha (which means Skull Hill) they offered him a drink of wine mixed with some bitter drug, but when he had tasted it he refused to drink. And when they had nailed him to the cross they shared out his clothes by drawing lots.

Then they sat down to keep guard over him. And over his head they put a placard with the charge against him :

THIS IS JESUS, THE KING OF THE JEWS

Now two bandits were crucified with Jesus at the same time, one on each side of him. The passers-by nodded their heads knowingly and called out to him in mockery, " Hi, you who could pull down the Temple and build it up again in three days—why don't you save yourself ? If you are the Son of God, step down from the cross ! " The Chief Priests also joined the Scribes and Elders in jeering at him, saying, " He saved others, but he can't save himself ! If this is the King of Israel, why doesn't he come down from the cross now, and we will believe him ! He trusted in God . . . let God rescue him if He will have anything to do with him ! For he said, ' I am God's son.' " Even the bandits who were crucified with him hurled abuse at him.

Then from midday until three o'clock darkness spread over the whole countryside, and then Jesus cried with a loud voice, " My God, my God, why did You forsake me ? " Some of those who were standing there heard these words which Jesus spoke in Aramaic (*Eli, Eli lama sabachthani ?*), and said, " This man is calling for Elijah ! " And one of them ran off and fetched a sponge, soaked it in vinegar and put it on a long stick and held it up for him to drink. But the others said, " Let him alone ! Let's see if Elijah will come and save him." But Jesus gave one more great cry, and died.

And the sanctuary curtain in the Temple was torn in two from top to bottom. The ground shook, rocks split and graves were opened. (A number of bodies of holy men who were asleep in death rose again. They left their graves after

Jesus' resurrection and entered the Holy City and appeared to many people.) When the centurion and his company who were keeping guard over Jesus saw the earthquake and all that was happening they were terrified. " Indeed he *was* a son of God ! " they said.

There were many women at the scene watching from a distance. They had followed Jesus from Galilee to minister to his needs. Among them was Mary of Magdala, Mary the mother of James and Joseph, and the mother of Zebedee's sons.

Jesus is buried and the tomb is guarded   27 : 57

That evening, Joseph, a wealthy man from Arimathaea, who was himself a disciple of Jesus, went to Pilate and asked for the body of Jesus, and Pilate gave orders for the body to be handed over to him. So Joseph took it, wrapped it in clean linen and placed it in his own new tomb which had been hewn in the rock. Then he rolled a large stone across the doorway of the tomb and went away. But Mary from Magdala and the other Mary remained there, sitting in front of the tomb.

Next day, which was the day after the Preparation, the Chief Priests and the Pharisees went in a body to Pilate and said, " Sir, we have remembered that while this impostor was alive, he said, ' After three days I shall rise again.' Will you give the order then to have the grave closely guarded until the third day, so that there can be no chance of his disciples' coming and stealing the body and telling people that he has risen from the dead ? We should then be faced with a worse fraud than the first one."

" You have a guard," Pilate told them. " Go and make it as safe as you think necessary." And they went and made the grave secure, putting a seal on the stone and leaving the soldiers on guard.

The first Lord's Day : Jesus rises   28 : 1

When the Sabbath was over, just as the first day of the week was dawning, Mary from Magdala and the other Mary went to look at the tomb. At that moment there was a great earthquake, for an angel of the Lord came down from Heaven, went forward and rolled back the stone, and took his seat upon it. His appearance was dazzling like lightning and his clothes were white as snow. The guards shook with terror at the sight of him and collapsed like dead men. But the angel spoke to the women, " Do not be afraid. I know that you are looking for Jesus Who was crucified. He is not here—He is risen, just as He said He would. Come and look at the place where He was lying. Then go quickly and tell His disciples that He has risen from the dead. And, listen, He goes before you into Galilee! You will see Him there! Now I have told you my message." Then the women went away quickly from the tomb, their hearts filled with awe and great joy, and ran to give the news to His disciples. But quite suddenly, Jesus stood before them in their path, and said, " Peace be with you!" And they went forward to meet Him and, clasping His feet, worshipped Him. Then Jesus said to them, " Do not be afraid. Go now and tell My brothers to go into Galilee and they shall see Me there."

And while they were on their way, some of the sentries went into the city and reported to the Chief Priests everything that had happened. They got together with the Elders, and after consultation gave the soldiers a considerable sum of money and told them, " Your story must be that his disciples came after dark, and stole him away while you were asleep. If by any chance this reaches the Governor's ears, we will put it right with him and see that you do not suffer for it." So they took the money and obeyed their instructions. The story was spread and is current among the Jews to this day.

Jesus gives His final commission   28 : 16

But the Eleven went to the hill-side in Galilee where Jesus had arranged to meet them, and when they had seen Him they worshipped Him, though some of them were doubtful. But Jesus came and spoke these words to them : " All power in Heaven and on earth has been given to Me. You, then, are to go and make disciples of all the nations and baptise them in the Name of the Father and of the Son and of the Holy Spirit. Teach them to observe all that I have commanded you and, remember, I am with you always, even to the end of the world."

THE GOSPEL OF
MARK

It is generally agreed that Mark's Gospel is the earliest. It probably appeared in 65, soon after the Great Fire of Rome which devastated a great part of the city in the winter of 64-65. The Christians were made the scapegoats of this disaster by the Emperor Nero, and it is quite probable that there is a definite connection between the appearance of this first-written Gospel and the monstrously false accusations which were being made against Christians. The original papyrus roll is traditionally supposed to have borne the title—" The Gospel of Jesus Christ the Son of God."

The author is generally thought to have been John Mark, a native of Jerusalem. The house of his mother Mary became one of the meeting places of the early Christians (Acts 12, 12). It has been suggested that perhaps John Mark is the mysterious young man who escaped from the soldiers' hands on the night of Jesus' arrest (Mark 14, 51). He is also linked with the early growth of the Church, working with Paul, Barnabas and Peter.

Eusebius, the fourth-century historian, quotes Papias (who wrote about 140) as saying that Mark was the " interpreter of Peter," and this seems to have been generally accepted by the early Church.

We may therefore reasonably assume that Mark, drawing on what Peter had told him personally, and being himself convinced of the Divinity of Christ, wrote down this Gospel, probably at Rome, with non-Jewish readers in mind. We notice, for instance, that he hardly quotes at all from the Old Testament, that he explains particular Jewish customs and that he translates any Aramaic expression by its Greek equivalent.

His style has no literary polish but it has the forceful vitality of the man who believes what he writes, and it is not without certain vivid flashes of realism. He draws with strong lines the portrait of a Man Who was thoroughly human but also unmistakably the Son of God.

The manuscript of Mark ends abruptly at 16, 8, and nearly all scholars regard the subsequent verses as a later addition.

How it began

The Gospel of Jesus Christ, the Son of God, begins with the fulfilment of this prophecy of Isaiah :

> Behold, I send my messenger before thy face,
> Who shall prepare thy way ;
> The voice of one crying in the wilderness,
> Make ye ready the way of the Lord,
> Make his paths straight.

For John came and began to baptize men in the desert, proclaiming baptism as the mark of a complete change of heart and of the forgiveness of sins. All the people of the Judean countryside and everyone in Jerusalem went out to him in the desert and received his baptism in the river Jordan, publicly confessing their sins.

John himself was dressed in camel-hair, with a leather belt round his waist, and he lived on locusts and wild honey. The burden of his preaching was, " There is someone coming after me who is stronger than I—indeed I am not good enough to kneel down and undo his shoes. I have baptized you with water, but he will baptize you with the Holy Spirit."

The arrival of Jesus   1 : 9

It was in those days that Jesus arrived from the Galilean village of Nazareth and was baptized by John in the Jordan. All at once, as he came up out of the water, he saw the heavens split open, and the Spirit coming down upon him like a dove. A Voice came out of Heaven, saying :

" You are My dearly-loved Son, in Whom I am well pleased ! "

Then the Spirit sent him out at once into the desert, and there he remained for forty days while Satan tempted him. During this time, no one was with him but wild animals, and only the angels were there to care for him.

Jesus begins to preach the gospel, and to call men to   1 : 14
follow him

It was after John's arrest that Jesus came into Galilee, proclaiming the Gospel of God, saying :

" The time has come at last—the Kingdom of God has

arrived. You must change your hearts and minds and believe the Good News."

As he walked along the shore of the Lake of Galilee, he saw two fishermen, Simon and his brother Andrew, casting their nets into the water.

"Come and follow me, and I will teach you to catch men!" he cried.

At once they dropped their nets, and followed him.

Then he went a little farther along the shore and saw James the son of Zebedee, aboard a boat with his brother John, overhauling their nets. At once he called them, and they left their father Zebedee in the boat with the hired men, and went off after him.

Jesus begins healing the sick   1 : 21

They arrived at Capernaum, and on the Sabbath day Jesus walked straight into the synagogue and began teaching. They were amazed at his way of teaching, for he taught with the ring of authority—quite unlike the Scribes. All at once, a man in the grip of an evil spirit appeared in the synagogue shouting out:

"What have you got to do with us, Jesus from Nazareth? Have you come to kill us? I know who you are—you're God's Holy one!"

But Jesus cut him short and spoke sharply:

"Hold your tongue and get out of him!"

At this the evil spirit convulsed the man, let out a loud scream and left him. Everyone present was so astounded that people kept saying to each other:

"What on earth has happened? This new teaching has authority behind it, Why, he even gives his orders to evil spirits and they obey him!"

And his reputation spread like wild-fire through the whole Galilean district.

Then he got up and went straight from the synagogue to the house of Simon and Andrew, accompanied by James and John. Simon's mother-in-law was in bed with a high fever, and they lost no time in telling Jesus about her. He went up to her, took her hand and helped her to her feet. The fever left her, and she began to see to their needs.

Late that evening, after sunset, they kept bringing to him

all who were sick or troubled by evil spirits. The whole
population of the town gathered round the doorway. And
he healed great numbers of people who were suffering from
various forms of disease. In many cases he expelled evil
spirits; but he would not allow them to say a word, for
they knew perfectly well who he was.

He retires for private prayer   I : 35

Then, in the early morning, while it was still dark, Jesus
got up, left the house and went off to a deserted place, and
there he prayed. Simon and his companions went in search
of him, and when they found him, they said :

" Everyone is looking for you."

" Then we will go somewhere else, to the neighbouring
towns," he replied, " so that I may give my message there
too—that is why I have come."

So he continued preaching in their synagogues and
expelling evil spirits throughout the whole of Galilee.

Jesus cures leprosy   I : 40

Then a leper came to Jesus, knelt in front of him and
appealed to him :

" If you want to, you can make me clean."

Jesus was filled with pity for him, and stretched out his
hand and placed it on the leper, saying :

" Of course I want to—be clean ! "

At once the leprosy left him and he was quite clean. Jesus
sent him away there and then, with the strict injunction :

" Mind you say nothing at all to anybody. Go straight
off and show yourself to the priest, and make the offerings
for your cleansing which Moses prescribed, as public proof
of your recovery."

But he went off and began to talk a great deal about it in
public, spreading his story far and wide. Consequently, it
became impossible for Jesus to show his face in the towns
and he had to stay outside in lonely places. Yet the people
still came to him from all quarters.

Faith at Capernaum   2 : 1

When he re-entered Capernaum some days later, a rumour
spread that he was in somebody's house. Such a large crowd

collected that while he was giving them his message it was impossible even to get near the doorway. Meanwhile a group of people arrived to see him, bringing with them a paralytic whom four of them were carrying. And when they found it was impossible to get near him because of the crowd, they removed the tiles from the roof over Jesus' head and let down the paralytic's bed through the opening. And when Jesus saw their faith, he said to the man on the bed:

"My son, your sins are forgiven."

But some of the Scribes were sitting their silently asking themselves:

"Why does this man talk such blasphemy? Who can possibly forgive sins but God?"

Jesus realised instantly what they were thinking, and said to them:

"Why must you argue like this in your minds? Which do you suppose is easier—to say to a paralysed man, 'Your sins are forgiven,' or 'Get up, pick up your bed and walk'? But to prove to you that the Son of Man has full authority to forgive sins on earth, I say to you,"—and here he spoke to the paralytic—"Get up, pick up your bed and go home."

At once the man sprang to his feet, picked up his bed and walked off in full view of them all. Everyone was amazed, praised God and said:

"We have never seen anything like this before."

Then Jesus went out again by the lake-side and the whole crowd came to him, and he continued to teach them.

Jesus now calls " a sinner " to follow him　　　2 : 14

As Jesus went on his way, he saw Levi the son of Alphaeus sitting at his desk in the tax-office, and he said to him:

"Follow me!"

Levi got up and followed him. Later, when Jesus was sitting at dinner in Levi's house, a large number of tax-collectors and disreputable folk came in and joined him and his disciples. For there were many such people among his followers. When the Scribes and Pharisees saw him eating in the company of tax-collectors and outsiders, they remarked to his disciples:

"Why does he eat with tax-collectors and sinners?"

When Jesus heard this, he said to them:

" It is not the fit and flourishing who need the doctor, but those who are ill. I did not come to invite the ' righteous,' but the ' sinners.' ''

The question of fasting   2 : 18

The disciples of John and those of the Pharisees were fasting. They came and said to Jesus :

" Why do those who follow John or the Pharisees keep fasts but your disciples do nothing of the kind ? "

Jesus told them :

" Can you expect wedding-guests to fast in the bride-groom's presence ? Fasting is out of the question as long as they have the bridegroom with them. But the day will come when the bridegroom will be taken away from them—that will be the time for them to fast.

" Nobody," he continued, " sews a patch of unshrunken cloth on to an old coat. If he does, the new patch tears away from the old and the hole is worse than ever. And nobody puts new wine into old wineskins. If he does, the new wine bursts the skins, the wine is spilt and the skins are ruined. No, new wine must go into new wineskins."

Jesus rebukes the Sabbatarians   2 : 23

One day he happened to be going through the corn-fields on the Sabbath day. And his disciples, as they made their way along, began to pick the ears of corn. The Pharisees said to him :

" Look at that ! Why should they do what is forbidden on the Sabbath day ? "

Then he spoke to them :

" Have you never read what David did, when he and his companions were hungry ? Haven't you read how he went into the House of God when Abiathar was High Priest, and ate the Presentation Loaves, which nobody is allowed to eat, except the priests—and gave some of the bread to his com-panions ? The Sabbath," he continued, " was made for man's sake ; man was not made for the sake of the Sabbath. That is why the Son of Man is master even of the Sabbath."

On another occasion when he went into the synagogue, there was a man there whose hand was shrivelled, and they were watching Jesus closely to see whether he would heal him on the Sabbath day, so that they might bring a charge against him. Jesus said to the man with the shrivelled hand:

"Stand up and come out here in front!"

Then he said to them:

"Is it right to do good on the Sabbath day, or to do harm? Is it right to save life or to kill?"

There was a dead silence. Then Jesus, deeply hurt as he sensed their inhumanity, looked round in anger at the faces surrounding him, and said to the man:

"Stretch out your hand!"

And he stretched it out, and the hand was restored as sound as the other one. The Phrarisees walked straight out and discussed with Herod's party how they could have Jesus put out of the way.

Jesus' enormous popularity   3 : 7

Jesus now retired to the lake-side with his disciples. A huge crowd of people followed him, not only from Galilee, but from Judaea, Jerusalem and Idumaea, some from the district beyond the Jordan and from the neighbourhood of Tyre and Sidon. This vast crowd came to him because they had heard about the sort of things he was doing. So Jesus told his disciples to have a small boat kept in readiness for him, in case the people should crowd him too closely. For he healed so many people that all those who were in pain kept pressing forward to touch him with their hands. Evil spirits, as soon as they saw him, acknowledged his authority and screamed:

"You are the Son of God!"

But he warned them repeatedly that they must not make him known.

Jesus chooses the twelve apostles   3 : 13

Later he went up on to the hill-side and summoned the men whom he wanted, and they went up to him. He appointed a band of Twelve to be his companions, whom he could send out to preach, with power to drive out evil spirits. These were the Twelve he appointed:

Peter (which was the new name he gave Simon), James the son of Zebedee, and John his brother. (He gave them the name of Boanerges, which means the "Thunderers.")

Andrew, Philip, Bartholomew, Matthew, Thomas, James
the son of Alphaeus, Thaddaeus, Simon the Patriot, and
Judas Iscariot, who betrayed him.

Jesus exposes an absurd accusation   3 : 20

Then he went indoors, but again such a crowd collected
that it was impossible for them even to eat a meal. When
his relatives heard of this, they set out to take charge of him,
for people were saying, " He must be mad ! "

The Scribes who had come down from Jerusalem were
saying that he was possessed by Beelzebub, and that he drove
out devils because he was in league with the prince of devils.
So Jesus called them to him and spoke to them in a parable :

" How can Satan be the one who drives out Satan ? If a
kingdom is divided against itself, then that kingdom cannot
last, and if a household is divided against itself, it cannot last
either. And if Satan leads a rebellion against Satan—his days
are certainly numbered. No one can break into a strong
man's house and steal his property, without first tying up
the strong man hand and foot. But if he did that, he could
ransack the whole house.

" Believe me, all men's sins can be forgiven and all their
blasphemies. But there can never be any forgiveness for
blasphemy against the Holy Spirit. That is an eternal sin."

He said this because they were saying, " He is in the
power of an evil spirit."

The new relationships in the Kingdom   3 : 31

Then his mother and his brothers arrived. They stood
outside the house and sent a message asking him to come
out to them. There was a crowd sitting round him when the
message was brought telling him, " Your mother and your
brothers are outside looking for you."

Jesus replied, " And who are really my mother and my
brothers ? "

And he looked round at the faces of those sitting in a circle
about him.

" Look ! " he said, " my mother and my brothers are here.
Anyone who does the Will of God is brother and sister and
mother to me."

The story of the sower   4 : 1

Then once again he began to teach them by the lake-side.
A bigger crowd than ever collected around him, so that he
got into the little boat on the lake and sat down, while the
crowd covered the ground right up to the water's edge. He
taught them a great deal in parables, and in the course of his
teaching he said :

" Listen ! A man once went out to sow his seed and as
he sowed, some seed fell by the roadside and the birds came
and gobbled it up. Some of the seed fell among the rocks
where there was not much soil, and sprang up very quickly
because there was no depth of earth. But when the sun rose,
it was scorched and because it had no root, it withered away.
And some of the seed fell among thorn-bushes and the thorns
grew up and choked the life out of it, and it bore no crop.
And there was some seed which fell on good soil, and when
it grew, produced a crop which yielded thirty or sixty or
even a hundred times as much as the seed."

Then he added :

" Every man who has ears should use them ! "

Then when they were by themselves, his close followers
and the Twelve asked him about the parables, and he told
them :

" The secret of the Kingdom of God has been given to
you. But to those who do not know the secret, everything
remains in parables, so that,

seeing they may see, and not percceive ;
and hearing they may hear, and not understand ;
lest haply they should turn again, and it should be forgiven
      them."

Then he continued :

" Do you really not understand this parable ? Then how
are you going to understand all the other parables ? The
man who sows sows the message. As for those who are by
the roadside where the message is sown, as soon as they hear
it Satan comes at once and takes away what has been sown
in their minds. Similarly, the seed sown among the rocks
represents those who hear the message without hesitation
and accept it joyfully. But they have no real roots and do

not last—when trouble or persecution arises because of the message, they give up their faith at once. Then there are the seeds which were sown among thorn-bushes. These are the people who hear the message, but the worries of this world and the false glamour of riches and all sorts of other ambitions creep in and choke the life out of what they have heard, and it produces no crop in their lives. As for the seed sown on good soil this means the men who hear the message and accept it and do produce a crop—thirty, sixty, even a hundred times as much as they received."

Truth is meant to be used   4 : 21

Then he said to them :

" Is a lamp brought into the room to be put under a bucket or underneath the bed ? Surely its place is on the lamp-stand ! There is nothing hidden which is not meant to be made perfectly plain one day, and there are no secrets which are not meant one day to be common knowledge. If a man has ears he should use them !

" Be careful how you listen," he said to them. " Whatever measure you use will be used towards you, and even more than that. For the man who has something will receive more. As for the man who has nothing, even his nothing will be taken away."

Jesus gives pictures of the Kingdom's growth   4 : 26

Then he said :

" The Kingdom of God is like a man scattering seed on the ground and then going to bed each night and getting up every morning, while the seed sprouts and grows up, though he has no idea how it happens. The earth produces a crop without any help from anyone : first a blade, then the ear of corn, then the full-grown grain in the ear. And as soon as the crop is ready, he sends his reapers in without delay, for the harvest-time has come."

Then he continued :

" What can we say the Kingdom of God is like ? How shall we put it in a parable ? It is like a tiny grain of mustard-seed which, when it is sown, is smaller than any seed that is ever sown. But after it is sown in the earth, it grows up and becomes bigger than any other plant. It shoots out

great branches so that birds can come and nest in its
shelter."

So he taught them his message with many parables such
as their minds could take in. He did not speak to them at
all without using parables, although in private he explained
everything to his disciples.

Jesus shows himself master of natural forces   4 : 35

On the evening of that day, he said to them :

" Let us cross over to the other side of the lake."

So they sent the crowd home and took him with them in
the little boat in which he had been sitting, accompanied by
other small craft. Then came a violent squall of wind which
drove the waves aboard the boat until it was almost swamped.
Jesus was in the stern asleep on the cushion. They awoke
him with the words :

" Master, don't you care that we're drowning ? "

And he woke up, rebuked the wind, and said to the waves :
" Hush now ! Be still ! "

The wind dropped and everything was very still.

" Why are you so frightened ? What has happened to
your faith ? " he asked them.

But sheer awe swept over them, and they kept saying to
each other :

" Who ever can he be ?—even the wind and the waves do
what he tells them ! "

Jesus meets a violent lunatic   5 : 1

So they arrived on the other side of the lake in the country
of the Gerasenes. As Jesus was getting out of the boat, a
man in the grip of an evil spirit rushed out to meet him from
among the tombs where he was living. It was no longer
possible for any human being to restrain him even with a
chain. Indeed he had frequently been secured with fetters
and lengths of chain, but he had simply snapped the chains
and broken the fetters in pieces. No one could do anything
with him. All through the night as well as in the day-time
he screamed among the tombs and on the hillside, and cut
himself with stones. Now, as soon as he saw Jesus in the
distance, he ran and knelt before him, yelling at the top of
his voice :

"What have you got to do with me, Jesus, Son of the Most High God? For God's sake, don't torture me!"

For Jesus had already said, "Come out of this man, you evil spirit!"

Then he asked him:

"What is your name?"

"My name is Legion," he replied, "for there are many of us."

Then he begged and prayed him not to send "them" out of the country.

A large herd of pigs was grazing there on the hill-side, and the evil spirits implored him, "Send us over to the pigs and we'll get into them!"

So Jesus allowed them to do this, and they came out of the man, made off and went into the pigs. The whole herd of about two thousand stampeded down the cliff into the lake and was drowned. The swineherds took to their heels and spread their story in the city and all over the countryside. Then the people came to see what had happened. As they approached Jesus, they saw the man who had been devil-possessed sitting there properly clothed and perfectly sane—the same man who had been possessed by "Legion"—and they were really frightened. Those who had seen the incident told them what had happened to the devil-possessed man and about the disaster to the pigs. Then they began to implore Jesus to leave their district. As he was embarking on the small boat, the man who had been possessed begged that he might go with him. But Jesus would not allow this.

"Go home to your own people," he told him, "and tell them what the Lord has done for you, and how kind he has been to you!"

So the man went off and began to spread throughout the Ten Towns the story of what Jesus had done for him. And they were all simply amazed.

Faith is followed by healing   5 : 21

When Jesus had crossed again in the boat to the other side of the lake, a great crowd collected around him as he stood on the shore. Then came a man called Jairus, one of the synagogue presidents. And when he saw Jesus, he knelt before him, pleading desperately for his help.

" My little girl is dying," he said. " Will you come and put your hands on her—then she will get better and live."

Jesus went off with him, followed by a large crowd jostling at his elbow. Among them was a woman who had had a hæmorrhage for twelve years and who had gone through a great deal at the hands of many doctors, spending all her money in the process. She had derived no benefit from them but, on the contrary, was getting worse. This woman had heard about Jesus and came up behind him under cover of the crowd, and touched his cloak :

" For if I can only touch his clothes," she kept saying, " I shall be all right."

The hæmorrhage stopped immediately, and she knew in herself that she was cured of her trouble. At once Jesus knew intuitively that power had gone out of him, and he turned round in the middle of the crowd and said :

" Who touched my clothes ? "

His disciples replied :

" You can see this crowd jostling you. How can you ask, ' Who touched me ' ? "

But he looked all round at their faces to see who had done so. Then the woman, scared and shaking all over because she knew that she was the one to whom this thing had happened, came and flung herself before him and told him the whole story. But he said to her :

" Daughter, it is your faith that has healed you. Go home in peace, and be free from your trouble."

While he was speaking, messengers arrived from the synagogue president's house, saying :

" Your daughter is dead—there is no need to bother the Master any further."

But when Jesus heard this, he said :

" Now don't be afraid, just go on believing ! "

Then he allowed no one to follow him except Peter and James and John, James's brother. They arrived at the president's house and Jesus noticed the hubbub and all the weeping and wailing, and as he went in, he said to the people of the house :

" Why are you making such a noise with your crying ? The child is not dead ; she is fast asleep."

They greeted this with a scornful laugh. But Jesus turned

them all out, and taking only the father and mother and his own companions with him, went into the room where the child was. Then he took the little girl's hand and said to her in Aramaic :

" Little girl, I tell you to get up ! "

At once she jumped to her feet and walked round the room, for she was twelve years old. This sight sent the others nearly out of their minds with joy. But Jesus gave them strict instructions not to let anyone know what had happened—and ordered food to be given to the little girl.

The " prophet without honour "   6 : 1

Then he left that district and came into his own native town, followed by his disciples. When the Sabbath day came, he began to teach in the synagogue. The congregation were astonished and remarked :

" Where does he get all this ? What is this wisdom that he has been given—and what about these marvellous things that he can do ? He's only the carpenter, Mary's son, the brother of James, Joses, Judas and Simon ; and his sisters are living here with us ! "

And they were deeply offended with him. But Jesus said to them :

" No prophet goes unhonoured—except in his native town or with his own relations or in his own home ! "

And he could do nothing miraculous there apart from laying his hands on a few sick people and healing them ; their lack of faith astonished him.

The Twelve are sent out to preach the gospel   6 : 6b

Then he made his way round the villages, continuing his teaching. He summoned the Twelve, and began to send them out in twos, giving them power over evil spirits. He instructed them to take nothing for the road except a staff— no satchel, no bread and no money in their pockets. They were to wear sandals and not to take more than one coat. And he told them :

" Wherever you are, when you go into a house, stay there until you leave that place. And wherever people will not welcome you or listen to what you have to say, leave them and shake the dust off your feet as a protest against them!"

So they went out and preached that men should change their whole outlook. They expelled many evil spirits and anointed many sick people with oil and healed them.

Herod's guilty conscience 6 : 14

All this came to the ears of King Herod, for Jesus' reputation was spreading, and people were saying that John the Baptist had risen from the dead, and that was why he was showing such miraculous powers. Others maintained that he was Elijah, and others that he was one of the prophets of the old days come back again. But when Herod heard of all this, he said:

"It must be John whom I beheaded, risen from the dead!"

For Herod himself had sent and arrested John and had him bound in prison, all on account of Herodias, wife of his brother Philip. He had married her, though John used to say to Herod, "It is not right for you to possess your own brother's wife." Herodias herself was furious with him for this and wanted to have him executed, but she could not do it, for Herod had a deep respect for John, knowing that he was a just and holy man, and protected him. He used to listen to him and be profoundly disturbed, and yet he enjoyed hearing him.

Then a good opportunity came, for Herod gave a birthday party for his courtiers and army commanders and for the leading people in Galilee. Herodias' daughter came in and danced, to the great delight of Herod and his guests. The king said to the girl:

"Ask me anything you like and I will give it to you!"

And he swore to her:

"I will give you whatever you ask me, up to half of my kingdom!"

And she went out and spoke to her mother:

"What shall I ask for?"

And she said:

"*The head of John the Baptist!*"

The girl rushed back to the king's presence, and made her request.

"I want you to give me, this minute, the head of John the Baptist on a dish!" she said.

Herod was aghast, but because of his oath and the presence of his guests, he did not like to refuse her. So he sent one of the palace guardsmen straight away to bring him John's head. He went off and beheaded him in the prison, brought back his head on the dish, and gave it to the girl who handed it to her mother. When his disciples heard what had happened, they came and took away the body and put it in a tomb.

The Apostles return : the huge crowds make rest impossible 6 : 30

The Apostles returned to Jesus and reported to him every detail of what they had done and taught.

"Now come along to some quiet place by yourselves, and rest for a little while," said Jesus, for there were people coming and going incessantly so that they had not even time for meals. They went off in the boat to a quiet place by themselves, but a great many saw them go and recognised them, and people from all the towns hurried around the shore on foot to forestall them. When Jesus disembarked he saw the large crowd and his heart was touched with pity for them because they seemed to him like sheep without a shepherd. And he settled down to teach them about many things. As the day wore on, his disciples came to him and said :

"We are right in the wilds here and it is getting late. Let them go now, so that they can buy themselves something to eat from the farms and villages around here."

But Jesus replied :

"You give them something to eat!"

"You mean we're to go and spend ten pounds on bread? Is that how you want us to feed them?"

"What bread have you got?" asked Jesus. "Go and have a look."

And when they had found out, they told him :

"We have five loaves and two fish."

Jesus miraculously feeds five thousand people   6 : 39

Then Jesus directed the people to sit down in parties on the fresh grass. And they threw themselves down in groups of fifty and a hundred. Then Jesus took the five loaves and the two fish, and looking up to Heaven, thanked God, broke the loaves and gave them to the disciples to distribute to the people. And he divided the two fish among them all. Everybody ate and was satisfied. Afterwards they collected twelve baskets full of pieces of bread and fish that were left over. There were five thousand men who ate the loaves.

Jesus' mastery over natural law   6 : 45

Directly after this, Jesus made his disciples get aboard the boat and go on ahead to Bethsaida on the other side of the lake, while he himself sent the crowds home. And when he had sent them all on their way, he went off to the hill-side to pray. When it grew late, the boat was in the middle of the lake, and he was by himself on land. He saw them straining at the oars, for the wind was dead against them. And in the small hours he went towards them, walking on the waters of the lake, intending to come alongside them. But when they saw him walking on the water, they thought he was a ghost, and screamed out. For they all saw him and they were absolutely terrified. But Jesus at once spoke quietly to them :

" It's all right, it is I myself; don't be afraid ! "

And he climbed aboard the boat with them, and the wind dropped. But they were scared out of their wits. They had not had the sense to learn the lesson of the loaves. Even that miracle had not opened their eyes to see who he was.

And when they had crossed over to the other side of the lake, they landed at Gennesaret and tied up there. As soon as they came ashore, the people recognised Jesus and rushed all over the country-side and began to carry the sick around on their beds to wherever they heard that he was. Wherever he went, in villages or towns or farms, they laid down their sick right in the road-way and begged him that they might " just touch the edge of his cloak." And all those who touched him were healed.

Jesus exposes the danger of man-made traditions   7 : 1

And now Jesus was approached by the Pharisees and some of the Scribes who had come from Jerusalem. They had noticed that his disciples ate their meals with " common " hands—meaning that they had not gone through a ceremonial washing. (The Pharisees, and indeed all the Jews, will never eat unless they have washed their hands in a particular way, following a traditional rule. And they will not eat anything bought in the market until they have first performed their " sprinkling." And there are many other things which they consider important, concerned with the washing of cups, jugs and basins.) So the Pharisees and the Scribes put this question to Jesus :

" Why do your disciples refuse to follow the ancient tradition, and eat their bread with ' common ' hands ? "

Jesus replied:

" You hypocrites, Isaiah described you beautifully when he wrote :

This people honoureth me with their lips,
But their heart is far from me.
But in vain do they worship me,
Teaching as doctrines the precepts of men.

You are so busy holding on to the traditions of men that you let go the Commandment of God ! "

Then he went on :

" It is wonderful to see how you can set aside the Commandment of God to preserve your own tradition ! For Moses said, ' *Honour thy father and thy mother* ' and ' *He that speaketh evil of father or mother, let him die the death.*' But you say, ' if a man says to his father or his mother, Korban— meaning, I have given God whatever duty I owed to you,' then he need not lift a finger any longer for his father or mother, so making the Word of God invalid for the sake of the tradition which you hold. And this is typical of much of what you do."

Then he called the crowd close to him again, and spoke to them :

" Listen to me now, all of you, and understand this. There is nothing outside a man which can enter into him and make him ' common.' It is the things which come out of a man that make him ' common ' ! "

Later, when he had gone indoors away from the crowd, his disciples asked him about this parable.

" Oh, are you as dull as they are ? " he said. " Can't you see that anything that goes into a man from outside cannot make him ' common ' or unclean ? You see, it doesn't go into his heart, but into his stomach, and passes out of the body altogether, so that all food is clean enough. But," he went on, " whatever comes out of a man, that is what makes a man ' common ' or unclean. For it is from inside, from men's hearts and minds, that evil thoughts arise—lust, theft, murder, adultery, greed, wickedness, deceit, sensuality, envy, slander, arrogance and folly ! All these evil things come from inside a man and make him unclean ! "

The faith of a Gentile is rewarded   7 : 24

Then he got up and left that place and went off to the neighbourhood of Tyre. There he went into a house and wanted no one to know where he was. But it proved impossible to remain hidden. For no sooner had he got there, than a woman who had heard about him, and who had a daughter possessed by an evil spirit, arrived and prostrated herself before him. She was a Greek, a Syrophoenician by birth, and she asked him to drive the evil spirit out of her daughter. Jesus said to her :

" You must let the children have all they want first. It is not right, you know, to take the children's food and throw it to the dogs."

But she replied :

" Yes, Lord, I know, but even the dogs under the table eat what the children leave."

" If you can answer like that," Jesus said to her, " you can go home ! The evil spirit has left your daughter."

And she went back to her home and found the child lying quietly on her bed, and the evil spirit gone.

Jesus restores speech and hearing   7 : 31

Once more Jesus left the neighbourhood of Tyre and passed through Sidon towards the Lake of Galilee, and crossed the Ten Towns territory. They brought to him a man who was deaf and unable to speak intelligibly, and they implored him to put his hand upon him. Jesus took him away from the crowd by himself. He put his fingers in the man's ears and touched his tongue with his own saliva.

Then, looking up to Heaven, he gave a deep sigh and said to him in Aramaic :

" Open ! "

And his ears were opened and immediately whatever had tied his tongue came loose and he spoke quite plainly. Jesus gave instructions that they should tell no one about this happening, but the more he told them, the more they broadcast the news. People were absolutely amazed, and kept saying :

" How wonderfully he has done everything ! He even makes the deaf hear and the dumb speak."

He again feeds the people miraculously   8 : 1

About this time it happened again that a large crowd collected and had nothing to eat. Jesus called the disciples over to him and said :

" My heart goes out to this crowd ; they have been with me three days now and they have no food left. If I send them off home without anything, they will collapse on the way—and some of them have come from a distance."

His disciples replied :

" Where could anyone find the food to feed them here in this deserted spot ? "

" How many loaves have you got ? " Jesus asked them.

" Seven," they replied.

So Jesus told the crowd to settle themselves on the ground. Then he took the seven loaves into his hands, and with a prayer of thanksgiving broke them, and gave them to the disciples to distribute to the people ; and this they did. They had a few small fish as well, and after blessing them, Jesus told the disciples to give these also to the people. They ate and they were satisfied. Moreover, they picked up seven baskets full of pieces left over. The people numbered about four thousand. Jesus sent them home, and then he boarded the boat at once with his disciples and went on to the district of Dalmanutha.

Jesus refuses to give a " sign "   8 : 11

Now the Pharisees came out and began an argument with him, wanting a sign from Heaven. Jesus gave a deep sigh, and then said :

" What makes this generation want a sign ? I can tell you this, they will certainly not be given one ! "

Then he left them and got aboard the boat again, and crossed the lake.

The disciples had forgotten to take any food and had only one loaf with them in the boat. Jesus spoke seriously to them, " Keep your eyes open ! Be on your guard against the ' yeast ' of the Pharisees and the ' yeast ' of Herod ! " And this sent them into an earnest consultation among themselves because they had brought no bread. Jesus knew it and said to them :

" Why all this discussion about bringing no bread ? Don't you understand or grasp what I say even yet ? Are you like the people who ' *having eyes, do not see ? and having ears, do not hear ?* ' Have you forgotten—when I broke five loaves for five thousand people, how many baskets full of pieces did you pick up ? "

" Twelve," they replied.

" And when there were seven loaves for four thousand people, how many baskets of pieces did you pick up ? "

" Seven," they said.

" And does that still mean nothing to you ? " he said.

Jesus restores sight   8 : 22

So they arrived at Bethsaida where a blind man was brought to him, with the earnest request that he should touch him. Jesus took the blind man's hand and led him outside the village. Then he moistened his eyes with saliva and putting his hands on him, asked :

" Can you see at all ? "

" I can see people. They look like trees—only they are walking about."

Then Jesus put his hands on his eyes once more and his sight came into focus, and he recovered and saw everything sharp and clear. And Jesus sent him off to his own house with the words :

" Don't even go into the village."

Jesus' question : Peter's inspired answer   8 : 27

Jesus then went away with his disciples to the villages of Caesarea Philippi. On the way he asked them :

G.M.E.   D

" Who are men saying that I am ? "

" John the Baptist," they answered. " But others say that you are Elijah or, some say, one of the prophets."

Then he asked them :

" But what about you—who do you say that I am ? "

" You are Christ ! " answered Peter.

Then Jesus impressed it upon them that they must not mention this to anyone.

Jesus speaks of the future and of the cost of discipleship   8 : 31

And he began to teach them that it was inevitable that the Son of Man should go through much suffering and be utterly repudiated by the Elders and Chief Priests and Scribes, and be killed, and after three days rise again. He told them all this quite bluntly.

This made Peter draw him on one side and take him to task about what he had said. But Jesus turned and faced his disciples and rebuked Peter.

" Out of my way, Satan ! " he said. " Peter, you are not looking at things from God's point of view, but from man's ! "

Then he called his disciples and the people around him, and said to them :

" If anyone wants to follow in my footsteps, he must give up all right to himself, take up his cross and follow me. The man who tries to save his life will lose it ; it is the man who loses his life for my sake and the Gospel's who will save it. What good can it do a man to gain the whole world at the price of his own soul ? What can a man offer to buy back his soul once he has lost it ? If anyone is ashamed of me and my words in this unfaithful and sinful generation, the Son of Man will be ashamed of him when he comes in the Father's glory with the holy angels around him."

Jesus foretells his glory   9 : 1

Then he added :

" Believe me, there are some of you standing here who will know nothing of death until you have seen the Kingdom of God coming in its power ! "

Six days later, Jesus took Peter and James and John with

him and led them up on a hill-side where they were entirely alone. His whole appearance changed before their eyes, while his clothes became white, dazzling white—whiter than any earthly bleaching could make them. Elijah and Moses appeared to the disciples and stood there in conversation with Jesus. Peter burst out to Jesus :

" Master, it is wonderful for us to be here. Shall we put up three shelters—one for you, one for Moses and one for Elijah ? "

He really did not know what to say, for they were very frightened. Then came a cloud which overshadowed them and a Voice spoke out of the cloud :

" This is My dearly-loved Son. Listen to Him ! "

Then, quite suddenly they looked all round them and saw nobody at all with them but Jesus. And as they came down from the hill-side, he warned them not to tell anybody what they had seen till " the Son of Man should have risen again from the dead." They treasured this remark and tried to puzzle out among themselves what " rising from the dead " could mean. Then they asked him this question :

" Why do the Scribes say that Elijah must come before Christ ? "

" It is quite true," he told them, " that Elijah does come first, and begins the restitution of all things. But what does the Scripture say about the Son of Man ? This : that he must go through much suffering and be treated with contempt ! Indeed I tell you that not only has Elijah come already but they have done to him exactly what they wanted —just as the Scripture says of him."

Jesus heals an epileptic boy   9 : 14

Then as they rejoined the other disciples, they saw that they were surrounded by a large crowd and that some of the Scribes were arguing with them. As soon as the people saw Jesus, they ran forward excitedly to welcome him.

" What is the trouble ? " Jesus asked them.

A man from the crowd answered :

" Master, I brought my son to you because he has a dumb spirit. Wherever he is, it gets hold of him, throws him down on the ground and there he foams at the mouth and grinds his teeth. It's simply wearing him out. I did speak to your disciples to get them to drive it out, but they hadn't the power to do it."

Jesus answered them :

" Oh, what a faithless people you are ! How long must I be with you, how long must I put up with you ? Bring him here to me."

So they brought the boy to him, and as soon as the spirit saw Jesus, it convulsed the boy, who fell to the ground and writhed there, foaming at the mouth.

" How long has he been like this ? " Jesus asked the father.

" Ever since he was a child," he replied. " Again and again it has thrown him into the fire or into water to finish him off. But if you can do anything, please take pity on us and help us."

" *If you can do anything !* " retorted Jesus. " Everything is possible to the man who believes."

" I do believe," the boy's father burst out. " Help me to believe more ! "

When Jesus noticed that a crowd was rapidly gathering, he spoke sharply to the evil spirit, with the words :

" I command you, deaf and dumb spirit, come out of this boy, and never go into him again ! "

The spirit gave a loud scream and after a dreadful convulsion left him. The boy lay there like a corpse, so that most of the bystanders said, " He is dead."

But Jesus grasped his hands and lifted him up, and then he stood on his own feet. When he had gone home, Jesus' disciples asked him privately :

" Why were we unable to drive it out ? "

" Nothing can drive out this kind of thing except prayer," replied Jesus.

Jesus privately warns his disciples of his own death   9 : 30

Then they left that district and went straight through Galilee. Jesus kept this journey secret for he was teaching his disciples that the Son of Man would be betrayed into the power of men, that they would kill him and that three days after his death he would rise again. But they were completely mystified by this saying, and were afraid to question him about it.

Jesus defines the new "greatness"   9 : 33

So they came to Capernaum. And when they were indoors he asked them :

" What were you discussing as we came along ? "

They were silent, for on the way they had been arguing about who should be the greatest. Jesus sat down and called the Twelve, and said to them :

" If any man wants to be first, he must be last and servant of all."

Then he took a little child and stood him in front of them all, and putting his arms round him, said to them :

" Anyone who welcomes one little child like this for my sake is welcoming me. And the man who welcomes me is welcoming not only me but the One Who sent me ! "

Then John said to him :

" Master, we saw somebody driving out evil spirits in your name, and we stopped him, for he is not one who follows us."

But Jesus replied :

" You must not stop him. No one who exerts such power in my name would readily say anything against me. For the man who is not against us is on our side. In fact, I assure you that the man who gives you a mere drink of water in my name, because you are followers of mine, will most certainly be rewarded. And I tell you too, that the man who disturbs the faith of one of the humblest of those who believe in me would be better off if he were thrown into the sea with a great millstone hung round his neck !

Entering the Kingdom may mean painful sacrifice   9 : 43

" Indeed, if it is your own hand that spoils your faith, you must cut it off. It is better for you to enter Life maimed than to keep both your hands and go to the rubbish-heap. If your foot spoils your faith, you must cut it off. It is better for you to enter Life on one foot than to keep both your feet and be thrown on to the rubbish-heap. And if your eye leads you astray, pluck it out. It is better for you to go one-eyed into the Kingdom of God than to keep both eyes and be thrown on to the rubbish-heap, where decay never stops and the fire never goes out. For everyone will be salted with fire. Salt is a very good thing ; but if it should lose its

saltiness, what can you do to restore its flavour ? You must
have salt in yourselves, and live at peace with each other."

The divine purpose in marriage   10 : 1

Then he got up and left Galilee and went off to the borders
of Judaea and beyond the Jordan. Again great crowds
assembled to meet him, and again, according to his custom,
he taught them. Then some Pharisees arrived to ask him
this test-question :

"Is it right for a man to divorce his wife ? "

Jesus replied by asking them :

"What has Moses commanded you to do ? "

"Moses allows men to write a divorce-notice and then to
dismiss her," they said.

"Moses gave you that commandment," returned Jesus,
"because you know so little of the meaning of love. But
from the beginning of the creation, God made them male
and female. '*For this cause shall a man leave his father and
mother, and shall cleave to his wife ; and the twain shall become one
flesh.*' So that in body they are no longer two people but one.
That is why man must never separate what God has joined
together."

On reaching the house, his disciples questioned him again
about this matter.

"Any man who divorces his wife and marries another
woman," he told them, "commits adultery against his wife.
And if she herself divorces her husband and marries someone
else, she commits adultery."

He welcomes small children   10 : 13

Then some people came to him bringing little children
for him to touch. The disciples tried to discourage them.
When Jesus saw this, he was indignant and told them :

"You must let little children come to me—never stop
them ! For the Kingdom of God belongs to such as these.
Indeed, I assure you that the man who does not accept the
Kingdom of God like a little child will never enter it."

Then he took the children in his arms and laid his hands
on them and blessed them.

Jesus shows the danger of riches   10 : 17

As he began to take the road again, a man came running up and fell at his feet, and asked him :

" Good Master, tell me please, what must I do to be sure of eternal life ? "

" I wonder why you call me good," returned Jesus. " No one is good—only God. You know the commandments, ' Do no murder, Do not commit adultery, Do not steal, Do not bear false witness, Do not cheat, Honour thy father and mother.' "

" Master," he replied, " I have carefully kept all these since I was quite young."

Jesus looked steadily at him, and his heart warmed towards him. Then he said :

" There is one thing you still want. Go and sell everything you have, give the money away to the poor,—you will have riches in Heaven. And then come back and follow me."

At these words his face fell and he went away in deep distress, for he was very rich. Then Jesus looked round at them all, and said to his disciples :

" How difficult it is for those who have great possessions to enter the Kingdom of God ! "

The disciples were staggered at these words, but Jesus continued :

" Children, you don't know how hard it can be to get into the Kingdom of Heaven. Why, a camel could more easily squeeze through the eye of a needle than a rich man get into the Kingdom of God."

At this their astonishment knew no bounds, and they said to each other :

" Then who can possibly be saved ? "

Jesus looked straight at them and said :

" Humanly speaking it is impossible, but not with God. Everything is possible with God."

Then Peter burst out :

" But look, we have left everything and followed you ! "

" I promise you," returned Jesus, " nobody leaves home or brothers or sisters or mother or father or children or property for my sake and the Gospel's without getting back a hundred times over, now in this present life, homes and brothers and sisters, mothers and children and land—though not without persecution—and in the next world eternal life. But many who are first now will then be last, and the last now will then be first."

The last journey to Jerusalem begins   10 : 32

They were now on their way going up to Jerusalem and Jesus walked on ahead. The disciples were dismayed at this, And those who followed were afraid. Then once more he took the Twelve aside and began to tell them what was going to happen to him.

"We are now going up to Jerusalem," he said, "as you can see. And the Son of Man will be betrayed into the power of the Chief Priests and Scribes. They are going to condemn him to death and hand him over to pagans who will jeer at him and spit at him and flog him and kill him. But after three days he will rise again."

An ill-timed request   10 : 35

Then Zebedee's two sons James and John approached him, saying :

"Master, we want you to grant us a special request."

"What do you want me to do for you?" answered Jesus.

"Give us permission to sit one on each side of you in the glory of your kingdom!"

"You don't know what you are asking," Jesus said to them. "Can you drink the cup I have to drink? Can you go through the baptism I have to bear?"

"Yes, we can," they replied.

Then Jesus told them :

"You will indeed drink the cup I am drinking, and you will undergo the baptism which I have to bear! But as for sitting on either side of me, that is not for me to give—such places belong to those for whom they are intended."

When the other ten heard about this, they began to be highly indignant with James and John; so Jesus called them all to him and said :

"You know that the so-called rulers in the heathen world lord it over them, and their great men have absolute power. But it must not be so among you. No, whoever among you wants to be great must become the servant of you all, and if he wants to be first among you he must be the slave of all men ! For the Son of Man himself has not come to be served but to serve, and to give his life to set many others free."

Then they came to Jericho, and he was leaving it accompanied by his disciples and a large crowd, Bartimaeus, (that is, the son of Timaeus) a blind beggar, was sitting in his usual place by the side of the road. When he heard that it was Jesus of Nazareth, he began to call out :

" Jesus, Son of David, have pity on me ! "

Many of the people told him sharply to keep quiet, but he shouted all the more :

" Son of David have pity on me ! "

Jesus stood quite still and said :

" Call him here."

So they called the blind man, saying :

" It's all right now, get up, he's calling you ! "

At this he threw off his coat, jumped to his feet and came to Jesus.

" What do you want me to do for you ? " he asked him.

" Oh, Master, let me see again ! "

" Go on your way then," returned Jesus, " your faith has healed you."

And he recovered his sight at once and followed Jesus along the road.

Jesus arranges for his entry into the city   11 : 1

When they were approaching Jerusalem and had come to Bethphage and Bethany on the slopes of the Mount of Olives, he sent off two of his disciples with these instructions :

" Go into the village just ahead of you and as soon as you enter it you will find a tethered colt on which no one has yet ridden. Untie it, and bring it here. If anybody asks you, ' Why are you doing this ? ', just say, ' The Lord needs it, and will send it back immediately.' "

So they went off and found the colt tethered by a doorway outside in the open street, and they untied it. Some of the bystanders did say, " What are you doing, untying this colt ? " but they made the reply Jesus told them to make, and the men raised no objection. So they brought the colt to Jesus, threw their coats upon its back, and he took his seat upon it.

Many of the people spread out their coats in his path as he

rode along, and others put down straw which they had cut from the fields. The whole crowd, both those who were in front and those who were behind Jesus, shouted:

"God save Him!—God bless the One Who comes in the Name of the Lord! God bless the coming kingdom of our father David! God save Him from on high!"

Jesus entered Jerusalem and went into the Temple and looked round on all that was going on. And then, since it was already late in the day, he went out to Bethany with the Twelve.

On the following day when they had left Bethany, Jesus felt hungry. He noticed a fig-tree in the distance covered with leaves, and he walked up to it to see if he could find any fruit on it, But when he got to it, he could find nothing but leaves, for it was not yet time for the figs. Then Jesus spoke to the tree:

"May nobody ever eat fruit from you!"

And the disciples heard him say it.

Then they came into Jerusalem and Jesus went into the Temple and began to drive out those who were buying and selling there. He overturned the tables of the money-changers and the benches of the dove-sellers, and he would not allow people to carry their water-pots through the Temple. And he taught them and said:

"Doesn't the Scripture say, '*My house shall be called a house of prayer for all nations*'? But you have turned it into a thieves' kitchen!"

The Chief Priests and Scribes heard him say this and tried to find a way of getting rid of him. But they were in fact afraid of him, for his teaching had captured the imagination of the people. And every evening he left the city.

Jesus talks of faith, prayer and forgiveness   11 : 20

One morning as they were walking along, they noticed that the fig-tree had withered away to the roots. Peter remembered it, and said:

"Master, look, the fig-tree that you cursed is all shrivelled up!"

"Have faith in God," replied Jesus to them. "I tell you that if anyone should say to this hill, 'Get up and throw yourself into the sea,' and without any doubt in his heart

believe that what he says will happen, then it *will* happen!
That is why I tell you, whatever you pray about and ask for,
believe that you have received it and it will be yours. And
whenever you stand praying, you must forgive anything that
you are holding against anyone else, and your Heavenly
Father will forgive you *your* sins."

Jesus' authority is directly challenged   11 : 27

So they came once more to Jerusalem, and while Jesus
was walking in the Temple, the Chief Priests, Elders and
Scribes approached him, and asked:

"What authority have you for what you're doing? And
who gave you permission to do these things?"

"I am going to ask you a question," replied Jesus, "and
if you answer me, I will tell you what authority I have for
what I do. The baptism of John, now—did it come from
Heaven or was it purely human? Tell me that."

At this they argued with each other, "If we say from
Heaven, he will say, ' then why didn't you believe in him?'
but if we say it was purely human, well . . ." For they were
frightened of the people, since all of them believed that
John was a real prophet. So they answered Jesus:

"We do not know."

"Then I cannot tell you by what authority I do these
things," returned Jesus.

Jesus tells a story, with a pointed application   12 : 1

Then he began to talk to them in parables.

"A man once planted a vineyard," he said, "fenced it
round, dug out the hole for the wine-press and built a watch-
tower. Then he let it out to some farm-workers and went
abroad. At the end of the season he sent a servant to the
tenants to receive his share of the vintage. But they got hold
of him, knocked him about and sent him off empty-handed.
The owner tried again. He sent another servant to them,
but this one they knocked on the head and generally insulted.
Once again he sent them another servant, but him they
murdered. He sent many others and some they beat up and
some they murdered. He had one man left—his own son
who was very dear to him. He sent him last of all to the
tenants, saying to himself, ' They will surely respect my own

son.' But they said to each other, ' This fellow is the future owner—come on, let's kill him, and the property will be ours.' So they got hold of him and murdered him, and threw his body out of the vineyard. What do you suppose the owner of the vineyard is going to do? He will come and destroy the men who were working his vineyard and will hand it over to others. Have you never read this Scripture:

The stone which the builders rejected,
The same was made the head of the corner;
This was from the Lord,
And it is marvellous in our eyes?"

Then they tried to get their hands on him, for they knew perfectly well that he had aimed this parable at them—but they were afraid of the people. So they left him and went away.

A test-question   12 : 13
Later they sent some of the Pharisees and some of the Herod-party to trap him in an argument. They came up and said to him:

" Master, we know that you are an honest man and that you are not swayed by men's opinion of you. Obviously you don't care for human approval but teach the way of God with the strictest regard for truth—*is it right to pay tribute to Caesar or not : are we to pay or not to pay?* "

But Jesus saw through their hypocrisy and said to them:

" Why try this trick on me? Bring me a coin and let me look at it."

So they brought one to him.

" Whose face is this? " asked Jesus, " and whose name is in the inscription? "

" Caesar's," they replied. And Jesus said:

" Then give to Caesar what belongs to Caesar, and to God what belongs to God!"—a reply which staggered them.

Jesus reveals the ignorance of the Sadducees   12 : 18
Then some of the Sadducees (a party which maintains that

there is no resurrection) approached him, and put this question to him :

"Master, Moses instructed us that if a man's brother dies leaving a widow but no child, then the man should marry the woman and raise children for his brother. Now there were seven brothers, and the first one married and died without leaving issue. Then the second one married the widow and died leaving no issue behind him. The same thing happened with the third, and indeed the whole seven died without leaving any child behind them. Finally the woman herself died. Now in this ' resurrection,' when men rise up again, whose wife is she going to be—for she was the wife of all seven of them ? "

Jesus replied, " Does not this show where you go wrong—and how you fail to understand both the Scriptures and the power of God ? When people rise from the dead they neither marry nor are they given in marriage ; they live like the angels in Heaven. But as for this matter of the dead being raised, have you never read in the book of Moses, in the passage about the Bush, how God spoke to him in these words, ' I am the God of Abraham and the God of Isaac and the God of Jacob ' ? God is not God of the dead but of living men ! That is where you make your great mistake ! "

The most important commandments   12 : 28

Then one of the Scribes approached him. He had been listening to the discussion, and noticing how well Jesus had answered them, he put this question to him :

" What are we to consider the greatest commandment of all ? "

" The first and most important one is this," Jesus replied— ' *Hear, O Israel : the Lord our God, the Lord is one : and thou shalt love the Lord thy God with all thy heart, and with all thy soul, and with all thy mind, and with all thy strength.*' The second is this, ' *Thou shalt love thy neighbour as thyself.*' No other commandment is greater than these."

" I am well answered," replied the Scribe. " You are absolutely right when you say that there is one God and no other God exists but Him ; and to love Him with the whole of our hearts, the whole of our intelligence and the whole of our energy, and to love our neighbours as ourselves is infinitely more important than all these burnt-offerings and sacrifices."

Then Jesus, noting the thoughtfulness of his reply, said to him:

" You are not far from the Kingdom of God ! "

After this nobody felt like asking him any more questions.

Jesus criticises the Scribes' teaching and behaviour   12 : 35

Later while Jesus was teaching in the Temple, he remarked:

" How can the Scribes make out that Christ is David's *son*, for David himself, inspired by the Holy Spirit, said :

The Lord said unto my *Lord*,
Sit thou on my right hand,
Till I make thine enemies the footstool of thy feet.

David is himself calling Christ ' Lord '—where do they get the idea that he is his son ? "

The vast crowd heard this with great delight, and Jesus continued in his teaching :

" Be on your guard against these Scribes who love to walk about in long robes and to be greeted respectfully in public and to have the front seats in the synagogue and the best places at dinner-parties ! These are the men who grow fat on widows' property and then cover up what they are doing by making lengthy prayers. They are only adding to their own punishment ! "

Then Jesus sat down opposite the Temple almsbox and watched the people putting their money into it. A great many rich people put in large sums. Then a poor widow came up and dropped in two little coins, worth together about a halfpenny. Jesus called his disciples to his side and said to them :

" Believe me, this poor widow has put in more than all the others. For they have all put in what they can easily afford, but she in her poverty who needs so much, has given away everything, her whole living ! "

Jesus prophesies the ruin of the Temple   13 : 1

Then as Jesus was leaving the Temple, one of his disciples said to him :

"Look, Master, what wonderful stonework, what a size these buildings are!"

Jesus replied:

"You see these great buildings? Not a single stone will be left standing on another; every one will be thrown down!"

Then while he was sitting on the slope of the Mount of Olives facing the Temple, Peter, James, John and Andrew said to him privately:

"Tell us when will these things happen. What sign will there be that all these things are going to be accomplished?"

So Jesus began to tell them:

"Be very careful that no one deceives you. Many are going to come in my name and say, 'I am He,' and will lead many astray. When you hear of wars and rumours of wars, don't be alarmed. Such things are bound to happen, but the end is not yet. Nation will take up arms against nation and kingdom against kingdom. There will be earth-quakes in different places and terrible famines. But this is only the beginning of 'the pains.' You yourselves must keep your wits about you, for men will hand you over to their councils, and will beat you in their synagogues. You will have to stand in front of rulers and kings for my sake to bear your witness to them—for before the end comes the Gospel must be proclaimed to all nations. But when they are taking you off to trial, do not worry beforehand about what you are going to say—simply say the words you are given when the time comes. For it is not really you who will speak, but the Holy Spirit.

Jesus foretells utter misery   13 : 12

"A brother is going to betray his own brother to death, and a father his own child. Children will stand up against their parents and condemn them to death. There will come a time when the whole world will hate you because you are known as my followers. Yet the man who holds out to the end will be saved.

"But when you see 'the abomination of desolation' standing where it ought not—(let the reader take note of this) —then those who are in Judaea must fly to the hills! The man on his house-top must not go down nor go into his house to fetch anything out of it, and the man in the field must not turn back to fetch his coat. Alas for the women who are pregnant at that time, and alas for those with babies at their breasts! Pray God that it may not be winter when that time comes, for there will be such utter misery in those days as has never been from the Creation until now—and never will be again. Indeed, if the Lord did not shorten those days, no human being would survive. But for the sake of the people whom He has chosen He has shortened those days.

He warns against false Christs, and commands vigilance   13 : 21
  " If anyone tells you at that time, ' Look, here is Christ,' or ' Look, there he is,' don't believe it! For false Christs and false prophets will arise and will perform signs and wonders, to deceive, if it be possible, even the men of God's choice. You must keep your eyes open! I am giving you this warning before it happens.

  " But when that misery is past, the light of the sun will be darkened and the moon will not give her light; stars will be falling from the sky and the powers of heaven will rock on their foundations. Then men shall see the Son of Man coming in the clouds with great power and glory. And then shall He send out His angels to summon His Chosen together from every quarter, from farthest earth to highest heaven. Let the fig-tree illustrate this for you: when its branches grow tender and produce leaves, you know that summer is near. So when you see these things happening, you may know that He is near, at your very doors! I tell you that this present age will not have passed until all these things have come true. Earth and sky will pass away, but what I have told you will never pass away! But no one knows the day or the hour of this Happening, not even the angels in Heaven, no, not even the Son—only the Father. Keep your eyes open, keep on the alert, for you do not know when the time will be. It is as if a man who is travelling abroad had left his house and handed it over to be managed by his servants. He has given each one his work to do and has ordered the doorkeeper to be on the look-out for his return. Just so must you keep a look-out, for you do not know when the Master of the House will come—it might be late evening, or midnight, or cockcrow, or early morning—otherwise He might come unexpectedly and find you sound asleep. What I am saying to you I am saying to all; keep on the alert!"

An act of love   14 : 1

In two days' time the Festival of the Passover and of Unleavened Bread was due. Consequently, the Chief Priests and the Scribes were trying to think of some trick by which they could get Jesus into their power and have him executed.

"But it must not be during the Festival," they said, "or there will be a riot."

Jesus himself was now in Bethany in the house of Simon the leper. As he was sitting at table, a woman approached him with an alabaster flask of very costly spikenard perfume. She broke the neck of the flask and poured the perfume on Jesus' head. Some of those present were highly indignant and muttered:

"What is the point of such wicked waste of perfume? It could have been sold for over thirty pounds and the money could have been given to the poor." And there was a murmur of resentment against her. But Jesus said:

"Let her alone, why must you make her feel uncomfortable? She has done a beautiful thing for me. You have the poor with you always and you can do good to them whenever you like, but you will not always have me. She has done all she could—for she has anointed my body in preparation for burial. I assure you that wherever the Gospel is preached throughout the whole world, this deed of hers will also be recounted, as her memorial to me."

Judas volunteers to betray Jesus   14 : 10

Then Judas Iscariot, who was one of the Twelve, went off to the Chief Priests to betray Jesus to them. And when they heard what he had to say, they were delighted and undertook to pay him for it. So he looked out for a convenient opportunity to betray him.

The Passover-supper prepared   14 : 12

On the first day of Unleavened Bread, the day when the Passover was sacrificed, Jesus' disciples said:

" Where do you want us to go and make the preparations for you to eat the Passover ? "

Jesus sent off two of them with these instructions :

" Go into the town and you will meet a man carrying a pitcher of water. Follow him and say to the owner of the house to which he goes, ' The Master says, where is the room for me to eat the Passover with my disciples ? ' And he will show you a large upstairs room all ready with the furnishings that we need. That is the place where you are to make our preparations."

So the disciples set off and went into the town, and found everything as he had told them, and prepared for the Passover.

The last supper together : the mysterious bread and wine   14 : 17

Late in the evening he arrived with the Twelve. And while they were sitting there, right in the middle of the meal, Jesus remarked :

" Believe me, one of you is going to betray me—someone who is now having his supper with me."

This shocked and distressed them and one after another they began to say to him :

" Surely, I'm not the one ? "

" It is one of the Twelve," Jesus told them, " a man who is dipping his hand into the dish with me. It is true that the Son of Man will follow the road foretold by the Scriptures, but alas for the man through whom he is betrayed ! It would be better for that man if he had never been born."

And while they were still eating Jesus took a loaf, blessed it and broke it and gave it to them, with the words :

" Take this, it is my body."

Then he took a cup, and after thanking God, he gave it to them, and they all drank from it, and he said to them :

" This is my blood which is shed for many in the New Agreement. I tell you truly I will drink no more wine until the day comes when I drink it fresh in the Kingdom of God ! "

Then they sang a hymn and went out to the Mount of Olives.

"Every one of you will lose your faith in me," Jesus told them, "as the Scripture says:

I will smite the shepherd,
And the sheep shall be scattered abroad.

Yet after I have risen, I shall go before you into Galilee!"

Peter's bold words—and Jesus' reply   14 : 29
Then Peter said to him:
"Even if everyone should lose his faith, I never will."
"Believe me, Peter," returned Jesus, "this very night before the cock crows twice, you will disown me three times."
But Peter protested violently.
"Even if it means dying with you, I will never disown you!"
And they all made the same protest.

The last desperate prayer in Gethsemane   14 : 32
Then they arrived at a place called Gethsemane, and Jesus said to his disciples:
"Sit down here while I pray."
He took with him Peter, James and John, and began to be horror-stricken and desperately depressed.
"My heart is nearly breaking," he told them. "Stay here and keep watch for me."
Then he walked forward a little way and flung himself on the ground, praying that, if it were possible, he might not have to face the ordeal.
"Dear Father," he said, "all things are possible to You. Please—let me not have to drink this cup! Yet it is not what I want but what You want."
Then he came and found them fast asleep. He spoke to Peter:
"Are you asleep, Simon? Couldn't you manage to watch for a single hour? Watch and pray, all of you, that you may not have to face temptation. Your spirit is willing, but human nature is weak."
Then he went away again and prayed in the same words, and once more he came and found them asleep. They could

not keep their eyes open and they did not know what to say for themselves. When he came back for the third time, he said :

"Are you still going to sleep and take your ease ? All right—the moment has come ; now you are going to see the Son of Man betrayed into the hands of evil men ! Get up, let us be going ! Look, here comes my betrayer ! "

Judas betrays Jesus   14 : 43

And indeed, while the words were still on his lips, Judas, one of the Twelve, arrived with a mob armed with swords and staves, sent by the Chief Priests and Scribes and Elders. The betrayer had given them a sign ; he had said, " The one I kiss will be the man. Get hold of him and you can take him away without any trouble." So he walked straight up to Jesus, cried, " Master ! " and kissed him affectionately. And so they got hold of him and held him. Somebody present drew his sword and struck at the High Priest's servant, slashing off his ear. Then Jesus spoke to them :

" So you've come out with your swords and staves to capture me like a bandit, have you ? Day after day I was with you in the Temple teaching, and you never laid a finger on me. But the Scriptures must be fulfilled."

Then all the disciples deserted him and made their escape. There happened to be a young man among Jesus' followers who wore nothing but a linen shirt. They seized him, but he left the shirt in their hands and took to his heels stark naked.

Jesus before the High Priest   14 : 53

So they marched Jesus away to the High Priest in whose presence all the Chief Priests and Elders and Scribes had assembled. (Peter followed him at a safe distance, right up to the High Priest's courtyard. There he sat in the firelight with the servants, keeping himself warm.) Meanwhile, the Chief Priests and the whole Council were trying to find some evidence against Jesus which would warrant the death penalty. But they failed completely. There were plenty of people ready to give false testimony against him, but their evidence was contradictory. Then some more perjurers stood up and said :

"We heard him say, 'I will destroy this Temple that was built by human hands and in three days I will build another made without human aid.'"

But even so their evidence conflicted. So the High Priest himself got up and took the centre of the floor.

"Have you no answer to make?" he asked Jesus. "What about all this evidence against you?"

But Jesus remained silent and offered no reply. Again the High Priest asked him:

"Are you Christ, Son of the Blessed One?"

And Jesus said:

"I am! Yes, you will all see the Son of Man sitting at the right hand of power, coming in the clouds of heaven."

Then the High Priest tore his robes and cried:

"Why do we still need witnesses? You heard the blasphemy; what is your opinion now?"

And their verdict was that he deserved to die. Then some of them began to spit at him. They blindfolded him and then slapped him, saying:

"Now prophesy who hit you!"

Even the servants who took him away slapped his face.

Peter, in fear, disowns his Master   14 : 66

In the meantime, while Peter was in the courtyard below, one of the High Priest's maids came and saw him warming himself. She looked closely at him, and said:

"You were with the Nazarene too—with Jesus!"

But he denied it, saying:

"I don't understand—I don't know what you're talking about."

And he walked out into the gateway, and a cock crew.

Again the maid who had noticed him began to say to the men standing there:

"This man is one of them!"

But he denied it again. A few minutes later the bystanders themselves said to Peter:

"You certainly are one of them. Why, you're a Galilean!"

But he started to curse and swear:

"I tell you I don't know the man you're talking about!"

Immediately the cock crew for the second time, and back into Peter's mind came the words of Jesus, " Before the cock crows twice, you will disown me three times."

And he broke down and wept.

Jesus before Pilate   15 : 1

The moment daylight came the Chief Priests called together a meeting of Elders, Scribes and members of the whole Council, bound Jesus and took him off and handed him over to Pilate. Pilate asked him straight out :

" Well, you—*are* you the King of the Jews ? "

" Yes, I am," he replied.

The Chief Priests brought many accusations. So Pilate questioned him again.

" Have you nothing to say ? Listen to all their accusations ! "

But Jesus made no further answer—to Pilate's astonishment.

Now it was Pilate's custom at festival-time to release a prisoner—anyone they asked for. There was in the prison at the time, with some other rioters who had committed murder in a recent outbreak, a man called Barabbas. The crowd surged forward and began to demand that Pilate should do what he usually did for them. So he spoke to them :

" Do you want me to set free the King of the Jews for you ? "

For he knew perfectly well that the Chief Priests had handed Jesus over to him through sheer malice. But the Chief Priests worked upon the crowd to get them to demand Barabbas' release instead. So Pilate addressed them once more :

" Then what am I to do with the man whom you call the King of the Jews ? "

They shouted back :

" Crucify him ! "

But Pilate replied :

" Why, what crime has he committed ? "

But their voices rose to a roar :

" Crucify him ! "

And as Pilate wanted to satisfy the crowd, he set Barabbas

free for them, and after having Jesus flogged handed him over to be crucified.

Then the soldiers marched him away inside the courtyard of the Governor's residence and called their whole company together. They dressed Jesus in a purple robe, and twisting some thorn-twigs into a crown, they put it on his head. Then they began to greet him :

" Hail, Your Majesty—king of the Jews ! "

They hit him on the head with a stick and spat at him, and then bowed low before him on bended knee. And when they had finished their fun with him, they took off the purple cloak and dressed him again in his own clothes. Then they led him outside to crucify him. They compelled Simon, a native of Cyrene in Africa, (the father of Alexander and Rufus), who was on his way from the fields at the time, to carry Jesus' cross.

The crucifixion   15 : 22

They took him to a place called Golgotha (which means Skull Hill) and they offered him some drugged wine, but he would not take it. Then they crucified him, and shared out his garments, drawing lots to see what each of them would get. It was about nine o'clock in the morning when they nailed him to the cross. Over his head the placard of his crime read, " THE KING OF THE JEWS." They also crucified two bandits at the same time, one on each side of him. And the passers-by jeered at him, shaking their heads in mockery, saying :

" Hi, you ! You could destroy the Temple and build it up again in three days, why not come down from the cross and save yourself ? "

The Chief Priests also made fun of him among themselves and the Scribes, and said :

" He saved others, he cannot save himself. If only this Christ, the King of Israel, would come down now from the cross, we should see it and believe ! "

And even the men who were crucified with him hurled abuse at him.

At midday darkness spread over the whole countryside and lasted until three o'clock in the afternoon, and at three o'clock Jesus cried out in a loud voice :

" My God, my God, why did You forsake me ? "

Some of the bystanders heard these words which Jesus spoke in Aramaic (*Eloi, Eloi, lama sabachthani ?*), and said :

" Listen, he's calling for Elijah ! "

One man ran off and soaked a sponge in vinegar, put it on a stick, and held it up for Jesus to drink, calling out :

" Let him alone ! Let's see if Elijah will come and take him down ! "

But Jesus let out a great cry, and died. The curtain of the Temple sanctuary was split in two from the top to the bottom. And when the centurion who stood in front of Jesus saw how he died, he said :

" This man was certainly a son of God ! "

There were some women there looking on from a distance, among them Mary of Magdala, Mary the mother of the younger James, and Joses, and Salome. These were the women who used to follow Jesus as he went about in Galilee and looked after him. And there were many other women there who had come up to Jerusalem with them.

The body of Jesus is reverently laid in a tomb   15 : 42

When the evening came, because it was the day of Preparation, that is the day before the Sabbath, Joseph from Arimathaea, a distinguished member of the Council, who was himself prepared [to accept the Kingdom of God, went boldly into Pilate's presence and asked for the body of Jesus Pilate was surprised that he should be dead already and he sent for the centurion and asked whether he had been dead long. On hearing the centurion's report, he gave Joseph the body of Jesus. So Joseph bought a linen winding-sheet, took Jesus down and wrapped him in it, and then put him in a tomb which had been hewn out of the solid rock, rolling a stone over the entrance to it. Mary of Magdala and Mary the mother of Joses were looking on and saw where he was laid.

Early on the first " Lord's Day " : the women are amazed   16 : 1

When the Sabbath was over, Mary of Magdala, Mary the mother of James, and Salome bought spices so that they could go and anoint him. And very early in the morning on the first day of the week, they came to the tomb, just as the sun was rising.

" Who is going to roll the stone back from the doorway of the tomb ? " they asked each other.

And then as they looked closer, they saw that the stone, which was a very large one, had been rolled back. So they went into the tomb and saw a young man in a white robe sitting on the right-hand side, and they were simply astonished. But he said to them :

" There is no need to be astonished. You are looking for Jesus of Nazareth Who was crucified. He has risen ; He is not here. Look, here is the place where they laid Him. But now go and tell His disciples, and Peter, that He will be in Galilee before you. You will see Him there just as He told you."

And they got out of the tomb and ran away from it. They were trembling with excitement. They did not dare to breathe a word to anyone.

An ancient appendix   16 : 9

When Jesus rose early on that first day of the week, He appeared first of all to Mary of Magdala, from whom He had driven out seven evil spirits. And she went and reported this to His sorrowing and weeping followers. They heard her say that He was alive and that she had seen Him, but they did not believe it.

Later, He appeared in a different form to two of them who were out walking, as they were on their way to the country. These two came back and told the others, but they did not believe them either. Still later He appeared to the Eleven themselves as they were sitting at table and reproached them for their lack of faith and reluctance to believe those who had seen Him after He had risen. Then He said to them :

" You must go out to the whole world and proclaim the Gospel to every creature. He who believes it and is baptized will be saved, but he who disbelieves it will be condemned. These signs will follow those who do believe : they will drive out evil spirits in My Name ; they will speak with new tongues ; they will pick up snakes, and if they drink anything poisonous it will do them no harm ;

they will lay their hands upon the sick and they will recover."

Jesus, His mission accomplished, returns to Heaven   16 : 19

After these words to them, the Lord Jesus was taken up into Heaven and was enthroned at the right hand of God. They went out and preached everywhere. The Lord worked with them, confirming their message by the signs that followed.

THE GOSPEL OF
LUKE

The author of this Gospel is beyond reasonable doubt Luke, "the beloved physician," companion and fellow-workers of Paul. This work is, of course, only the first of his "two volumes," the second being what we know as The Acts of the Apostles. It is generally recognised that he was not a Jew and that he was a doctor by profession.

This Gospel is thought by many to be the most beautiful of the Four, both because of its style and of the imaginative sympathy with which Luke paints the portrait of his Master. There is a persistent legend that he was an artist, and while this is a matter of uncertainty, we owe him a definite enrichment and enlargement of the story of Jesus which gives the impression of an artist's sensitivity.

On his own admission Luke has carefully compared and edited existing narratives, but it would seem that he had access to a good deal of additional material, and we can reasonably guess at some of the sources from which he drew it. He would almost certainly know Mark's Gospel ; he would be able to draw from the mysterious "Q," which scholars believe to have existed, although there is no trace of it ; and he had his own reminiscences and material collected in Caesarea (Acts 24, 27).

Though it is impossible to state accurately how the work was composed, a great many scholars think that there was a first version, possibly written during his travels with Paul, and that later material —the birth stories and the preface, for example—was incorporated later. Luke, like Mark, is writing primarily for the non-Jewish reader. A Gentile centurion, for example, is singled out as having more faith than Jesus had found in Israel ; more than once, Samaritans, who were anathema to the Jews, are singled out for praise. Jesus' ancestry is traced back, not to Abraham the father of the Jewish race, but to Adam the father of all mankind.

None of the other evangelists shows so clearly the love and sympathy of Jesus for the sinner, the outcast and the unfortunate. And there is a reverence for women as the story unfolds, which shows the writer, through his understanding of his Master, far ahead of his time. The

*graphic, but always careful and accurate, style conveys a strong
impression of veracity. Many scholars nowadays would place the
writing of Luke's Gospel and of The Acts of the Apostles soon
after Paul's death and before the Fall of Jerusalem, i.e. between
65 and 70.*

Prefatory Note

DEAR THEOPHILUS,[1]

Since many people have already written an account of the
events which have happened among us, basing their work
on the evidence of those whom we know were eye-witnesses
as well as teachers of the Message, I have decided, since I
have traced the course of these happenings carefully from
the beginning, to set them down for you myself in their
proper order, so that you may have reliable information about
the matters in which you have already had instruction.

A vision comes to an old priest of God   1 : 5

The story begins, in the days when Herod was King of
Judaea, with a priest called Zacharias (who belonged to the
Abijah section of the priesthood), whose wife, Elisabeth,
was like him, a descendant of Aaron. They were both truly
religious people, blamelessly observing all God's commandments and requirements. They were childless through
Elisabeth's infertility, and both of them were getting on in
years. One day, while Zacharias was performing his priestly
functions (it was the turn of his division to be on duty), it
fell to him to go into the sanctuary and burn the incense.
The crowded congregation outside was praying at the actual
time of the incense-burning, when an angel of the Lord
appeared on the right side of the incense-altar. When
Zacharias saw him, he was terribly agitated and a sense of
awe swept over him. But the angel spoke to him:

" Do not be afraid, Zacharias ; your prayers have been
heard. Elisabeth your wife will bear you a son, and you are
to call him John. This will be joy and delight to you and
many more will be glad because he is born. He will be one
of God's great men ; he will touch neither wine nor strong
drink and he will be filled with the Holy Spirit from the

[1] *Theophilus :* either a convert from Paganism or a general term,
meaning in Greek " Loved by God."

moment of his birth. He will turn many of Israel's children to the Lord their God. He will go out before God in the spirit and power of Elijah—to reconcile fathers and children, and bring back the disobedient to the wisdom of good men— and he will make a people fully ready for their Lord."

But Zacharias replied to the angel :

" How can I know that this is true ? I am an old man myself and my wife is getting on in years . . ."

" I am Gabriel," the angel answered. " I stand in the presence of God, and I have been sent to speak to you and tell you this good news. Because you do not believe what I have said, you shall live in silence, and you shall be unable to speak a word until the day that it happens. But be sure that everything that I have told you will come true at the proper time."

Meanwhile, the people were waiting for Zacharias, won- dering why he stayed so long in the sanctuary. But when he came out and was unable to speak a word to them—for although he kept making signs, not a sound came from his lips—they realised that he had seen a vision in the Temple. Later, when his days of duty were over, he went back home, and soon afterwards his wife Elisabeth became pregnant and kept herself secluded for five months.

" How good the Lord is to me," she would say, " now that He has taken away the shame that I have suffered."

A vision comes to a young woman in Nazareth   1 : 26

Then, six months after Zacharias' vision, the angel Gabriel was sent from God to a Galilean town, Nazareth by name, to a young woman who was engaged to a man called Joseph (a descendant of David). The girl's name was Mary. The angel entered her room and said :

" Greetings to you, Mary. O favoured one !—the Lord be with you ! "

Mary was deeply perturbed at these words and wondered what such a greeting could possibly mean. But the angel said to her :

" Do not be afraid, Mary ; God loves you dearly. You are going to be the mother of a son, and you will call him Jesus. He will be great and will be known as the Son of the Most High. The Lord God will give him the throne of his

forefather, David, and he will be King over the people of
Jacob for ever. His reign shall never end."

Then Mary spoke to the angel:

"How can this be," she said, "I am not married!"

But the angel made this reply to her:

"The Holy Spirit will come upon you, the power of the
Most High will overshadow you. Your child will therefore
be called Holy—the Son of God. Your cousin Elisabeth
has also conceived a son, old as she is. Indeed, this is the
sixth month for her, a woman who was called barren. For
no promise of God can fail to be fulfilled."

"I belong to the Lord, body and soul," replied Mary,
"let it happen as you say." And at this the angel left her.

With little delay Mary got ready and hurried off to the
hill-side town in Judaea where Zacharias and Elisabeth lived.
She went into their house and greeted her cousin. When
Elisabeth heard her greeting, the unborn child stirred inside
her and she herself was filled with the Holy Spirit, and cried
out:

"Blessed are you among women, and blessed is your
child! What an honour it is to have the mother of my Lord
come to see me! Why, as soon as your greeting reached
my ears, the child within me jumped for joy! Oh how happy
is the woman who believes in God, for He does make His
promises to her come true."

Then Mary said, "My heart is overflowing with praise of
my Lord, my soul is full of joy in God my Saviour. For He
has deigned to notice me, His humble servant and, after this,
all the people who ever shall be will call me the happiest of
women! The One Who can do all things has done great
things for me—oh, Holy is His Name! Truly, His mercy
rests on those who fear Him in every generation. He has
shown the strength of His arm, He has swept away the high
and mighty. He has set kings down from their thrones and
lifted up the humble. He has satisfied the hungry with good
things and sent the rich away with empty hands. Yes, He
has helped Israel, His child: He has remembered the mercy
that He promised to our forefathers, to Abraham and his
sons for evermore!"

The old woman's son, John, is born   1 : 56

So Mary stayed with Elisabeth about three months, and then went back to her own home. Then came the time for Elisabeth's child to be born, and she gave birth to a son. Her neighbours and relations heard of the great mercy the Lord had shown her and shared her joy.

When the eighth day came, they were going to circumcise the child and call him Zacharias, after his father, but his mother said :

"Oh no ! He must be called John."

"But none of your relations is called John," they replied. And they made signs to his father to see what name he wanted the child to have. He beckoned for a writing-tablet and wrote the words, "His name is John," which greatly surprised everybody. Then his power of speech suddenly came back, and his first words were to thank God. The neighbours were awe-struck at this, and all these incidents were reported in the hill-country of Judaea. People turned the whole matter over in their hearts, and said :

"What is this child's future going to be?" For the Lord's blessing was plainly upon him.

Then Zacharias, his father, filled with the Holy Spirit and speaking like a prophet, said :

"Blessings on the Lord, the God of Israel, because He has turned His face towards His people and has set them free ! And He has raised up for us a standard of salvation in His servant David's house ! Long, long ago, through the words of His holy prophets, He promised to do this for us, so that we should be safe from our enemies and secure from all who hate us. So does He continue the mercy He showed to our forefathers. So does He remember the holy agreement He made with them and the oath which He swore to our father Abraham, to make us this gift : that we should be saved from the hands of our enemies, and in His Presence should serve Him unafraid in holiness and righteousness all our lives.

"And you, little child, will be called the Prophet of the Most High, for you will go before the Lord to prepare the way for His coming. It will be for you to give His people knowledge of their salvation through the forgiveness of their sins. Because the heart of our God is full of mercy towards us, the first light of Heaven shall come to visit us—to shine on those who lie in darkness and under the shadow of death, and to guide our feet into the path of peace."

The little child grew up and became strong in spirit. He lived in lonely places until the day came for him to show himself to Israel.

The census brings Mary and Joseph to Bethlehem   2 : 1

At that time a proclamation was made by Caesar Augustus that all the inhabited world should be registered. This was the first census, undertaken while Cyrenius was governor of Syria ; and everybody went to the town of his birth to be registered. Joseph went up from the town of Nazareth in Galilee to David's town, Bethlehem, in Judaea, because he was a direct descendant of David, to be registered with his future wife, Mary, now in the later stages of her pregnancy. So it happened that it was while they were there in Bethlehem that she came to the end of her time. She gave birth to her first child, a son. And as there was no place for them inside the inn, she wrapped him up and laid him in a manger.

A vision comes to shepherds on the hill-side   2 : 8

There were some shepherds living in the same part of the country, keeping guard throughout the night over their flock in the open fields. Suddenly an angel of the Lord stood by their side, the splendour of the Lord blazed around them, and they were terror-stricken. But the angel said to them :

" Do not be afraid ! Listen, I bring you glorious news of great joy which is for all the people. This very day, in David's town, a Saviour has been born for you. He is Christ, the Lord. Let this prove it to you : you will find a baby, wrapped up and lying in a manger."

And in a flash there appeared with the angel a vast host of the armies of Heaven, praising God, saying :

" Glory to God in the highest Heaven ! Peace upon earth among men of goodwill ! "

When the angels left them and went back into Heaven, the shepherds said to each other :

" Now let us go straight to Bethlehem and see this thing which the Lord has made known to us."

So they came as fast as they could and they found Mary and Joseph—and the baby lying in the manger. And when they had seen this sight, they told everybody what had been said to them about the little child. And those who heard them were amazed at what the shepherds said. But Mary treasured all these things and turned them over in her mind. The shepherds went back to work, glorifying and praising God for everything that they had heard and seen, which had happened just as they had been told.

Mary and Joseph bring their newly-born son to the Temple   2 : 21

At the end of the eight days, the time came for circumcising the child and he was called Jesus, the name given to him by the angel before his conception.

When the " purification " time, stipulated by the Law of Moses, was completed, they brought Jesus to Jerusalem to present him to the Lord. This was to fulfil a requirement of the Law :

Every male that openeth the womb shall be called holy to the Lord.

They also offered the sacrifice prescribed by the Law :

A pair of turtle-doves, or two young pigeons.

In Jerusalem was a man by the name of Simeon. He was an upright man, devoted to the service of God, living in expectation of the " salvation of Israel." His heart was open to the Holy Spirit, and it had been revealed to him that he would not die before he saw the Lord's Christ. He had been led by the Spirit to go into the Temple, and when Jesus' parents brought the child in to have done to him what the Law required, he took him up in his arms, blessed God and said :

" At last, Lord, You can dismiss Your servant in peace, as You promised ! For with my own eyes I have seen Your Salvation which You have made ready for every people— a light to show truth to the Gentiles and bring glory to Your people Israel."

Joseph and Jesus' mother were surprised at what Simeon

said about the child. And he gave them his blessing and said to Mary, the child's mother :

" This child is destined to make many fall and many rise in Israel and to set up a standard which many will attack—for he will expose the secret thoughts of many hearts. And for you ... your very soul will be pierced by a sword."

There was also present, Anna, the daughter of Phanuel of the tribe of Asher, who was a prophetess. She was a very old woman, having had seven years' married life and was now a widow of eighty-four. She spent her whole life in the Temple and worshipped God night and day with fastings and prayers. She came up at this very moment, praised God and spoke about Jesus to all those in Jerusalem who were expecting redemption.

When they had completed all the requirements of the Law of the Lord, they returned to Galilee, to their own town of Nazareth. The child grew up and became strong and full of wisdom. And God's blessing was upon him.

Twelve years later : the boy Jesus goes with his parents to   2 : 41
Jerusalem

Every year at the Passover Festival, Jesus' parents used to go to Jerusalem. When he was twelve years old they went up to the City as usual for the Festival. When it was over they started back home, but the boy Jesus stayed behind in Jerusalem, without his parents' knowledge. They went a day's journey assuming that he was somewhere in their company, and then they began to look for him among their relations and acquaintances. They failed to find him, however, and turned back to the City, looking for him as they went. Three days later, they found him—in the Temple, sitting among the teachers, listening to them and asking them questions. All those who heard him were astonished at his powers of comprehension and at the answers that he gave. When Joseph and Mary saw him, they could hardly believe their eyes, and his mother said to him :

" Why have you treated us like this, my son ? Here have your father and I been very worried, looking for you everywhere ! "

And Jesus replied :

"But why were you looking for me? Did you not know that I must be in my Father's House?"

But they did not understand his reply. Then he went home with them to Nazareth and was obedient to them. And his mother treasured all these things in her heart. And as Jesus continued to grow in body and mind, he grew also in the love of God and of those who knew him.

Several years later : John prepares the way of Christ   3 : 1

In the fifteenth year of the reign of the Emperor Tiberius (a year when Pontius Pilate was governor of Judaea, Herod tetrarch of Galilee, Philip, his brother, tetrarch of the territory of Ituraea and Trachonitis, and Lysanias tetrarch of Abilene, while Annas and Caiaphas were the High Priests), the word of God came to John, the son of Zacharias, while he was in the desert. He went into the whole country round about the Jordan proclaiming baptism as a mark of a complete change of heart and of the forgiveness of sins, as the book of the prophet Isaiah says :

The voice of one crying in the wilderness,
Make ye ready the way of the Lord,
Make his paths straight.
Every valley shall be filled,
And every mountain and hill shall be brought low :
And the crooked shall become straight,
And the rough ways smooth :
And all flesh shall see the salvation of God.

So John used to say to the crowds who came out to be baptized by him :

"Who warned you, you serpent's brood, to escape from the wrath to come? See that you do something to show that your hearts are really changed! Don't start thinking that you can say to yourselves, 'We are "Abraham's children," ' for I tell you that God could produce children of Abraham out of these stones! The axe already lies at the root of the tree, and the tree that fails to produce good fruit is cut down and thrown into the fire."

Then the crowds would ask him, "Then what shall we do?"

And his answer was, "The man who has two shirts must share with the man who has none, and the man who has food must do the same."

Some of the tax-collectors also came to him to be baptized and they asked him:

"Master, what are we to do?"

"You must not demand more than you are entitled to," he replied.

And the soldiers asked him, "And what are we to do?"

"Don't bully people, don't bring false charges, and be content with your pay," he replied.

The people were in a great state of expectation and were inwardly discussing whether John could possibly be Christ. But John answered them all in these words:

"It is true that I baptize you with water, but the one who follows me is stronger than I am—indeed I am not fit to undo his shoe-laces—he will baptize you with the fire of the Holy Spirit. He will come all ready to separate the wheat from the chaff, and to clear the rubbish from his threshing-floor. The wheat he will gather into his barn and the chaff he will burn with a fire that cannot be put out."

These and many other things John said to the people as he exhorted them and announced the Good News. But the tetrarch Herod, who had been condemned by John in the affair of Herodias, his brother's wife, as well as for the other evil things that he had done, crowned his misdeeds by putting John in prison.

Jesus is himself baptized   3 : 21

When all the people had been baptized, and Jesus was praying after his own baptism, Heaven opened and the Holy Spirit came down upon him in the bodily form of a dove. Then there came a Voice from Heaven, saying:

"You are my dearly-loved Son, in Whom I am well pleased."

Jesus himself was about thirty years old at this time when he began his work.

The ancestry of Jesus traced to Adam   3 : 23b

People assumed that Jesus was the son of Joseph, who was the son of Heli, who was the son of Matthat, who was the son of Levi, who

was the son of Melchi, who was the son of Jannai, who was the son
of Joseph, who was the son of Mattathias, who was the son of Amos,
who was the son of Nahum, who was the son of Esli, who was the
son of Naggai, who was the son of Maath, who was the son of
Mattathias, who was the son of Semein, who was the son of Josech,
who was the son of Joda, who was the son of Joanan, who was the son
of Rhesa, who was the son of Zerubbabel, who was the son of Shealtiel,
who was the son of Neri, who was the son of Melchi, who was the
son of Addi, who was the son of Cosam, who was the son of Elmadam,
who was the son of Er, who was the son of Jose, who was the son of
Eliezer, who was the son of Jorim, who was the son of Matthat,
who was the son of Levi, who was the son of Symeon, who was the
son of Judas, who was the son of Joseph, who was the son of Jonam,
who was the son of Eliakim, who was the son of Melea, who was the
son of Menna, who was the son of Mattatha, who was the son of
Nathan, who was the son of David, who was the son of Jesse, who
was the son of Obed, who was the son of Boaz, who was the son of
Salmon, who was the son of Nahshon, who was the son of Amminadab,
who was the son of Arni, who was the son of Hezron, who was the
son of Perez, who was the son of Judah, who was the son of Jacob,
who was the son of Isaac, who was the son of Abraham, who was the
son of Terah who, was the son of Nahor, who was the son of Serug,
who was the son of Reu, who was the son of Peleg, who was the son
of Eber, who was the son of Shelah, who was the son of Cainan, who
was the son of Arphaxad, who was the son of Shem, who was the
son of Noah, who was the son of Lamech, who was the son of
Methuselah, who was the son of Enoch, who was the son of Jared,
who was the son of Mahalaleel, who was the son of Cainan, who was
the son of Enos, who was the son of Seth, who was the son of Adam,
who was the son of God.

Jesus faces temptation   4 : 1

Jesus returned from the Jordan full of the Holy Spirit and
he was led by the Spirit to spend forty days in the desert,
where he was tempted by the devil. He ate nothing during
that time and afterwards he felt very hungry.

"If you really are the Son of God," the devil said to him,
"tell this stone to turn into a loaf."

Jesus answered:

"The Scripture says, '*Man shall not live by bread alone.*'"

Then the devil took him up and showed him all the

kingdoms of mankind in a sudden vision, and said to him :

"I will give you all this power and magnificence, for it belongs to me and I can give it to anyone I please. It shall all be yours if you will fall down and worship me."

To this Jesus replied :

"It is written, '*Thou shalt worship the Lord thy God and Him only shalt thou serve.*'"

Then the devil took him to Jerusalem and set him on the highest ledge of the Temple.

"If you really are the Son of God," he said, "throw yourself down from here, for the Scripture says, '*He shall give His angels charge concerning thee, to guard thee,*' and '*On their hands they shall bear thee up, lest haply thou dash thy foot against a stone.*'"

To which Jesus replied :

"It is also said, '*Thou shalt not tempt the Lord thy God.*'"

And when he had exhausted every kind of temptation, the devil withdrew until his next opportunity.

Jesus begins his ministry in Galilee   4 : 14

And now Jesus returned to Galilee in the power of the Spirit, and news of him spread through all the surrounding district. He taught in their synagogues, to everyone's great admiration.

Then he came to Nazareth where he had been brought up and, according to his custom, went to the synagogue on the Sabbath day. He stood up to read the Scriptures and the book of the prophet Isaiah was handed to him. He opened the book and found the place where these words are written :

The Spirit of the Lord is upon me,
Because he anointed me to preach good tidings to the
    poor :
He hath sent me to proclaim release to the captives,
And recovering of sight to the blind,
To set at liberty them that are bruised,
To proclaim the acceptable year of the Lord.

Then he shut the book, handed it back to the attendant and resumed his seat. Every eye in the synagogue was fixed upon him and he began to tell them, "This very day this Scripture has been fulfilled, while you have been listening to it!"

Everybody noticed what he said and was amazed at the beautiful words that came from his lips, and they kept saying:

"Isn't this Joseph's son?"

So he said to them:

"I expect you will quote this proverb to me, 'Cure yourself, doctor!' Let us see you do in your own country all that we have heard that you did in Capernaum!" Then he added, "I assure you that no prophet is ever welcomed in his own country. I tell you the plain fact that in Elijah's time, when the heavens were shut up for three and a half years and there was a great famine through the whole country, there were plenty of widows in Israel, but Elijah was not sent to any of them. But he *was* sent to Sarepta, to a widow in the country of Sidon. In the time of Elisha the prophet, there were a great many lepers in Israel, but not one of them was healed—only Naaman, the Syrian."

But when they heard this, everyone in the synagogue was furiously angry. They sprang to their feet and drove him right out of the town, taking him to the brow of the hill on which it was built, intending to hurl him down bodily. But he walked straight through the whole crowd and went on his way.

Jesus heals in Capernaum   4 : 31

So he came down to Capernaum, a town in Galilee, and taught them on the Sabbath day. They were astonished at his teaching, for his words had the ring of authority.

There was a man in the synagogue under the influence of some evil spirit and he yelled at the top of his voice, "Hi! What have you got to do with us, Jesus, you Nazarene— have you come to kill us? I know who you are all right, you're God's Holy One!"

Jesus cut him short and spoke sharply:

"Be quiet! Get out of him!"

And after throwing the man down in front of them, the devil did come out of him without hurting him in the slightest. At this, everybody present was amazed and they kept saying to each other:

" What sort of words are these ? He speaks to these evil spirits with authority and power and out they come."

And his reputation spread over the whole surrounding district.

When Jesus got up and left the synagogue he went into Simon's house. Simon's mother-in-law was suffering from a high fever, and they asked Jesus about her. He stood over her as she lay in bed, brought the fever under control and it left her. At once she got up and began to see to their needs.

Then, as the sun was setting, all those who had friends suffering from every kind of disease brought them to Jesus and he laid his hands on each one of them separately and healed them. Evil spirits came out of many of these people, shouting, " You are the Son of God ! "

But he spoke sharply to them and would not allow them to say any more, for they knew perfectly well that he was Christ.

Jesus attempts to be alone—in vain   4 : 42

At daybreak, he went off to a deserted place, but the crowds tried to find him and when they did discover him, tried to prevent him from leaving them. But he told them, " I must tell the good news of the Kingdom of God to other towns as well—that is my mission."

And he continued proclaiming his message in the synagogues of Judaea.

Simon, James and John become Jesus' followers   5 : 1

One day the people were crowding closely round Jesus to hear God's message, as he stood on the shore of Lake Gennesaret. Jesus noticed two boats drawn up on the beach, for the fishermen had left them there while they were cleaning their nets. He went aboard one of the boats, which belonged to Simon, and asked him to push out a little from the shore. Then he sat down and continued his teaching of the crowds from the boat.

When he had finished speaking, he said to Simon, " Push out now into deep water and let down your nets for a catch."

Simon replied, " Master ! We've worked all night and never caught a thing, but if you say so, I'll let the nets down."

And when they had done this, they caught an enormous

shoal of fish—so big that the nets began to tear. So they signalled to their friends in the other boat to come and help them. They came and filled both the boats to sinking point. When Simon Peter saw this, he fell on his knees before Jesus and said :

" Keep away from me, Lord, for I'm only a sinful man ! "

For he and his companions (including Zebedee's sons, James and John, Simon's partners) were staggered at the haul of fish that they had made.

Jesus said to Simon, " Don't be afraid, Simon. From now on your catch will be *men*."

So they brought the boats ashore, left everything and followed him.

Jesus cures leprosy   5 : 12

While he was in one of the towns, Jesus came upon a man who was a mass of leprosy. When he saw Jesus, he prostrated himself before him and begged :

" If you want to, Lord, you can make me clean."

Jesus stretched out his hand, placed it on the leper, saying : " Certainly I want to. Be clean ! "

Immediately the leprosy left him and Jesus warned him not to tell anybody, but to go and show himself to the priest and to make the offerings for his recovery that Moses prescribed, as evidence to the authorities.

Yet the news about him spread all the more, and enormous crowds collected to hear Jesus and to be healed of their diseases. But he slipped quietly away to deserted places for prayer.

Jesus cures a paralytic in soul and body   5 : 17

One day while Jesus was teaching, some Pharisees and experts in the Law were sitting near him. They had come out of every village in Galilee and Judaea as well as from Jerusalem. God's power to heal people was with him. Soon some men arrived carrying a paralytic on a small bed and they kept trying to carry him in to put him down in front of Jesus. When they failed to find a way of getting him in because of the dense crowd, they went up on to the top of the house and let him down, bed and all, through the tiles, into the middle of the crowd in front of Jesus. When Jesus saw their faith, he said to the man :

" My friend, your sins are forgiven."

The Scribes and the Pharisees began to argue about this, saying, " Who is this man who talks blasphemy ? Who can forgive sins ? Only God can do that."

Jesus realised what was going on in their minds and spoke straight to them.

" Why must you argue like this in your minds ? Which do you suppose is easier—to say, ' Your sins are forgiven ' or to say, ' Get up and walk ' ? But to make you realise that the Son of Man has full authority on earth to forgive sins— I tell *you*," he said to the man who was paralysed, " get up, pick up your bed and go home ! "

Instantly before their eyes the man sprang to his feet, picked up the bedding on which he used to lie, and went off home, praising God. Sheer amazement gripped every man present, and they praised God and said in awed voices, " We have seen incredible things to-day."

Jesus calls Levi to be his disciple   5 : 27

Later on, Jesus went out and looked straight at a tax-collector called Levi, as he sat at his office desk.

" Follow me," he said to him.

And he got to his feet at once, left everything behind and followed him.

Then Levi gave a big reception for Jesus in his own house, and there was a great crowd of tax-collectors and others at table with them. The Pharisees and their companions the Scribes kept muttering indignantly about this to Jesus' disciples, saying :

" Why do you have your meals with tax-collectors and sinners ? "

Jesus answered them :

" It is not the healthy who need the doctor, but those who are ill. I have not come to invite the ' righteous ' but the ' sinners '—to change their ways."

Jesus hints at who he is   5 : 33

Then people said to him :

" Why is it that John's disciples are always fasting and

praying, just like the Pharisees' disciples, but yours both eat and drink ? "

Jesus answered :

" Can you expect wedding-guests to fast while they have the bridegroom with them ? The day will come when they will lose the bridegroom ; that will be the time for them to fast ! "

Then he gave them this illustration.

" Nobody tears a piece from a new coat to patch up an old one. If he does, he ruins the new one and the new piece does not match the old.

" Nobody puts new wine into old wine-skins. If he does, the new wine will burst the skins—the wine will be spilt and the skins ruined. No, new wine must be put into new wine-skins. Of course, nobody who has been drinking old wine will want the new at once. He is sure to say, ' The old is a good sound wine.' "

Jesus speaks of the Sabbath—   6 : 1

One Sabbath day, as Jesus happened to be passing through the cornfields, his disciples began picking the ears of corn, rubbing them in their hands, and eating them. Some of the Pharisees remarked :

" Why are you doing what the Law forbids men to do on the Sabbath day ? "

Jesus answered them and said :

" Have you never read what David and his companions did when they were hungry ? How he went into the House of God, took the Presentation Loaves, ate some bread himself and gave some to his companions, even though the Law does not permit anyone except the priests to eat it ? "

Then he added, " The Son of Man is master even of the Sabbath."

—and provokes violent antagonism   6 : 6

On another Sabbath day when he went into a synagogue to teach, there was a man there whose right hand was wasted away. The Scribes and the Pharisees were watching Jesus closely to see whether he would heal on the Sabbath day, which would, of course, give them grounds for an accusation.

But he knew exactly what was going on in their minds and said to the man with the wasted hand :

"Stand up and come out in front."

And he got up and stood there. Then Jesus said to them :

"I am going to ask you a question. Does the Law command us to do good on Sabbath days or do harm—to save life or destroy it ? "

He looked round, meeting all their eyes, and said to the man :

"Now stretch out your hand."

He did so, and his hand was restored as sound as the other one. But they were filled with insane fury and kept discussing with each other what they could do to Jesus.

After a night of prayer Jesus selects the Twelve   6 : 12

It was in those days that he went up the hill-side to pray, and spent the whole night in prayer to God. When daylight came, he summoned his disciples to him and out of them he chose twelve whom he called Apostles. They were :

Simon (whom he called Peter),
Andrew, his brother,
James,
John,
Philip,
Bartholomew,
Matthew,
Thomas,
James, the son of Alphaeus,
Simon, called the Patriot,
Judas, the brother of James, and
Judas Iscariot, who later betrayed him.

Then he came down with them and stood on a level piece of ground, surrounded by a large crowd of his disciples and a great number of people from all parts of Judaea and Jerusalem and the coastal district of Tyre and Sidon, who had come to hear him and to be healed of their diseases. (And even those who were troubled with evil spirits were cured.) The whole crowd were trying to touch him with their hands, for power was going out from him and he was healing them all.

Jesus declares who is happy and who is to be pitied, and   6 : 20
defines a new attitude towards life

Then Jesus looked steadily at his disciples and said :

" How happy are you who own nothing, for the Kingdom of God is yours !

" How happy are you who are hungry now, for you will be satisfied !

" How happy are you who weep now, for you are going to laugh !

" How happy you are when men hate you and turn you out of their company ; when they slander you and detest all that you stand for because you are loyal to the Son of Man. Be glad when that happens and jump for joy—your reward in Heaven is magnificent. For that is exactly how their fathers treated the prophets.

" But how miserable for you who are rich, for you have had all your comforts !

" How miserable for you who have all you want, for you are going to be hungry !

" How miserable for you who are laughing now, for you will know sorrow and tears !

" How miserable for you when everybody says nice things about you, for that is exactly how their fathers treated the false prophets.

" But I say to all of you who will listen to me : love your enemies, do good to those who hate you, bless those who curse you, and pray for those who treat you badly.

" As for the man who hits you on one cheek, offer him the other one as well ! And if a man is taking away your coat, do not stop him from taking your shirt as well. Give to everyone who asks you, and when a man has taken what belongs to you, don't demand it back.

" Treat men exactly as you would like them to treat you. If you love only those who love you, what credit is that to you ? Even sinners love those who love them ! And if you do good only to those who do good to you, what credit is that to you ? Even sinners do that. And if you lend to those from whom you hope to get your money back, what credit is that to you ? Even sinners lend to sinners and expect to get their money back. No, you are to love your *enemies* and do good and lend without hope of return. Your

reward will be wonderful and you will be sons of the Most
High. For He is kind to the ungrateful and the wicked!

" You must be merciful, as your Father in Heaven is merciful. Don't judge other people and you will not be judged
yourselves. Don't condemn and you will not be condemned.
Make allowances for others and people will make allowances
for you. Give and men will give to you—yes, good measure,
pressed down, shaken together and running over will they
pour into your lap. For whatever measure you use with
other people, they will use in their dealings with you."

The need for thorough-going sincerity   6 : 39

Then he gave them an illustration :

" Can one blind man be guide to another blind man ?
Surely they will both fall into the ditch together. A disciple
is not above his teacher, but when he is fully trained he will
be like his teacher.

" Why do you look at the speck of sawdust in your
brother's eye and fail to notice the plank in your own ? How
can you say to your brother, ' Let me take the speck out of
your eye ' when you cannot see the plank in your own ?
You fraud, take the plank out of your own eye first and then
you can see clearly enough to remove your brother's speck.

" It is impossible for a good tree to produce bad fruit—as
impossible as it is for a bad tree to produce good fruit. Do
not men know what a tree is by its fruit ? You cannot pick
figs from briars, or gather a bunch of grapes from a black-
berry bush ! A good man produces good things from the
good stored up in his heart, and a bad man produces evil
things from his own stores of evil. For a man's words will
always express what has been treasured in his heart.

" And what is the point of calling me, ' Lord, Lord,'
without doing what I tell you to do ? Let me show you
what the man who comes to me, hears what I have to say,
and puts it into practice, is really like. He is like a man
building a house, who dug down to rock-bottom and made
the foundation of his house upon it. Then when the flood
came and the flood-water swept down upon that house, it
could not shift it because it was properly built. But the man
who hears me and does nothing about it is like a man who
built his house with its foundation upon soft earth. When the

flood-water swept down upon it, it collapsed and the whole house crashed down in ruins."

A Roman centurion's extraordinary faith in Jesus 7 : 1

When Jesus had finished these talks to the people, he came to Capernaum, where it happened that there was a man very seriously ill and in fact at the point of death. He was the slave of a centurion who thought very highly of him. When the centurion heard about Jesus, he sent some Jewish Elders to him with the request that he would come and save his servant's life. When they came to Jesus, they urged him strongly to grant this request, saying that the centurion deserved to have this done for him. " He loves our nation and has built us a synagogue out of his own pocket," they said.

So Jesus went with them, but as he approached the house, the centurion sent some of his personal friends with the message :

" Don't trouble yourself, sir ! I'm not important enough for you to come into my house—I didn't think I was fit to come to you in person. Just give the order, please, and my servant will recover. I am used to working under orders, and I have soldiers under me. I can say to one, ' Go,' and he goes, or I can say to another, ' Come here,' and he comes ; or I can say to my slave, ' Do this job,' and he does it."

These words amazed Jesus and he turned to the crowd who were following behind him, and said :

" I have never found faith like this anywhere even in Israel ! "

Then those who had been sent by the centurion returned to the house and found the slave perfectly well.

Jesus brings a dead youth back to life 7 : 11

Not long afterwards, Jesus went into a town called Nain, accompanied by his disciples and a large crowd. As they approached the city gate, it happened that some people were carrying out a dead man, the only son of his widowed mother. The usual crowd of fellow-townsmen was with her. When the Lord saw her, his heart went out to her and he said :

" Don't cry."

Then he walked up and put his hand on the bier while the bearers stood still. Then he said :

" Young man, *wake up !* "

And the dead man sat up and began to talk, and Jesus handed him to his mother. Everybody present was awe-struck and they praised God, saying :

" A great prophet has arisen among us and God has turned His face towards His people."

And this report of him spread through the whole of Judaea and the surrounding countryside.

Jesus sends John a personal message   7 : 18

John's disciples reported all these happenings to him. Then he summoned two of them and sent them to the Lord with this message :

" Are you the One Who was to come, or are we to look for someone else ? "

When the men came to Jesus, they said :

" John the Baptist has sent us to you with this message, ' Are you the One Who was to come, or are we to look for someone else ? "

At that very time Jesus was healing many people of their diseases and ailments and evil spirits, and he restored sight to many who were blind. Then he answered them :

" Go and tell John what you have seen and heard. The blind are recovering their sight, cripples are walking again, lepers being healed, the deaf hearing, dead men are being brought to life again, and the Good News is being given to those in need. *And happy is the man who never loses his faith in me.*"

Jesus emphasises the greatness of John—and the greater   7 : 24
importance of the Kingdom of God

When these messengers had gone back, Jesus began to talk to the crowd about John.

" What did you go out into the desert to look at ? Was it a reed waving in the breeze ? Well, *what* was it you went out to see ? A man dressed in fine clothes ? But the men who wear fine clothes live luxuriously in palaces. But what *did* you really go to see ? A prophet ? Yes, I tell you, **a** prophet and far more than a prophet! This is the man of whom the Scripture says :

Behold, I send my messenger before thy face,
Who shall prepare thy way before thee.

Believe me, no one greater than John has ever been born, and yet a humble member of the Kingdom of God is greater than he.

"All the people, yes, even the tax-collectors, when they heard John, acknowledged God and were baptized by his baptism. But the Pharisees and the experts in the Law frustrated God's purpose for them, for they refused John's baptism.

"What can I say that the men of this generation are like— what sort of men are they? They are like children sitting in the market-place and calling out to each other, 'We played at weddings for you, but you wouldn't dance, and we played at funerals for you, and you wouldn't cry'! For John the Baptist came in the strictest austerity and you say he is crazy. Then the Son of Man came, enjoying life, and you say, 'Look, a drunkard and a glutton, a bosom-friend of the tax-collector and the outsider!' Ah well, Wisdom's reputation is entirely in the hands of her children!"

Jesus contrasts unloving righteousness with loving penitence　7 : 36

Then one of the Pharisees asked Jesus to a meal with him. When Jesus came into the house, he took his place at the table and a woman, known in the town as a bad woman, found out that Jesus was there and brought an alabaster flask of perfume and stood behind him crying, letting her tears fall on his feet and then drying them with her hair. Then she kissed them and anointed them with the perfume. When the Pharisee who had invited him saw this, he said to himself, "If this man were really a prophet, he would know who this woman is and what sort of a person is touching him. He would have realised that she is a bad woman." Then Jesus spoke to him :

"Simon, there is something I want to say to you."

"Very well, Master," he returned, "say it."

"Once upon a time, there were two men in debt to the

same money-lender. One owed him fifty pounds and the other five. And since they were unable to pay, he generously cancelled both their debts. Now, which one of them do you suppose will love him more?"

"Well," returned Simon, "I suppose it will be the one who has been more generously treated."

"Exactly," replied Jesus, and then turning to the woman, he said to Simon:

"You can see this woman? I came into your house but you provided no water to wash my feet. But she has washed my feet with her tears and dried them with her hair. There was no warmth in your greeting, but she, from the moment I came in, has not stopped covering my feet with kisses. You gave me no oil for my head, but she has put perfume on my feet. That is why I tell you, Simon, that her sins, many as they are, are forgiven; for she has shown me so much love. But the man who has little to be forgiven has only a little love to give."

Then he said to her:

"Your sins are forgiven."

And the men at table with him began to say to themselves:

"And who is this man, who even forgives sins?"

But Jesus said to the woman:

"It is your faith that has saved you. Go in peace."

Not long after this incident, Jesus went through every town and village preaching and telling the people the good news of the Kingdom of God. He was accompanied by the Twelve and some women who had been cured of evil spirits and illnesses—Mary, known as "the woman from Magdala" (who had once been possessed by seven evil spirits), Joanna the wife of Chuza, Herod's agent, Susanna, and many others who used to look after his comfort from their own resources.

Jesus' parable of the mixed reception given to the truth   8 : 4

When a large crowd had collected and people were coming to him from one town after another, he spoke to them and gave them this parable:

"A sower went out to sow his seed, and while he was sowing, some of the seed fell by the roadside and was trodden down and the birds gobbled it up. Some fell on the rock, and when it sprouted it withered for lack of moisture. Some fell among thorn-bushes which grew up with the seeds and choked the life out of them. But some seed fell on good soil and grew and produced a crop—a hundred times what had been sown."

And when he had said this, he called out :

" Let the man who has ears to hear use them ! "

Then his disciples asked him the meaning of the parable. To which Jesus replied :

" You have been given the chance to understand the secrets of the Kingdom of God, but the others are given parables so that they may go through life with their eyes open and see nothing, and with their ears open and understand nothing of what they hear.

" This is what the parable means. The seed is the message of God. The seed sown by the roadside represents those who hear the message, and then the devil comes and takes it away from their hearts so that they cannot believe it and be saved. That sown on the rock represents those who accept the message with great delight when they hear it, but have no real root. They believe for a little while but when the time of temptation comes, they lose faith. And the seed sown among the thorns represents the people who hear the message and go on their way, and with the worries and riches and pleasures of living, the life is choked out of them, and in the end they produce nothing. But the seed sown on good soil means the men who hear the message and accept it with a good and honest heart, and go on steadily producing a good crop.

Truth is not a secret to be hidden but a gift to be used   8 : 16

" Nobody lights a lamp and covers it with a basin or puts it under the bed. No, a man puts his lamp on a lamp-stand so that those who come in can see the light. For there is nothing hidden now which will not become perfectly plain and there are no secrets now which will not become as clear as daylight. So take care how you listen—more will be given to the man who has something already, but the man who has nothing will lose even what he thinks he has."

Then his mother and his brothers arrived to see him, but could not get near him because of the crowd. So a message was passed to him :

"Your mother and your brothers are standing outside wanting to see you."

To which he replied:

"My mother and my brothers? That means those who listen to God's message and obey it."

Jesus' mastery of wind and water   8 : 22

It happened on one of these days that he embarked on a boat with his disciples and said to them:

"Let us cross over to the other side of the lake."

So they set sail, and when they were under way he dropped off to sleep. Then a squall of wind swept down upon the lake and they were being swamped and were in grave danger. Coming forward, they woke him up, saying:

"Master, Master, we're drowning!"

Then he got up and reprimanded the wind and the stormy waters, and they died down, and everything was still. Then he said to them:

"What has happened to your faith?"

But they were frightened and bewildered and kept saying to each other:

"Who ever can this be? He gives orders even to the winds and waters and *they obey him*."

Jesus encounters and heals a dangerous lunatic   8 : 26

They sailed on to the country of the Gerasenes which is on the opposite side of the lake to Galilee. And as Jesus disembarked, a man from the town who was possessed by evil spirits met him. He had worn no clothes for a long time and did not live inside a house, but among the tombs. When he saw Jesus, he let out a howl and fell down in front of him, yelling:

"What have you got to do with me, you Jesus, Son of the Most High God? Please, please, don't torment me."

For Jesus was commanding the evil spirit to come out of the man. Again and again the evil spirit had taken control of him, and though he was bound with chains and fetters and closely watched, he would snap his bonds and go off into the desert with the devil at his heels. Then Jesus asked him:

"What is your name?"

"Legion!" he replied. For many evil spirits had gone into him, and were now begging Jesus not to order them off to the bottomless pit. It happened that there was a large herd of pigs feeding on the hill-side, so they implored him to allow them to go into the pigs, and he let them go. And when the evil spirits came out of the man and went into the pigs, the whole herd rushed down the cliff into the lake and were drowned. When the swineherds saw what had happened, they took to their heels, pouring out the story to the people in the town and countryside. These people came out to see what had happened, and approached Jesus. They found the man, whom the evil spirits had left, sitting down at Jesus' feet, properly clothed and quite sane. That frightened them. Those who had seen it told the others how the man with the evil spirits had been cured. And the whole crowd of people from the district surrounding the Gerasenes' country begged Jesus to go away from them, for they were thoroughly frightened. Then he re-embarked on the boat and turned back. The man who had had the evil spirits kept begging to go with Jesus, but he sent him away with the words:

"Go back home and tell them all what wonderful things God has done for you."

So the man went away and told the marvellous story of what Jesus had done for him, all over the town.

On Jesus' return, the crowd welcomed him back, for they had all been looking for him.

Jesus heals in response to faith   8 : 41

Then up came Jairus (he was president of the synagogue), and fell at Jesus' feet, begging him to come into his house, for his daughter, an only child about twelve years old, was dying.

But as he went, the crowds nearly suffocated him. Among them was a woman who had had a hæmorrhage for twelve years and who had derived no benefit from anybody's treatment. She came up behind Jesus and touched the edge of his cloak, with the result that her hæmorrhage stopped at once.

"Who was that who touched me?" said Jesus.

And when everybody denied it, Peter remonstrated:

"Master, the crowds are all round you and are pressing you on all sides. . . ."

But Jesus said:

"Somebody touched me, for I felt that power went out from me."

When the woman realised that she had not escaped notice she came forward trembling, and fell at his feet and admitted before everybody why she had had to touch him, and how she had been instantaneously cured.

"Daughter," said Jesus, "it is your faith that has healed you—go in peace."

While he was still speaking, somebody came from the synagogue president's house to say:

"Your daughter is dead—there is no need to trouble the Master any further."

But when Jesus heard this, he said to him:

"Now don't be afraid, go on believing and she will be all right."

Then when he came to the house, he would not allow anyone to go in with him except Peter, John and James, and the child's parents. All those already there were weeping and wailing over her, but he said:

"Stop crying! She is not dead, she is fast asleep."

This drew a scornful laugh from them, for they were quite certain that she had died. But he turned them all out, took the little girl's hand and called out to her:

"Wake up, my child!"

And her spirit came back and she got to her feet at once, and Jesus ordered food to be given to her. Her parents were nearly out of their minds with joy, but Jesus told them not to tell anyone what had happened.

Jesus commissions the Twelve to preach and heal   9 : 1

Then he called the Twelve together and gave them power and authority over all evil spirits and the ability to heal disease. He sent them out to preach the Kingdom of God and to heal the sick, with these words:

"Take nothing for your journey—neither a stick nor a purse nor food nor money, nor even extra clothes! When you come to stay at a house, remain there until you go on your way again. And where they will not welcome you, leave that town, and shake the dust off your feet as a protest against them!"

So they set out, and went from village to village preaching the Gospel and healing people everywhere.

Herod's uneasy conscience after his execution of John   9 : 7

All these things came to the ears of Herod the tetrarch and caused him acute anxiety, because some people were saying that John had risen from the dead, some maintaining that the prophet Elijah had appeared, and others that one of the old-time prophets had come back.

"I beheaded John," said Herod. "Who can this be that I hear all these things about?"

And he tried to find a way of seeing Jesus.

The Twelve return and tell their story   9 : 10

Then the Apostles returned, and when they had made their report to Jesus of what they had done, he took them with him privately and retired into a town called Bethsaida.

Jesus welcomes the crowds, teaches, heals and feeds them   9 : 11

But the crowds observed this and followed him. And he welcomed them and talked to them about the Kingdom of God, and cured those who were in need of healing. As the day drew to its close the Twelve came to him and said :

"Please dismiss the crowd now so that they can go to the villages and country round about and find some food and shelter, for we're quite in the wilds here."

"You give them something to eat!" returned Jesus.

"But we've nothing here," they replied, "except five loaves and two fish, unless you want us to go and buy food for all this crowd?" (There were approximately five thousand men there.)

Then Jesus said to the disciples :

"Get them to sit down in groups of about fifty."

This they did, making them all sit down. Then he took the five loaves and the two fish and looked up to Heaven, blessed them, broke them into pieces and passed them to his disciples to serve to the crowd. Everybody ate and was satisfied. Afterwards they collected twelve baskets full of broken pieces which were left over.

Jesus asks a question and receives Peter's momentous   9 : 18
answer

Then came this incident. While Jesus was praying by
himself, having only the disciples near him, he asked them
this question :

" Who are the crowd saying that I am ? "

" Some say that you are John the Baptist," they replied.
" Others that you are Elijah, and others think that one of the
old-time prophets has come to life again."

Then he said :

" And who do you say that I am ? "

" *God's Christ !* " said Peter.

Jesus foretells his own suffering : the paradox of losing   9 : 21
life to find it

But Jesus expressly told them not to say a word to anybody, at the same time warning them of the inevitability of
the Son of Man's great suffering, of his repudiation by the
Elders, Chief Priests and Scribes, and of his death and of
being raised to life again on the third day. Then he spoke
to them all :

" If anyone wants to follow in my footsteps, he must give
up all right to himself, carry his cross every day and keep
close behind me. For the man who wants to save his life
will lose it, but the man who loses his life for my sake will
save it. For what is the use of a man gaining the whole
world if he loses or forfeits his own soul ? If anyone is
ashamed of me and my words, the Son of Man will be
ashamed of him, when he comes in his glory and the
glory of the Father and the holy angels. I tell you the
simple truth—there are men standing here to-day who
will not taste death until they have seen the Kingdom of
God ! "

Peter, John and James are allowed to see the glory of Jesus   9 : 28

About eight days after these sayings, Jesus took Peter,
James and John and went off with them to the hill-side to
pray. And then, while he was praying, the whole appearance
of his face changed and his clothes became white and dazzling.
And two men were talking with Jesus. They were Moses
and Elijah—revealed in heavenly splendour and their talk

was about the way he must take and the end he must fulfil
in Jerusalem. But Peter and his companions had been overcome by sleep and it was as they struggled into wakefulness
that they saw the glory of Jesus and the two men standing
with him. Just as they were parting from him, Peter said
to Jesus :

"Master, it is wonderful for us to be here! Let us put up
three shelters,—one for you, one for Moses and one for
Elijah." But he did not know what he was saying. While
he was still talking, a cloud overshadowed them and awe
swept over them as it enveloped them. A Voice came out
of the cloud, saying :

"This is My Son, My Chosen! Listen to Him!"

And while the Voice was speaking, they found there was
no one there at all but Jesus. The disciples were reduced to
silence, and in those days never breathed a word to anyone
of what they had seen.

Jesus heals an epileptic boy 9 : 37

Then on the following day, as they came down the hill-
side, a great crowd met him. And now we have a man from
the crowd shouting out :

"Master, please come and look at my son! He's my only
child, and without any warning some spirit gets hold of him
and he calls out suddenly. Then it convulses him until he
foams at the mouth, and only after a fearful struggle does
it go away and leave him bruised all over. I begged your
disciples to get rid of it, but they couldn't."

"You really are an unbelieving and difficult people,"
replied Jesus. "How long must I be with you, how long
must I put up with you? Bring him here to me."

But even while the boy was on his way, the spirit hurled
him to the ground in a dreadful convulsion. Then Jesus
reprimanded the evil spirit, healed the lad and handed him
back to his father. And everybody present was amazed at
this demonstration of the power of God.

The realism of Jesus in the midst of enthusiasm 9 : 43^b

And while everybody was full of wonder at all the things
they saw him do, Jesus said to the disciples :

"Store up in your minds what I tell you nowadays, for

the Son of Man is going to be handed over to the power of men."

But they made no sense of this saying—something made it impossible for them to understand it, and they were afraid to ask him what he meant.

Jesus and " greatness "   9 : 46
Then an argument arose among them as to who should be the greatest. But Jesus, knowing what they were arguing about, took a little child and made him stand by his side. And then he said to them :

" Anyone who accepts a little child in my name is really accepting me, and the man who accepts me is really accepting the One Who sent me. It is the humblest among you all who is really the greatest."

Then John broke in :

" Master, we saw a man driving out evil spirits in your name, but we stopped him, for he is not one of us who follow you."

But Jesus told him :

" You must not stop him. The man who is not against you is on your side."

He sets off for Jerusalem to meet inevitable death   9 : 51
Now as the days before he should be taken back into Heaven were running out, he resolved to go to Jerusalem, and sent messengers in front of him. They set out and entered a Samaritan village to make preparations for him. But the people there refused to welcome him because he was obviously intending to go to Jerusalem. When the disciples James and John saw this, they said :

" Master, do you want us to call down fire from heaven and burn them all up ? "

But Jesus turned and reproved them, and they all went on to another village.

As the little company made its way along the road, a man said to him :

" I'm going to follow you wherever you go."

And Jesus replied :

" Foxes have earths, birds have nests, but the Son of Man has nowhere that he can call his own."

But he said to another man :

"Follow me."

And he replied :

"Let me go and bury my father first."

But Jesus told him :

"Leave the dead to bury their own dead. You must come away and preach the Kingdom of God."

Another man said to him :

"I am going to follow you, Lord, but first let me bid farewell to my people at home."

But Jesus told him :

"Anyone who puts his hand to the plough and then looks behind him is useless for the Kingdom of God."

Jesus now despatches thirty-five couples to preach and heal the sick   10 : 1

Later on the Lord commissioned seventy other disciples, and sent them off in two's as advance-parties into every town and district where he intended to go.

"There is a great harvest," he told them, "but only a few are working in it—which means you must pray to the Lord of the harvest that he will send out more reapers.

"Now go on your way. I am sending you out like lambs among wolves. Don't carry a purse or a bag or a pair of shoes, and don't stop to pass the time of day with anyone you meet on the road. When you go into a house, say first of all, 'Peace be to this household !' If there is a lover of peace there, he will accept your words of blessing, and if not, they will come back to you. Stay in the same house and eat and drink whatever they put before you—a workman deserves his wages. But don't move from one house to another.

"Whatever town you go into and the people welcome you, eat the meals they give you and heal the people who are ill there. Tell them, 'The Kingdom of God is very near to you now.' But whenever you come into a town and they will not welcome you, you must go into the streets and say, 'We brush off even the dust of your town from our feet as a protest against you. But it is still true that the Kingdom of God has arrived !' I assure you that it will be better for Sodom in 'that Day' than for that town.

" Alas for you, Chorazin, and also for you, Bethsaida ! For if Tyre and Sidon had seen the demonstrations of God's power that you have seen, they would have repented long ago and sat in sackcloth and ashes. It will be better for Tyre and Sidon in the Judgment than for you ! As for you, Capernaum, are you on your way up to heaven ? I tell you you will go hurtling down among the dead ! "

Then he added to the Seventy :

" Whoever listens to you is listening to me, and the man who has no use for you has no use for me either. And the man who has no use for me has no use for the One Who sent me ! "

Jesus tells the returned missioners not to be enthusiastic   10 : 17
over mere power

Later the Seventy came back full of joy.

" Lord," they said, " even evil spirits obey us when we use your name ! "

" Yes," returned Jesus, " I was watching and saw Satan fall from heaven like a flash of lightning ! It is true that I have given you the power to tread on snakes and scorpions and to overcome all the enemy's power—there is nothing at all that can do you any harm. Yet it is not your power over evil spirits which should give you such joy, but the fact that your names are written in Heaven."

Jesus prays aloud to his Father   10 : 21

At that moment Jesus himself was inspired with joy, and exclaimed :

" O Father, Lord of Heaven and earth, I thank You for hiding these things from the clever and intelligent and for showing them to mere children ! Yes, I thank You, Father, that this was Your Will." Then he went on :

" Everything has been put in my hands by my Father ; and nobody knows who the Son really is except the Father. Nobody knows Who the Father really is except the Son—and the man to whom the Son chooses to reveal Him ! "

Then he turned to his disciples and said to them quietly :

" How fortunate you are to see what you are seeing ! I tell you that many prophets and kings have wanted to see what you are seeing but they never saw it, and to hear what you are hearing but they never heard it."

Jesus shows the relevance of the Law to actual living   10 : 25

Then one of the experts in the Law stood up to test him and said :

" Master, what must I do to be sure of eternal life ? "

" What does the Law say and what has your reading taught you ? " said Jesus.

" The Law says, ' Thou shalt love the Lord thy God with all thy heart and with all thy soul and with all thy strength and with all thy mind—and thy neighbour as thyself,' " he replied.

" Quite right," said Jesus. " Do that and you will live."

But the man, wanting to justify himself, continued :

" But who is my ' neighbour ' ? "

And Jesus gave him the following reply :

" A man was once on his way down from Jerusalem to Jericho. He fell into the hands of bandits who stripped off his clothes, beat him up, and left him half dead. It so happened that a priest was going down that road, and when he saw him, he passed by on the other side. A Levite also came on the scene and when he saw him, he too passed by on the other side. But then a Samaritan traveller came along to the place where the man was lying, and at the sight of him he was touched with pity. He went across to him and bandaged his wounds, pouring on oil and wine. Then he put him on his own mule, brought him to an inn and did what he could for him. Next day he took out two silver coins and gave them to the inn-keeper with the words, ' Look after him, will you ? I will pay you back whatever more you spend, when I come through here on my return.' Which of these three seems to you to have been a neighbour to the bandits' victim ? "

" The man who gave him practical sympathy," he replied.

" Then you go and give the same," returned Jesus.

Yet emphasises the need for quiet listening to his words   10 : 38

As they continued their journey, Jesus came to a village and a woman called Martha welcomed him to her house. She had a sister by the name of Mary who settled down at the Lord's feet and was listening to what he said. But Martha was very worried about her elaborate preparations and she burst in, saying:

"Lord, don't you *mind* that my sister has left me to do everything by myself? Tell her to get up and help me!"

But the Lord answered her:

"Martha, my dear, you are worried and bothered about providing so many things. Only a few things are really needed, perhaps only one. Mary has chosen the best part and you must not tear it away from her!"

Jesus gives a model prayer   11 : 1

One day it happened that Jesus was praying and after he had finished, one of his disciples said:

"Lord, teach us how to pray, as John used to teach his disciples."

"When you pray," returned Jesus, "you should say, 'Father, may Your Name be honoured—may Your Kingdom come! Give us each day the bread we need, and forgive us our sins, for we forgive anyone who owes anything to us; and keep us clear of temptation.'"

The willingness of the Father to answer prayer   11 : 5

Then he added:

"If any of you has a friend, and goes to him in the middle of the night and says, 'Lend me three loaves, my dear fellow, for a friend of mine has just arrived after a journey and I have no food to put in front of him'; and then he answers from inside the house, 'Don't bother me with your troubles. The front door is locked and my children and I have gone to bed. I simply cannot get up now and give you anything!' Yet, I tell you, that even if he won't get up and give him what he wants simply because he is his friend, yet if he persists, he will rouse himself and give him everything he needs. And so I tell you, ask and it will be given you, search and you will find, knock and the door will be opened to you. The one who asks will always receive; the one who is searching will always find, and the door is opened to the man who knocks. Some of you are fathers, and if your son asks you for some fish, would you give him a snake instead, or if he asks you for an egg, would you make him a present of a scorpion? So, if you, for all your evil, know how to give good things to your children, how much more likely is it that your Heavenly Father will give the Holy Spirit to those who ask Him!"

Jesus shows the absurdity of "his being in league with   11 : 14
the devil"

Another time, Jesus was expelling an evil spirit which was preventing a man from speaking, and as soon as the evil spirit left him, the dumb man found his speech, to the amazement of the crowds.

But some of them said:

"He expels these spirits because he is in league with Beelzebub, the chief of the evil spirits."

Others among them, to test him, tried to get a sign from Heaven out of him. But he knew what they were thinking and told them:

"Any kingdom divided against itself is doomed and a disunited household will collapse. And if Satan disagrees with Satan, how does his kingdom continue?—for I know you are saying that I expel evil spirits because I am in league with Beelzebub. But if I do expel devils because I am an ally of Beelzebub, who is your own sons' ally when they do the same thing? They can settle that question for you. But if it is by the finger of God that I am expelling evil spirits, *then the Kingdom of God has swept over you unawares!*

"When a strong man armed to the teeth guards his own house, his property is in peace. But when a stronger man comes and conquers him, he removes all the arms on which he pinned his faith and divides the spoil among his friends.

"Anyone who is not with me is against me, and the man who does not gather with me is really scattering.

The danger of a spiritual vacuum in a man's soul   11 : 24
"When the evil spirit comes out of a man, it wanders through waterless places looking for rest, and when it fails to find any, it says, 'I will go back to my house from which I came.' When it arrives, it finds it clean and all in order. Then it goes and collects seven other spirits more evil than

itself to keep it company, and they all go in and make themselves at home. The last state of that man is worse than the
first."

Jesus brings sentimentality down to earth   11 : 27

And while he was still saying this, a woman in the crowd
called out and said :

" Oh, what a blessing for a woman to have brought you
into the world and nursed you ! "

But Jesus replied :

" Yes, but a far greater blessing to hear the word of God
and obey it."

His scathing judgment on his contemporary generation   11 : 29

Then as the people crowded closely around him, he continued :

" This is an evil generation ! It looks for a sign and it
will be given no sign except that of Jonah. Just as Jonah
was a sign to the people of Nineveh, so will the Son of Man
be a sign to this generation. When the Judgment comes,
the Queen of the South will rise up with the men of this
generation and she will condemn them. For she came from
the ends of the earth to listen to the wisdom of Solomon,
and there is more than the wisdom of Solomon with you
now ! The men of Nineveh will stand up at the Judgment
with this generation and will condemn it. For they did
repent when Jonah preached to them, and there is something
more than Jonah's preaching with you now !

The need for complete sincerity   11 : 33

" No one takes a lamp and puts it in a cupboard or under
a bucket, but on a lamp-stand, so that those who come in
can see the light. The lamp of your body is your eye. When
your eye is sound, your whole body is full of light, but
when your eye is evil, your whole body is full of darkness.
So be very careful that your light never becomes darkness.
For if your whole body is full of light, with no part of it in
shadow, it will all be radiant,—it will be like having a bright
lamp to give you light."

While he was talking, a Pharisee invited him to dinner.
So he went into his house and sat down at table. The Pharisee

noticed with some surprise that he did not wash before the meal. But the Lord said to him :

"You Pharisees are fond of cleaning the outside of your cups and dishes, but inside yourselves you are full of greed and wickedness! Have you no sense? Don't you realise that the One Who made the outside is the Maker of the inside as well? If you would only make the inside clean by doing good to others, the outside things become clean as a matter of course! But alas for you Pharisees, for you pay out your tithe of mint and rue and every little herb, and lose sight of the justice and the love of God. Yet these are the things you ought to have been concerned with—it need not mean leaving the lesser duties undone. Yes, alas for you Pharisees, who love the front seats in the synagogues and having men bow down to you in public! Alas for you, for you are like unmarked graves—men walk over your corruption without ever knowing it is there."

Jesus denounces the learned for obscuring the truth   11 : 45

Then one of the experts in the Law said to him :

"Master, when you say things like this, you are insulting us as well."

And he returned.

"Yes, and I do blame you experts in the Law! For you pile up back-breaking burdens for men to bear, but you yourselves will not raise a finger to lift them. Alas for you, for you build memorial tombs for the prophets—the very men whom your fathers murdered. You show clearly enough how you approve your fathers' actions. They did the actual killing and you put up a memorial to it. That is why the Wisdom of God has said, 'I will send them prophets and apostles, some they will kill and some they will persecute!' So that the blood of all the prophets shed from the foundation of the earth, from Abel to Zachariah who died between the altar and the sanctuary, shall be charged to this generation!

"Alas for you experts in the Law, for you have taken away the key of knowledge. You have never gone in yourselves and you have hindered everyone else who was at the door!"

And when he left the house, the Scribes and the Pharisees began to regard him with bitter animosity and tried to draw him out on a great many subjects, waiting to pounce on some incriminating remark.

Meanwhile, the crowds had gathered in thousands, so that they were actually treading on each other's toes, and Jesus, speaking primarily to his disciples, said :

" Be on your guard against yeast—I mean the yeast of the Pharisees, which is sheer pretence. For there is nothing covered up which is not going to be exposed, nor anything private which is not going to be made public. Whatever you may say in the dark will be heard in daylight, and whatever you whisper within four walls will be shouted from the house-tops.

Man need only fear God   12 : 4

" I tell you, as friends of mine, that you need not be afraid of those who can kill the body, but afterwards cannot do anything more. I will show you the only One you need to fear—the One Who after He has killed, has power to throw you into destruction ! Yes, I tell you, it is right to stand in awe of Him. The market-price of five sparrows is two farthings, isn't it ? Yet not one of them is forgotten in God's sight. Why, the very hairs of your heads are all numbered ! Don't be afraid, then, you are worth more than a great many sparrows ! I tell you that every man who publicly acknowledges me, I, the Son of Man, will acknowledge in the presence of the angels of God. But the man who publicly disowns me will find himself disowned before the angels of God !

" Anyone who speaks against the Son of Man will be forgiven, but there is no forgiveness for the man who speaks evil against the Holy Spirit. And when they bring you before the synagogues and magistrates and authorities, don't worry as to what defence you are going to put up or what words you are going to use. For the Holy Spirit will tell you at the time what is the right thing for you to say."

Jesus gives a warning about the love of material security   12 : 13

Then someone out of the crowd said to him :

" Master, tell my brother to share his legacy with me."

But Jesus replied :

" My dear man, who appointed me a judge or arbitrator in your affairs ? "

And then, turning to the disciples, he said to them :

" Notice that, and be on your guard against covetousness in any shape or form. For a man's real life in no way depends upon the number of his possessions."

Then he gave them a parable in these words :

" Once upon a time a rich man's farmland produced heavy crops. So he said to himself, ' What shall I do, for I have no room to store this harvest of mine ? ' Then he said, ' I know what I'll do. I'll pull down my barns and build bigger ones where I can store all my grain and my goods and I can say to my soul, Soul, you have plenty of good things stored up there for years to come. Relax ! Eat, drink and have a good time ! ' But God said to him, ' You fool, this very night you will be asked for *your soul* ! Then who is going to possess all that you have prepared ? ' That is what happens to the man who hoards things for himself and is not rich where God is concerned."

And then he added to the disciples :

" That is why I tell you, don't worry about life, wondering what you are going to eat. And stop bothering about what clothes you will need. Life is much more important than food, and the body more important than clothes. Think of the ravens. They neither sow nor reap, and they have neither store nor barn, but God feeds them. And how much more valuable do you think you are than birds ? Can any of you make himself an inch taller however much he worries about it ? And if you can't manage a little thing like this, why do you worry about anything else ? Think of the wild flowers, and how they neither work nor weave. Yet I tell you that Solomon in all his glory was never arrayed like one of these. If God so clothes the grass, which flowers in the field to-day and is burnt in the stove to-morrow, is He not much more likely to clothe you, you little-faiths ? You must not set your heart on what you eat or drink, nor must you live in a state of anxiety. The whole heathen world is busy about getting food and drink, and your Father knows well enough that you need such things. No, set your heart on His King-dom, and your food and drink will come as a matter of course. Don't be afraid, you tiny flock ! Your Father plans

to give you the Kingdom. Sell your possessions and give
the money away. Get yourselves purses that never grow
old, inexhaustible treasure in Heaven, where no thief can
ever reach it, or moth ruin it. For wherever your treasure is, you may be certain that your heart will be there
too!

Jesus' disciples must be on the alert   12 : 35

" You must be ready dressed and have your lamps alight,
like men who wait to welcome their lord and master on his
return from the wedding-feast, so that when he comes and
knocks at the door, they may open it for him at once. Happy
are the servants whom their lord finds on the alert when he
arrives. I assure you that he will then take off his outer clothes,
make them sit down to dinner, and come and wait on them.
And if he should come just after midnight or in the very early
morning and find them still on the alert, their happiness is
assured. But be certain of this, that if the householder had
known the time when the burglar would come, he would
not have let his house be broken into. So you must be on
the alert, for the Son of Man is coming at a time when you
may not expect him."

Then Peter said to him :

" Lord, do you mean this parable for us or for everybody ? "

But the Lord continued :

" Well, who will be the faithful, sensible steward whom
his master will put in charge of his household to give them
their supplies at the proper time ? Happy is the servant if
his master finds him so doing when he returns. I tell
you he will promote him to look after all his property. But
suppose the servant says to himself, ' My master takes his
time about returning,' and then begins to beat the men
and women servants and to eat and drink and get drunk,
that servant's lord and master will return suddenly and
unexpectedly, and he will punish him severely and send him
to share the penalty of the unfaithful. The slave who knows
his master's plan but does not get ready or act upon it will
be severely punished, but the servant who did not know
the plan, though he has done wrong, will be let off lightly.
Much will be expected from the one who has been given

much, and the more a man is trusted, the more people will expect of him.

" It is fire that I have come to bring upon the earth—how I could wish it were already ablaze ! There is a baptism that I must undergo and how strained I am until it is over !

Jesus declares that his coming is bound to bring division   12 : 51

" Do you think I have come to bring peace on the earth ? No, I tell you, not peace, but division ! For from now on, there will be five people divided against each other in one house, three against two, and two against three. It is going to be father against son, and son against father, and mother against daughter, and daughter against mother ; mother-in-law against daughter-in-law, and daughter-in-law against mother-in-law ! "

Intelligence should be used not only about the weather but   12 : 54
about the times in which men live

Then he said to the crowds :

" When you see a cloud arising in the west, you say at once that it is going to rain, and so it does. And when you feel the south wind blowing, you say that it is going to be hot, and so it is. You frauds ! You know how to interpret the look of the earth and the sky. Why can't you interpret the meaning of the times in which you live ?

" And why can't you decide for yourselves what is right ? For instance, when you are going before the magistrate with your opponent, do your best to come to terms with him while you have the chance, or he may rush you off to the judge, and the judge hand you over to the police-officer, and the police-officer throw you into prison. I tell you you will never get out again until you have paid your last farthing."

Jesus is asked about the supposed significance of disasters   13 : 1

It was just at this moment that some people came up to tell him the story of the Galileans whose blood Pilate had mixed with that of their own sacrifices. Jesus made this reply to them :

" Are you thinking that these Galileans were worse sinners than any other men of Galilee because this happened to them ? I assure you that is not so. You will all die just as miserable a death unless your hearts are changed! You remember those eighteen people who were killed at Siloam when the tower collapsed upon them? Are you imagining that they were worse offenders than any of the other people who lived in Jerusalem? I assure you they were not. You will all die just as tragically unless your whole outlook is changed!"

And hints at God's patience with the Jewish nation   13 : 6

Then he gave them this parable:

"Once upon a time a man had a fig-tree growing in his garden, and when he came to look for the figs, he found none at all. So he said to his gardener, 'Look, I have come expecting fruit on this fig-tree for three years running and never found any. Better cut it down. Why should it use up valuable space?' And the gardener replied, 'Master, don't touch it this year till I have had a chance to dig round it and give it a bit of manure. Then, if it bears after that, it will be all right. But if it doesn't then you can cut it down.'"

Jesus reduces the Sabbatarians to silence   13 : 10

It happened that he was teaching in one of the synagogues on the Sabbath day. In the congregation was a woman who for eighteen years had been ill from some psychological cause; she was bent double and was quite unable to straighten herself up. When Jesus noticed her, he called her and said:

"You are set free from your illness!"

And he put his hands upon her, and at once she stood upright and praised God. But the president of the synagogue, in his annoyance at Jesus' healing on the Sabbath, announced to the congregation:

"There are six days in which men may work. Come on one of them and be healed, and not on the Sabbath day!"

But the Lord answered him, saying:

"You hypocrites, every single one of you unties his ox or his ass from the stall on the Sabbath and leads him away to water! This woman, a daughter of Abraham, whom you all know Satan has kept bound for eighteen years—surely she should be released from such bonds on the Sabbath day!"

These words reduced his opponents to shame, but the crowd was thrilled at all the glorious things he did.

Then he went on:

"What is the Kingdom of God like? What illustration can I use to make it plain to you? It is like a grain of mustard seed which a man took and dropped in his own garden. It grew and became a tree and the birds came and nested in its branches."

Then he said again:

"What can I say the Kingdom of God is like? It is like the yeast which a woman took and covered up in three measures of flour until the whole lot had risen."

The Kingdom is not entered by drifting but by decision   13 : 22

So he went on his way through towns and villages, teaching as he went and making his way towards Jerusalem. Someone remarked:

"Lord, are only a few men to be saved?"

And Jesus told them:

"You must do your utmost to get in through the narrow door, for many, I assure you, will try to do so and will not succeed, once the master of the house has got up and shut the door. Then you may find yourselves standing outside and knocking at the door crying, 'Lord, please open the door for us.' He will reply to you, 'I don't know who you are or where you come from.' 'But . . .' you will protest, 'we have had meals with you, and you taught in our streets!' Yet he will say to you, 'I tell you I do not know where you have come from. Be off, you scoundrels!' At that time there will be tears and bitter regret—to see Abraham and Isaac and Jacob and all the prophets inside the Kingdom of God, and you yourselves excluded, outside! Yes, and people will come from the east and the west, and from the north and the south, and take their seats in the Kingdom of God. There are some at the back now who will be in front then, and there are some in front now who will then be far behind."

The Pharisees warn Jesus of Herod ; he replies   13 : 31

Just then some Pharisees arrived to tell him:

"You must get right away from here, for Herod intends to kill you."

"Go and tell that fox," returned Jesus, "to-day and to-morrow I am expelling evil spirits and continuing my

work of healing, and on the third day my work will be
finished. But I must journey on to-day, to-morrow and the
next day, for it would never do for a prophet to meet his
death outside Jerusalem!

" Oh Jerusalem, Jerusalem, you murder the prophets and
stone the messengers that are sent to you! How often have
I longed to gather your children round me like a bird gathering her brood together under her wings, but you would never
have it. Now, all that is left is yourselves, and your house.
For I tell you that you will never see me again till the day
when you cry, ' Blessed is He Who comes in the Name of
the Lord!'"

Strict Sabbatarianism is again rebuked   14 : 1

One Sabbath day he went into the house of one of the
leading Pharisees for a meal, and they were all watching him
closely. Right in front of him was a man afflicted with
dropsy. So Jesus spoke to the Scribes and Pharisees and
said :

" Well, is it right to heal on the Sabbath day or not? "

But there was no reply. So Jesus took the man and healed
him and let him go. Then he said to them :

" If an ass or a cow belonging to one of you fell into a
well, wouldn't you rescue him without the slightest hesitation
even though it were the Sabbath? "

And this again left them quite unable to reply.

A lesson in humility   14 : 7

Then he gave a little word of advice to the guests when
he noticed how they were choosing the best seats.

" When you are invited to a wedding reception, don't sit
down in the best seat. It might happen that a more distinguished man than you has also been invited. Then your
host might say, ' I am afraid you must give up your seat
for this man.' And then, with considerable embarrassment,
you will have to sit in the humblest place. No, when you
are invited, go and take your seat in an inconspicuous place,
so that when your host comes in he may say to you, ' Come
on, my dear fellow, we have a much better seat than this for
you.' That is the way to be important in the eyes of all your
fellow guests! For everyone who makes himself important

will become insignificant, while the man who makes himself
insignificant will find himself important."

Then, addressing his host, Jesus said:

"When you give a luncheon or dinner party, don't invite
your friends or your brothers or relations or wealthy neighbours, for the chances are they will invite you back, and you
will be fully repaid. No, when you give a party, invite the
poor, the lame, the crippled and the blind. That way lies
real happiness for you. They have no means of repaying
you, but you will be repaid when good men are rewarded—
at the Resurrection."

Then, one of the guests, hearing these remarks of Jesus,
said:

"What happiness for a man to eat a meal in the Kingdom
of God!"

Men who are " too busy " for the Kingdom of God   14 : 16

But Jesus said to him:

"Once upon a time, a man planned a big dinner party
and invited a great many people. At dinner-time, he sent his
servant out to tell those who were invited, 'Please come,
everything is ready now.' But they all, as one man, began
to make their excuses. The first one said to him, 'I have
bought some land. I must go and look at it. Please excuse
me.' Another one said, 'I have bought five yoke of oxen
and am on my way to try them out. Please convey my
apologies.' And another one said, 'I have just got married
and I am sure you will understand I cannot come.' So the
servant returned and reported all this to his master. The
master of the house was extremely annoyed and said to his
servant, 'Hurry out now into the streets and alleys of the
town, and bring here the poor and crippled and blind and
lame.' Then the servant said, 'I have done what you told
me, sir, and there are still empty places.' Then the master
replied, 'Now go out to the roads and hedgerows and make
them come inside, so that my house may be full. For I tell
you that not one of the men I invited shall have a taste of
my dinner.' "

Now as Jesus proceeded on his journey, great crowds
accompanied him, and he turned and spoke to them:

"If anyone comes to me without 'hating' his father and

mother and wife and children and brothers and sisters, and even his own life, he cannot be a disciple of mine. The man who will not take up his cross and follow in my footsteps cannot be my disciple.

"If any of you wanted to build a tower, wouldn't he first sit down and work out the cost of it, to see if he can afford to finish it? Otherwise, when he has laid the foundation and found himself unable to complete the building, everyone who sees it will begin to jeer at him, saying, 'This is the man who started to build a tower but couldn't finish it!' Or, suppose there is a king who is going to war with another king, doesn't he sit down first and consider whether he can engage the 20,000 of the other king with his own 10,000. And if he decides he can't, then, while the other king is still a long way off, he sends messengers to him to ask for conditions of peace. So it is with you; only the man who says good-bye to all his possessions can be my disciple.

"Salt is a very good thing, but if salt loses its flavour, what can you use to restore it? It is no good for the ground and no good as manure. People just throw it away, Every man who has ears should use them!"

Jesus speaks of the love of God for " the lost "   15 : 1

Now all the tax-collectors and "outsiders" were crowding round to hear what he had to say. The Pharisees and the Scribes complained of this, remarking:

"This man accepts sinners and even eats his meals with them."

So Jesus spoke to them, using this parable:

"Wouldn't any man among you who owned a hundred sheep, and lost one of them, leave the ninety-nine to themselves in the open and go after the one which is lost until he finds it? And when he has found it, he will put it on his shoulders with great joy, and as soon as he gets home, he will call his friends and neighbours together. 'Come and celebrate with me,' he will say, 'for I have found that sheep of mine which was lost.' I tell you that it is the same in Heaven—there is more joy over one sinner whose heart is changed than over ninety-nine righteous people who have no need for repentance.

"Or if there is a woman who has ten silver coins, if she

should lose one, won't she take a lamp and sweep and search the house from top to bottom until she finds it? And when she has found it, she calls her friends and neighbours together. 'Come and celebrate with me,' she says, 'for I have found that coin I lost.' I tell you, it is the same in Heaven—there is rejoicing among the angels of God over one sinner whose heart is changed."

Then he continued:

"Once there was a man who had two sons. The younger one said to his father, 'Father, give me my share of the property that will come to me.' So he divided up his property between the two of them. Before very long, the younger son collected all his belongings and went off to a foreign land, where he squandered his wealth in the wildest extravagance. And when he had run through all his money, a terrible famine arose in that country, and he began to feel the pinch. Then he went and hired himself out to one of the citizens of that country who sent him out into the fields to feed the pigs. He got to the point of longing to stuff himself with the food the pigs were eating, and not a soul gave him anything. Then he came to his senses and cried aloud, 'Why, dozens of my father's hired men have got more food than they can eat and here am I dying of hunger! I will get up and go back to my father, and I will say to him, "Father, I have done wrong in the sight of Heaven and in your eyes. I don't deserve to be called your son any more. Please take me on as one of your hired men."' So he got up and went to his father. But while he was still some distance off, his father saw him and his heart went out to him, and he ran and fell on his neck and kissed him. But his son said, 'Father, I have done wrong in the sight of Heaven and in your eyes. I don't deserve to be called your son any more. ...' 'Hurry!' called out his father to the servants, 'fetch the best clothes and put them on him! Put a ring on his finger and shoes on his feet, and get that calf we've fattened and kill it, and we will have a feast and a celebration! For this is my son—I thought he was dead, and he's alive again. I thought I had lost him, and he's found!' And they began to get the festivities going.

"But his elder son was out in the fields, and as he came near the house, he heard music and dancing. So he called one of the servants across to him and enquired what was the meaning of it all. ' Your brother has arrived, and your father has killed the calf we fattened because he has got him home again safe and sound,' was the reply. But he was furious and refused to go inside the house. So his father came outside and called him. Then he burst out, ' Look, how many years have I slaved for you and never disobeyed a single order of yours, and yet you have never given me so much as a young goat, so that I could give my friends a dinner? But when that son of yours arrives, who has spent all your money on prostitutes, for *him* you kill the calf we've fattened!' But the father replied, ' My dear son, you have been with me all the time and everything I have is yours. But we *had* to celebrate and show our joy' For this is your brother; I thought he was dead—and he's alive. I thought he was lost—and he is found!'"

A clever rogue, and the right use of money[1]   16 : 1

Then there is this story he told his disciples :

" Once there was a rich man whose agent was reported to him to be mismanaging his property. So he summoned him and said, ' What's this that I hear about you? Give me an account of your stewardship—you're not fit to manage my household any longer.' At this the agent said to himself, ' What am I going to do now that my employer is taking away the stewardship from me? I am not strong enough to dig and I can't sink to begging. Ah, I know what I'll do so that when I lose my position people will welcome me into their homes!' So he sent for each one of his master's debtors. ' How much do you owe my master?' he said to the first. ' A hundred barrels of oil,' he replied. ' Here,' replied the agent, ' take your bill, sit down, hurry up and write in fifty.' Then he said to another, ' And what's the size of your debt?' ' A thousand bushels of wheat,' he replied. ' Take your bill,' said the agent, ' and write in eight hundred.' Now the master praised this rascally steward because he had been so careful for his own future. For the children of this world are considerably more shrewd in dealing with their contemporaries than the children of light. Now my advice to you is to use ' Money,' tainted as it is, to

[1] See Appendix, Note 4.

make yourselves friends, so that when it comes to an end, they may welcome you into eternal habitations.

"The man who is faithful in the little things will be faithful in the big things, and the man who cheats in the little things will cheat in the big things too. So that if you are not fit to be trusted to deal with the wicked wealth of this world, who will trust you with the true riches? And if you are not trustworthy with someone else's property, who will give you property of your own? No servant can serve two masters. He is bound to hate one and love the other, or give his loyalty to one and despise the other. You cannot serve God and the power of money at the same time."

Now the Pharisees, who were very fond of money, heard all this with a sneer. But he said to them:

"You are the people who advertise your goodness before men, but God knows your hearts. Remember, there are things men consider perfectly splendid which are detestable in the sight of God!

Jesus states that the Kingdom of God has superseded   16 : 16
"The Law and the Prophets"

"The Law and the Prophets were in force until John's day. From then on the Good News of the Kingdom of God has been proclaimed and men are forcing their way into it.

"Yet it would be easier for Heaven and earth to disappear than for a single point of the Law to become a dead letter.

"Any man who divorces his wife and marries another woman commits adultery. And so does any man who marries the woman who was divorced from her husband.

Jesus shows the fearful consequence of social injustice   16 : 19

"There was once a rich man who used to dress in purple and fine linen and lead a life of daily luxury. And there was a poor man called Lazarus who was put down at his gate. He was covered with sores. He used to long to be fed with the scraps from the rich man's table. Yes, and the dogs used to come and lick his sores. Well, it happened that the poor man died, and was carried by the angels into Abraham's bosom. The rich man also died and was buried. And from among the dead he looked up and saw Abraham a long way away, and Lazarus in his arms. 'Father Abraham!' he cried out, 'please pity me. Send Lazarus to dip the tip of his finger in water and cool my tongue, for I am in agony in these flames.' But Abraham replied, 'Remember, my son, you used to have the good things in your lifetime, while Lazarus suffered the bad. Now he is being comforted here, while you are in agony. And besides this, a great chasm has been set between you and us, so that those who want to go to you from this side cannot do so, and people cannot come to us from your side.' At this he said, 'Then I beg you, Father, to send him to my father's house, for I have five brothers. He could warn them about all this and prevent their coming to this place of torture.' But Abraham said, 'They have Moses and the Prophets : they can listen to them.' 'Ah no, Father Abraham,' he said, 'if only someone were to go to them from the dead, they would change completely.' But Abraham told him, 'If they will not listen to Moses and the Prophets, they would not be convinced even if somebody were to rise from the dead.'"

Jesus warns his disciples about spoiling the spirit of the   17 : 1
new Kingdom

Then Jesus said to his disciples :

"It is inevitable that there should be pitfalls, but alas for the man who is responsible for them! It would be better for that man to have a millstone hung round his neck and be thrown into the sea, than that he should trip up one of these little ones. So be careful how you live. If your brother offends you, take him to task about it, and if he is sorry, forgive him. Yes, if he wrongs you seven times in one day and turns to you and says, 'I am sorry' seven times, you must forgive him."

And the Apostles said to the Lord,

"Give us more faith."

And he replied :

"If your faith were as big as a grain of mustard-seed, you could say to this fig-tree, 'Pull yourself up by the roots and plant yourself in the sea,' and it would do what you said!

Work in the Kingdom must be taken as a matter of course   17 : 7

"If any of you has a servant ploughing or looking after the sheep, are you likely to say to him when he comes in from the fields, 'Come straight in and sit down to your meal'? Aren't you more likely to say, 'Get my supper ready: change your coat, and wait while I eat and drink: and then, when I've finished, you can have your meal'? Do you feel particularly grateful to your servant for doing what you tell him? I don't think so. It is the same with yourselves—when you have done everything that you are told to do, you can say, 'We are not much good as servants, for we have only done what we ought to do.'"

Jesus heals ten men of leprosy : only one shows his gratitude
17 : 11

In the course of his journey to Jerusalem, Jesus crossed the boundary between Samaria and Galilee, and as he was approaching a village, ten lepers met him. They kept their distance but shouted out :

"Jesus, Master, have pity on us!"

When Jesus saw them, he said :

"Go and show yourselves to the priests."

And it happened that as they went on their way they were cured. One of their number, when he saw that he was cured, turned round and praised God at the top of his voice, and then fell on his face before Jesus and thanked him. This man was a Samaritan. And at this Jesus remarked :

"Weren't there ten men healed? Where are the other nine? Is nobody going to turn and praise God for what has been done, except this stranger?"

And he said to the man :

"Stand up now, and go on your way. It is your faith that has made you well."

Jesus tells the Pharisees that the Kingdom is here and now
17 : 20

Later, he was asked by the Pharisees when the Kingdom of God was coming, and he gave them this reply :

"The Kingdom of God never comes by watching for it. Men cannot say, 'Look, here it is,' or 'there it is,' for the Kingdom of God is inside you."

Jesus tells his disciples about the future
17 : 22

Then he said to the disciples :

"The time will come when you will long to see again a

single day of the Son of Man, but you will not see it. People will say to you, 'Look, there he is,' or 'Look, here he is.' Stay where you are and don't go off looking for him! For the Day of the Son of Man will be like lightning flashing from one end of the sky to the other. But before that happens, he must go through much suffering and be utterly rejected by this generation. In the time of the coming of the Son of Man, life will be as it was in the days of Noah. People ate and drank, married and were given in marriage, right up to the day when Noah entered the Ark—and then came the Flood and destroyed them all. It will be just the same as it was in the days of Lot. People ate and drank, bought and sold, planted and built, but on the day that Lot left Sodom, it rained fire and brimstone from heaven, and destroyed them all. That is how it will be on the day when the Son of Man is revealed. When that Day comes, the man who is on the roof of his house, with his goods inside it, must not come down to get them. And the man out in the fields must not turn back for anything. Remember what happened to Lot's wife. Whoever tries to preserve his life will lose it, and the man who is prepared to lose his life will preserve it. I tell you, that night there will be two men in one bed; one man will be taken and the other will be left. Two women will be turning the grinding-mill together; one will be taken and the other left."

"But when, Lord?" they asked him.

"'Wherever there is a dead body, there the vultures will flock,'" he replied.

Jesus urges his disciples to persist in prayer   18 : 1

Then he gave them an illustration to show that they must always pray and never lose heart.

"Once upon a time," he said, "there was a magistrate in a town who had neither fear of God nor respect for his fellow men. There was a widow in the town who kept coming to him, saying, 'Please protect me from the man who is trying to ruin me.' And for a long time he refused. But later he said to himself, 'Although I don't fear God and have no respect for men, yet this woman is such a nuisance that I shall give judgment in her favour, or else her continual visits will be the death of me!'"

Then the Lord said :

" Notice how this dishonest magistrate behaved. Do you suppose God, patient as He is, will not see justice done for His chosen, who appeal to him day and night ? I assure you He will not delay in seeing justice done. Yet, when the Son of Man comes, will he find men on earth who believe in him ? "

Jesus tells a story against the self-righteous   18 : 9

Then he gave this illustration to certain people who were confident of their own goodness and looked down on others :

" Two men went up to the Temple to pray, one was a Pharisee, the other was a tax-collector. The Pharisee stood and prayed like this with himself, ' O God, I do thank Thee that I am not like the rest of mankind, greedy, dishonest, impure, or even like that tax-collector over there. I fast twice every week ; I give away a tenth-part of all my income.' But the tax-collector stood in a distant corner, scarcely daring to look up to Heaven, and with a gesture of despair, said, ' God, have mercy on a sinner like me.' I assure you that he was the man who went home justified in God's sight, rather than the other one. For everyone who sets himself up as somebody will become a nobody, and the man who makes himself nobody will become somebody."

Jesus welcomes babies   18 : 15

Then people began to bring babies to him for him to put his hands on them. But when the disciples noticed it, they frowned on them. But Jesus called them to him, and said :

" You must let little children come to me, and you must never prevent their coming. The Kingdom of Heaven belongs to little children like these. I tell you, the man who will not accept the Kingdom of God like a little child will never get into it at all."

Jesus and riches   18 : 18

Then one of the Jewish rulers put this question to him :

" Master, I know that you are good ; tell me, please, what must I do to be sure of eternal life ? "

" I wonder why you call me good ? " returned Jesus.

"No one is good—only the One God. You know the Commandments :

"Thou shalt not commit adultery.

"Thou shalt not commit murder.

"Thou shalt not steal.

"Thou shalt not bear false witness.

"Honour thy father and thy mother."

"All these," he replied, "I have carefully kept since I was quite young."

And when Jesus heard that, he said to him :

"There is still one thing you have missed. Sell everything you have and give the money away to the poor, and you will have riches in Heaven. Then come and follow me."

But when he heard this, he was greatly distressed for he was very rich.

And when Jesus saw how his face fell, he remarked :

"How difficult it is for those who have great possessions to enter the Kingdom of God! A camel could squeeze through the eye of a needle more easily than a rich man could get into the Kingdom of God."

Those who heard Jesus say this, exclaimed :

"Then who can possibly be saved ? "

Jesus replied :

"What men find impossible is perfectly possible with God."

"Well," rejoined Peter, "we have left all that we ever had and followed you."

And Jesus told them :

"Believe me, nobody has left his home or wife, or brothers or parents or children for the sake of the Kingdom of God, without receiving very much more in this present life,—and eternal life in the world to come."

Jesus foretells his death and resurrection   18 : 31

Then Jesus took the Twelve on one side and spoke to them :

"Listen to me. We are now going up to Jerusalem and everything that has been written by the prophets about the Son of Man will come true. For he will be handed over to the heathen, and he is going to be jeered at and insulted and spat upon, and then they will flog him and kill him. But he will rise again on the third day."

But they did not understand any of this. His words were quite obscure to them and they had no idea of what he meant.

On the way to Jericho he heals a blind beggar 18 : 35

Then, as he was approaching Jericho, it happened that there was a blind man sitting by the roadside, begging. He heard the crowd passing and enquired what it was all about. And they told him, Jesus the man from Nazareth is going past you. So he shouted out :

" Jesus, Son of David, have pity on me ! "

Those who were in front tried to hush his cries. But that made him call out all the more :

" Son of David, have pity on me ! "

So Jesus stood quite still and ordered the man to be brought to him. And when he was quite close, he said to him :

" What do you want me to do for you ? "

" Lord, make me see again," he cried.

" You can see again ! Your faith has cured you," returned Jesus.

And his sight was restored at once, and he followed Jesus, praising God. All the people who saw it thanked God too.

The chief tax-collector is converted to faith in Jesus 19 : 1

Then he went into Jericho and was making his way through it. And here we find a wealthy man called Zacchaeus, a chief collector of taxes, wanting to see what sort of person Jesus was. But the crowd prevented him from doing so, for he was very short. So he ran ahead and climbed up into a sycamore tree to get a view of Jesus as he was heading that way. When Jesus reached the spot, he looked up and saw the man and said :

" Zacchaeus, hurry up and come down. I must be your guest to-day."

So Zacchaeus hurriedly climbed down and gladly welcomed him. But the bystanders muttered their disapproval, saying :

" Now he has gone to stay with a real sinner."

But Zacchaeus himself stopped and said to the Lord :

" Look, sir, I will give half my property to the poor. And if I have swindled anybody out of anything I will pay him back four times as much."

Jesus said to him :

" Salvation has come to this house to-day ! Zacchaeus is a descendant of Abraham, as much as you are, and it was the lost that the Son of Man came to seek—and to save."

Life requires courage, and is hard on those who dare not   19 : 11
use their gifts

Then as the crowd still listened attentively, Jesus went on to give them this parable. For the fact that he was nearing Jerusalem made them imagine that the Kingdom of God was on the point of appearing.

" Once upon a time a man of good family went abroad to accept a kingdom and then return. He summoned ten of his servants and gave them each ten pounds, with the words, ' Use this money to trade with until I come back.' But the citizens detested him and they sent a delegation after him, to say, ' We will not have this man to be our king.' Then later, when he had received his kingdom, he returned and gave orders for the servants to whom he had given the money to be called to him, so that he could find out what profit they had made. The first came into his presence, and said, ' Sire, your ten pounds have made a hundred pounds more.' ' Splendid, my good fellow,' he said, ' since you have proved trustworthy over this small amount, I am going to put you in charge of ten towns.' The second came in and said, ' Sire, your ten pounds have made fifty pounds.' And he said to him, ' Good, you're appointed governor of five towns.' When the last came, he said, ' Sire, here are your ten pounds, which I have been keeping wrapped up in a handkerchief. I have been scared—I know you're a hard man, getting something for nothing and reaping where you never sowed.' To which he replied, ' You scoundrel, your own words condemn you ! You knew perfectly well, did you, that I am a hard man who gets something for nothing and reaps where he never sowed ? Then why didn't you put my money into the bank, and then when I returned I could have had it back with interest ? ' Then he said to those who were standing by, 'Take away his ten pounds and give it to the fellow who has a hundred.'

" ' But, Sire, he has a hundred pounds already,' they said to him. ' Yes,' he replied, ' and I tell you that the man who has something will get more given to him. But as for the man who has nothing, even his " nothing " will be taken away. And as for these enemies of mine who objected to my being their king, bring them here and execute them in my presence.' "

After these words, Jesus walked on ahead of them on his way to Jerusalem.

Jesus arranges his own entrance into Jerusalem   19 : 29

Then as he was approaching Bethphage and Bethany, near the hill called the Mount of Olives, he sent off two of his disciples, telling them :

" Go into the village just ahead of you, and there you will find a colt tied on which no one has ever yet ridden. Untie it and bring it here. And if anybody asks you, ' Why are you untying it ? ' just say, ' The Lord needs it.' "

So the messengers went off and found things just as he had told them. In fact, as they were untying the colt, the owners did say, " Why are you untying it ? " and they replied, " The Lord needs it." So they brought it to Jesus and, throwing their cloaks upon it, mounted Jesus on its back. Then as he rode along, people spread out their coats in the roadway. And as he approached the City, where the road slopes down from the Mount of Olives, the whole crowd of his disciples joyfully shouted praises to God for all the marvellous things that they had seen him do.

" God bless the King Who comes in the Name of the Lord ! " they cried. " There is peace in Heaven and glory on high ! "

There were some Pharisees in the crowd who said to Jesus :

" Master, restrain your disciples ! "

To which he replied :

" I tell you that if they kept quiet, the very stones in the road would burst out cheering ! "

The sight of the city moves him to tears   19 : 41

And as he came still nearer to the City, he caught sight of it and wept over it, saying :

"Ah, if you only knew, even at this eleventh hour, on what your peace depends—but you cannot see it. The time is coming when your enemies will encircle you with ramparts, surrounding you and hemming you in on every side. And they will hurl you and all your children to the ground—yes, they will not leave you one stone standing upon another—all because you did not know when God Himself was visiting you ! "

Then he went into the Temple, and proceeded to throw out the traders there.

"It is written," he told them, "' *My house shall be a house of prayer*,' but you have turned it into a thieves' kitchen ! "

Jesus teaches daily in the Temple   19 : 47

Then day after day he was teaching inside the Temple. The Chief Priests, the Scribes and the national leaders were all the time trying to get rid of him, but they could not find any way to do it since all the people hung upon his words.

Then one day as he was teaching the people in the Temple, and preaching the gospel to them, the Chief Priests, the Scribes and Elders confronted him in a body and asked him this direct question :

"Tell us by whose authority you act as you do—who gave you such authority ? "

"I have a question for you, too," replied Jesus. "John's baptism, now—tell me, did it come from Heaven or was it purely human ? "

At this they began arguing with each other, saying :

"If we say, ' from Heaven,' he will say to us, ' Then why didn't you believe in him ? ' but if we say it was purely human, this mob will stone us to death, for they are convinced that John was a prophet." So they replied that they did not know where it came from.

"Then," returned Jesus, "neither will I tell you by what authority I do what I am doing."

He tells the people a pointed story   20 : 9

Then he turned to the people and told them this parable :

" There was once a man who planted a vineyard, let it out
to farm-workers, and went abroad for some time. Then,
when the season arrived, he sent a servant to the farm-
workers so that they could give him the proceeds of the vineyard. But the farm-workers beat him up and sent him back
empty-handed. So he sent another servant, and they beat
him up as well, manhandling him disgracefully, and sent
him back empty-handed. Then he sent a third servant, but
after wounding him severely they threw him out. Then the
owner of the vineyard said, ' What shall I do now ? I will
send them my son who is so dear to me. Perhaps they will
respect *him*.' But when the farm-workers saw him, they
talked the matter over with each other and said, ' This man
is the heir—come on, let's kill him, and we shall get everything that he would have had.' And they threw him outside
the vineyard and killed him. What then do you suppose the
owner will do to them ? He will come and destroy the men
who were working his property, and hand it over to others."

When they heard this, they said :

" God forbid ! "

But he looked them straight in the eyes and said :

" Then what is the meaning of this Scripture :

The stone which the builders rejected,
The same was made the head of the corner ?

The man who falls on that stone will be broken, and the
man on whom it falls will be crushed to powder."

The authorities resort to trickery   20 : 19

The Scribes and Chief Priests longed to get their hands on
him at that moment, but they were afraid of the people.
They knew well enough that his parable referred to them.
They watched him, however, and sent some spies into the
crowd, pretending that they were honest men, to fasten on
something that he might say which could be used to hand
him over to the authority and power of the Governor.

These men asked him :

" Master, we know that what you say and teach is right,
and that you teach the way of God truly without fear or
favour. Now, *is it right for us to pay taxes to Caesar or not ?* "

But Jesus saw through their cunning and said to them :

" Show me one of the coins. Whose face is this, and whose name is in the inscription ? "

" Caesar's," they said.

" Then give to Caesar," he replied, " what belongs to Caesar, and to God what belongs to God."

So his reply gave them no sort of handle that they could use against him publicly. And in fact they were so taken aback by his answer that they had nothing more to say.

Jesus exposes the ignorance of the Sadducees   20 : 27

Then up came some of the Sadducees (who deny that there is any resurrection) and they asked him,

" Master, Moses told us in the Scripture, ' If a man's brother should die without any children, he should marry the widow and raise up a family for his brother.' Now, there were once seven brothers. The first got married and died childless, and the second and the third married the woman, and in fact all the seven married her and died without leaving any children. Lastly, the woman herself died. Now, in this ' resurrection ' whose wife is she of these seven men, for she belonged to all of them ? "

" People in this world," Jesus replied, " marry and are given in marriage. But those who are considered worthy of reaching that world, which means rising from the dead, neither marry nor are they given in marriage. They cannot die any more but live like the angels ; for being children of the resurrection, they are the sons of God. But that the dead are raised, even Moses showed this to be true in the story of the Bush, when he calls the Lord the God of Abraham, the God of Isaac and the God of Jacob. For God is not God of the dead, but of the living. For all men are alive to Him."

To this some of the Scribes replied :

" Master, that was a good answer."

And indeed nobody had the courage to ask him any more questions. But Jesus went on to say :

" How can they say that Christ is David's *son* ? For David himself says in the book of Psalms :

The Lord said unto my *Lord*,
Sit thou on my right hand,
Till I make thine enemies the footstool of thy feet.

David is plainly calling him ' Lord.' How then can he be
his *son* ? "

Jesus warns his disciples against religious pretentiousness   20 : 45
Then while everybody was listening, Jesus remarked to
his disciples :

" Be on your guard against the Scribes, who enjoy walking
round in long robes and love having men bow to them in
public, getting front seats in the synagogue, and the best
places at dinner parties—while all the time they are battening
on widows' property and covering it up with long prayers.
These men are only heading for deeper damnation."

Then he looked up and saw the rich people dropping their
gifts into the treasury, and he noticed a poor widow drop
in two coppers, and he commented :

" I assure you that this poor widow has put in more than
all of them, for they have all put in what they can easily
spare, but she in her poverty has given away her whole
living."

Jesus foretells the destruction of the Temple   21 : 5
Then when some of them were talking about the Temple
and pointing out the beauty of its lovely stonework and the
various ornaments that people had given, he said :

" Yes, you can gaze on all this to-day, but the time is
coming when not a single stone will be left upon another,
without being thrown down."

So they asked him :

" Master, when will this happen, and what sign will there
be that these things are going to take place ? "

" Be careful that you are not deceived," he replied. " There
will be many coming in my name, saying ' I am He ' and
' The Time is very near now.' Never follow men like that.
And when you hear about wars and disturbances, don't be
alarmed. These things must indeed happen first, but the end
will not come immediately."

And prophesies world-wide suffering   21 : 10

Then he continued :

" Nation will rise up against nation, and kingdom against
kingdom ; there will be great earthquakes and famines and
plagues in this place or that. There will be dreadful sights,
and great signs from Heaven. But before all this happens,
men will arrest you and persecute you, handing you over to
synagogue or prison, or bringing you before kings and
governors, for my name's sake. This will be your chance to
witness for me. So make up your minds not to think out
your defence beforehand. I will give you such eloquence
and wisdom that none of your opponents will be able to
resist or contradict it. But you will be betrayed, even by
parents and brothers and kinsfolk and friends, and there will
be some of you who will be killed and you will be hated
everywhere for my name's sake. Yet, not a hair of your head
will perish. Hold on, and you will win your souls !

" But when you see Jerusalem surrounded by armed
forces, then you will know that the time of her devastation
has arrived. Then is the time for those who are in Judaea
to fly to the hills. And those who are in the city itself must
get out of it, and those who are already in the country must
not try to get into the city. For these are the days of
vengeance, when all that the Scriptures have said will come
true. Alas for those who are pregnant and those who have
tiny babies in those days ! For there will be bitter misery in
the land and a great anger against this people. They will die
by the sword. They will be taken off as prisoners into all
nations. Jerusalem will be trampled under foot by the
heathen until the heathen's day is over. There will be signs
in the sun and moon and stars, and on the earth there will
be dismay among the nations and bewilderment at the roar
of the surging sea. Men's courage will fail completely as
they realise what is threatening the world, for the very powers
of Heaven will be shaken. Then men will see the Son of
Man coming in a cloud with great power and splendour !
But when these things begin to happen, look up, hold your
heads high, for you will soon be free."

Vigilance is essential   21 : 29

Then he gave them a parable.

" Look at a fig-tree, or indeed any tree, when it begins to burst its buds, and you realise without anybody telling you that summer is nearly here. So, when you see these things happening, you can be equally sure that the Kingdom of God has nearly come. Believe me, this generation will not disappear until all this has taken place. Earth and heaven will pass away, but my words will never pass away.

" Be on your guard—see to it that your minds are never clouded by dissipation or drunkenness or the worries of this life, or else that Day may catch you like the springing of a trap—for it will come upon every inhabitant of the whole earth.

" You must be vigilant at all times, praying that you may be strong enough to come safely through all that is going to happen, and stand in the presence of the Son of Man."

And every day he went on teaching in the Temple, and every evening he went off and spent the night on the hill which is called the Mount of Olives. And the people used to come early in the morning to listen to him in the Temple.

Judas Iscariot becomes the tool of the authorities   22 : 1

Now as the Feast of Unleavened Bread, called the Passover, was approaching, fear of the people made the Chief Priests and Scribes try desperately to find a way of getting rid of Jesus. Then a diabolical plan came into the mind of Judas Iscariot, who was one of the Twelve. He went and discussed with the Chief Priests and officers a method of getting Jesus into their hands. They were delighted and arranged to pay him for it. He agreed, and began to look for a suitable opportunity for betrayal when there was no crowd present.

Jesus makes arrangements for his last Passover with his   22 : 7
disciples

Then the day of Unleavened Bread arrived, on which the Passover Lamb had to be sacrificed, and Jesus sent off Peter and John with the words, " Go and make all the preparations for us to eat the Passover."

" Where would you like us to do this ? " they asked.

And he replied :

" Listen, just as you're going into the city a man carrying

a jug of water will meet you. Follow him to the house he is making for. Then say to the owner of the house, ' The Master has this message for you—which is the room where my disciples and I may eat the Passover ? ' And he will take you upstairs and show you a large room furnished for our needs. Make all the preparations there."

So they went off and found everything exactly as he had told them it would be, and they made the Passover preparations.

Then, when the time came, he took his seat at table with the Apostles, and spoke to them :

" With all my heart I have longed to eat this Passover with you before the time comes for me to suffer. Believe me, I shall not eat the Passover again until all that it means is fulfilled in the Kingdom of God."

Then taking a cup from them, he thanked God and said :

" Take this and share it amongst yourselves, for I tell you that I shall drink no more wine until the Kingdom of God comes."

The mysterious words which were remembered later   22 : 19

Then he took a loaf and after thanking God he broke it and gave it to them, with these words :

" This is my body which is given for you : do this in remembrance of me."

So too, he gave them a cup after supper with the words :

" This cup is the New Agreement made in my own blood which is shed for you. Yet the hand of the man who is betraying me lies with mine at this moment on the table. The Son of Man goes on his appointed way : yet alas for the man by whom he is betrayed ! "

Jesus again teaches humility   22 : 23

And at this they began to debate among themselves as to which of them would do this thing.

And then a dispute arose among them as to who should be considered the most important.

But Jesus said to them :

" Among the heathen it is their kings who lord it over them, and their rulers are given the title of ' benefactors.' But it must not be so with you ! *Your* greatest man must

become like a junior and your leader must be a servant.
Who is the greater, the man who sits down to dinner or the
man who serves him ? Obviously, the man who sits down to
dinner—yet *I* am the one who is the servant among you.
But you are the men who have stood by me in all that I
have gone through, and as surely as my Father has given
me my Kingdom, so I give you the right to eat and drink
at my table in that Kingdom. Yes, you will sit on thrones
and rule the twelve tribes of Israel !

The personal warning to Simon   22 : 31
   " Oh Simon, Simon, do you know that Satan has asked to
have you all to sift like wheat ? But I have prayed for *you*
that you may not lose your faith. Yes, when you have turned
back to me, you must strengthen these brothers of yours."
   Peter said to him :
   " Lord, I am ready to go to prison, or even to die with
you ! "
   " I tell you, Peter," returned Jesus, " before the cock
crows to-day you will deny three times that you know
me ! "

Jesus tells his disciples that the crisis has arrived   22 : 35
   Then he continued to them all :
   " That time when I sent you out without any purse or
wallet or shoes—did you find you needed anything ? "
   " No, not a thing," they replied.
   " But now," Jesus continued, " if you have a purse or
wallet, take it with you, and if you have no sword, sell your
coat and buy one ! For I tell you that this Scripture must be
fulfilled in me—

   And he was reckoned with transgressors.

So comes the end of what they wrote about me."
   Then the disciples said :
   " Lord, look here are two swords."
   And Jesus returned :
   " That is enough."
Then he went out of the city and up on to the Mount of
Olives, as he had often done before, with the disciples

following him. And when he reached his usual place, he said
to them :

"Pray that you may not have to face temptation!"

Then he went off by himself, about a stone's throw away,
and falling on his knees, prayed in these words :

"Father, if You are willing, take this cup away from me—
but it is not my will, but Yours, that must be done."

And an angel from Heaven appeared strengthening him.
He was in agony and prayed even more intensely so that his
sweat was like great drops of blood falling to the ground.
Then he got to his feet from his prayer and walking back
to the disciples, he found them sleeping through sheer grief.

"Why are you sleeping ?" he said to them. "You must
get up and go on praying that you may not have to face
temptation."

The mob arrives and Judas betrays   22 : 47

While he was still speaking a crowd of people arrived, led
by the man called Judas, one of the Twelve. He stepped up
to Jesus to kiss him.

"Judas, would you betray the Son of Man with a kiss ?"
said Jesus to him.

And the disciples, seeing what was going to happen,
cried :

"Lord, shall we use our swords ?"

And one of them did slash at the High Priest's servant,
cutting off his right ear. But Jesus retorted :

"That will do!"

And he touched his ear and healed him. Then he spoke
to the Chief Priests, Temple officers and Elders who were
there to arrest him :

"So you have come out with your swords and staves as if
I were a bandit. Day after day I was with you in the Temple
and you never laid a finger on me—but this is your hour and
the power of darkness is yours!"

Jesus is arrested : Peter follows but denies his master   22 : 54
three times

Then they arrested him and marched him off to the High
Priest's house. Peter followed at a distance, and sat down
among some people who had lighted a fire in the middle of

the courtyard and were sitting round it. A servant-maid saw him sitting there in the firelight, peered into his face and said :

" This man was with him too."

But he denied it and said :

" I don't know him, girl ! "

A few minutes later someone else noticed Peter, and said :

" You're one of these men too."

But Peter said :

" Man, I am not ! "

Then about an hour later someone else insisted :

" I am convinced this fellow was with him. Why he is a Galilean ! "

" Man," returned Peter, " I don't know what you're talking about."

And immediately, while he was still speaking, the cock crew. The Lord turned his head and looked straight at Peter, and into his mind flashed the words that the Lord had said to him . . . " You will disown me three times before the cock crows to-day." And he went outside and wept bitterly.

Then the men who held Jesus made a great game of knocking him about. And they blindfolded him and asked him :

" Now, prophet, guess who hit you that time ! "

And that was only the beginning of the way they insulted him.

In the early morning Jesus is formally interrogated   22 : 66

Then when daylight came, the assembly of the Elders of the people, which included both Chief Priests and Scribes, met and marched him off to their own Council. There they asked him :

" If you really are Christ, tell us ! "

" If I tell you, you will never believe me, and if I ask you a question, you will not answer me. But from now on the Son of Man will take his seat at the right hand of Almighty God."

Then they all said :

" So you are the Son of God then ? "

" You are right ; I am," Jesus told them.

Then they said :

"Why do we need to call any more witnesses, for we ourselves have heard this thing from his own lips?"

Jesus is taken before Pilate and Herod   23 : 1

Then they rose up in a body and took him off to Pilate,
and began their accusation in these words:

"Here is this man whom we have found corrupting our
people, and telling them that it is wrong to pay taxes to
Caesar, claiming that he himself is Christ, a king."

But Pilate addressed his question to Jesus:

"Are you the king of the Jews?"

"Yes, I am," he replied.

Then Pilate spoke to the Chief Priests and the crowd:

"I find nothing criminal about this man."

But they pressed their charge, saying:

"He's a trouble-maker among the people. He teaches
through the whole of Judaea, all the way from Galilee to
this place."

When Pilate heard this, he enquired whether the man were
a Galilean, and when he discovered that he came under
Herod's jurisdiction, he passed him on to Herod who happened to be in Jerusalem at that time. When Herod saw
Jesus, he was delighted, for he had been wanting to see him
for a long time. He had heard a lot about Jesus and was
hoping to see him perform a miracle. He questioned him
very thoroughly, but Jesus gave him absolutely no reply,
though the Chief Priests and Scribes stood there making the
most violent accusations. So Herod joined his own soldiers
in scoffing and jeering at Jesus. Finally, they dressed him
up in a gorgeous cloak, and sent him back to Pilate. On that
day Herod and Pilate became firm friends, though previously
they had been at daggers drawn.

Pilate declares Jesus' innocence   23 : 13

Then Pilate summoned the Chief Priests, the officials and
the people, and addressed them in these words:

"You have brought this man to me as a mischief-maker
among the people, and I want you all to realise that, after
examining him in your presence, I have found nothing
criminal about him, in spite of all your accusations. And
neither has Herod, for he has sent him back to us. Obviously

then, he has done nothing to deserve the death penalty. I propose, therefore, to teach him a sharp lesson and let him go."

But they all yelled as one man:

"Take this man away! We want Barabbas set free!"

(Barabbas was a man who had been put in prison for causing a riot in the city and for murder.) But Pilate wanted to set Jesus free and he called out to them again, but they shouted back at him:

"Crucify, crucify him!"

Then he spoke to them, for the third time:

"What is his crime, then? I have found nothing in him that deserves execution; I am going to teach him his lesson and let him go."

But they shouted him down, yelling their demand that he should be crucified.

Their shouting won the day, and Pilate pronounced the official decision that their request should be granted. He released the man for whom they asked, the man who had been imprisoned for rioting and murder, and surrendered Jesus to their demands.

And as they were marching him away, they caught hold of Simon, a native of Cyrene in Africa, who was on his way home from the fields, and put the cross on his back for him to carry behind Jesus.

On the way to the cross   23 : 27

A huge crowd of people followed him, including women who wrung their hands and wept for him. But Jesus turned to them and said:

"Women of Jerusalem, do not shed your tears for me, but for yourselves and for your children! For the days are coming when men will say, 'Lucky are the women who are childless—the bodies which have never borne, and the breasts which have never given nourishment.' Then men will begin to say to the mountains, 'Fall upon us!' and will say to the hills, 'Cover us up!' For if this is what men do when the wood is green, what will they do when it is seasoned?"

Jesus is crucified with two criminals   23 : 32

Two criminals were also led out with him for execution, and when they came to the place called The Skull, they crucified him with the criminals, one on each side of him. But Jesus himself was saying:

" Father, forgive them; they do not know what they are doing."

Then they shared out his clothes by casting lots.

The people stood and stared while their rulers continued to scoff, saying, " He saved other people, let's see him save himself, if he is really God's Christ—His Chosen ! "

The soldiers also mocked him by coming up and presenting sour wine to him, saying:

" If you are the king of the Jews, why not save yourself? "

For there was a placard over his head which read:

" THIS IS THE KING OF THE JEWS."

One of the criminals hanging there covered him with abuse.

" Aren't you Christ ? Why don't you save yourself— and us ? "

But the other one checked him with the words:

" Aren't you afraid of God even when you're getting the same punishment as he is ? And it's fair enough for us, for we've only got what we deserve, but this man never did anything wrong in his life."

Then he said:

" Jesus, remember me when you come into your kingdom."

And Jesus answered:

" I tell you truly, this very day you will be with me in Paradise."

The darkness, and the death of Jesus   23 : 44

It was now about midday, but darkness came over the whole countryside until three in the afternoon, for there was an eclipse of the sun. The veil in the Temple sanctuary was split in two. Then Jesus gave a great cry and said:

" Father, I commend my spirit into Your hands."

And with these words, he died.

When the centurion saw what had happened, he exclaimed reverently:

"That was indeed a good man!"

And the whole crowd who had collected for the spectacle, when they saw what had happened, went home in deep distress. And those who had known him, as well as the women who had followed him from Galilee, remained standing at a distance and saw all this happen.

Joseph from Arimathaea lays the body of Jesus in a tomb 23 : 50

Now there was a man called Joseph, a member of the Jewish Council. He was a good and just man, and had neither agreed with this plan nor voted for their decision. He came from the Jewish city of Arimathaea and was awaiting the Kingdom of God. He went to Pilate and asked for Jesus' body. He took it down and wrapped it in linen and placed it in a rock-hewn tomb which had not been used before.

It was now the day of the Preparation and the Sabbath was beginning to dawn, so the women who had accompanied Jesus from Galilee followed Joseph, noted the tomb and the position of the body, and then went home to prepare spices and perfumes. On the Sabbath they rested, in obedience to the commandment.

The first day of the week : the empty tomb   24 : 1

But at the first signs of dawn on the first day of the week, they went to the tomb, taking with them the aromatic spices they had prepared. They discovered that the stone had been rolled away from the tomb, but on going inside, the body of the Lord Jesus was not to be found. While they were still puzzling over this, two men suddenly stood at their elbow, dressed in dazzling light. The women were terribly frightened, and turned their eyes away and looked at the ground. But the two men spoke to them :

"Why do you look for the Living among the dead? He is not here : He has risen! Remember that He said to you, while He was still in Galilee—that the Son of Man must be betrayed into the hands of sinful men, and must be crucified, and must rise again on the third day."

Then they did remember what he had said, and they turned their backs on the tomb and went and told all this to the Eleven and the others who were with them.

It was Mary of Magdala, Joanna, Mary, the mother of

James, and their companions who made this report to the
Apostles. But it struck them as sheer imagination, and they
did not believe the women. Only Peter got up and ran to
the tomb. He stooped down and saw the linen clothes lying
there all by themselves, and he went home wondering at the
thing that had happened.

The walk to Emmaus   24 : 13

Then on the same day we find two of them going off to
Emmaus, a village about seven miles from Jerusalem. As
they went they were deep in conversation about everything
that had happened. While they were absorbed in their serious
talk and discussion, Jesus Himself approached and walked
along with them, but something prevented them from
recognising Him. Then He spoke to them:

"What is all this discussion that you are having on your
walk?"

They stopped, their faces drawn with misery, and the one
called Cleopas replied:

"You must be the only stranger in Jerusalem who hasn't
heard all the things that have happened there recently!"

"What things?" asked Jesus.

"Oh, all about Jesus, from Nazareth. There was a man—
a prophet strong in what he did and what he said, in God's
eyes as well as the people's. Haven't you heard how our
Chief Priests and rulers handed him over for execution, and
had him crucified? But we were hoping he was the one
who was to come and set Israel free. . . .

"Yes, and as if that were not enough, it's getting on for
three days since all this happened; and some of our women-
folk have disturbed us deeply. For they went to the tomb at
dawn, and then when they couldn't find his body they said
that they had had a vision of angels who said that he was
alive. Some of our people went straight off to the tomb and
found things just as the women had described them—but
they didn't see *him*!"

Then He Himself spoke to them:

"Aren't you being unintelligent, and slow to believe in all
the things the prophets have said? Was it not inevitable
that Christ should suffer like that and so find His glory?"

Then, beginning with Moses and all the prophets, He

explained to them everything in the Scriptures that referred to Himself.

They were by now approaching the village to which they were going. He gave the impression that He meant to go on farther, but they stopped Him with the words:

"Do stay with us. It is nearly evening and soon the day will be over."

So He went indoors to stay with them. *Then it happened!* While He was sitting at table with them He took the loaf, gave thanks, broke it and passed it to them. Their eyes opened wide and *they knew Him!* But He vanished from their sight. Then they said to each other:

"Weren't our hearts glowing while He was with us on the road, and when He made the Scriptures so plain to us?"

And they got to their feet without delay and turned back to Jerusalem. There they found the Eleven and their friends all together, full of the news—

"The Lord is really risen—He has appeared to Simon now!"

Then they told the story of their walk, and how they recognised Him when He broke the loaf.

Jesus suddenly appears to the disciples   24 : 36

And while they were still talking about these things, Jesus Himself stood among them and said:

"Peace be to you all!"

But they shrank back in terror for they thought they were seeing a ghost.

"Why are you so worried?" said Jesus, "and why do doubts arise in your minds? Look at My hands and My feet—it is really I Myself! Feel Me and see; ghosts have no flesh or bones as you can see that I have."

But while they still could not believe it through sheer joy and were quite bewildered, Jesus said to them:

"Have you anything to eat?"

They gave Him a piece of broiled fish and part of a honeycomb, which He took and ate before their eyes. Then He said:

"Here and now are fulfilled the words that I told you when I was with you: that everything written about Me in the Law of Moses and in the prophets and psalms must come true."

Then He opened their minds so that they could understand the Scriptures, and added :

" That is how it was written, and that is why it was inevitable that Christ should suffer, and rise from the dead on the third day. So must the change of heart which leads to the forgiveness of sins be proclaimed in His Name to all nations, beginning at Jerusalem.

Jesus commissions them with the new Message   24 : 48

" You are eye-witnesses of these things. Now I hand over to you the Message of the Father. Stay in the City, then, until you are clothed with power from on high."

Then He led them outside as far as Bethany, where He blessed them with uplifted hands. While He was in the act of blessing them He was parted from them and was carried up to Heaven. They worshipped Him and turned back to Jerusalem with great joy, and spent their days in the Temple, praising and blessing God.

THE GOSPEL OF
JOHN

It is quite plain that in this Gospel we are breathing a very different atmosphere from that of Matthew, Mark and Luke. The story itself shows great differences, almost the whole of the " action " taking place in Jerusalem ; while a large amount of both the teaching and the healing ministries described by Mark, for example, find no place in " John " at all. There is also the remarkable difference that in this Gospel Jesus is recognised as the Messiah in the very first chapter by John, Andrew and Philip. Consequently John's version lacks the note of mounting tension which is very strong in the other three. The discourses of Jesus differ remarkably from those in the other three Gospels, where they consist for the most part of parables or short memorable rules of the way in which life is meant to be lived. In John's Gospel the discourses are long and different in style ; they deal almost entirely with the great themes of Life, Light, Love, Truth and Christ's relationship with the Father. There are many similes and metaphors but no parables at all.

Naturally, this and many other sharp differences have given rise to an enormous amount of study and research. There is a vast body of literature commenting on the situation, and offering widely different explanations. To mention but one basic problem : in view of the difference of style between this and the other three Gospels, are we to suppose that Jesus spoke in different styles on different occasions, or are we to suppose that John is re-writing in his own style of Greek what Jesus spoke in Aramaic? The subject is obviously much too large to be more than introduced here, and the reader in search of further information is referred to the List of Recommended Books at the end of the Preface.

Whether this Gospel was written as a conscious supplement (or even a deliberate corrective) to the other three, we simply do not know. But the majority of Christian scholars, for all their disagreements, would not deny the enormous spiritual value of this document. It seems probable that the author knew Jesus personally, and although modern scholarship is mostly against considering him to be

*the apostle John, there can be no doubt that the author had close
spiritual acquaintance with Christ, and had reflected long and deeply
on the nature of the divine Word. Here he gives to the world the
results of his thoughts, prayers and meditations about the Life which
is the Light of men.*

*Modern scholarship has gradually set the probable date of the
Gospel earlier and earlier, and it is now fairly generally agreed that
it was written at Ephesus between 90 and 110.*

Prologue

At the beginning God expressed Himself. That Personal
Expression, that Word, was with God and was God, and He
existed with God from the beginning. All creation took
place through Him, and none took place without Him. In
Him appeared Life and this Life was the Light of mankind.
The Light still shines in the darkness, and the darkness has
never put it out.

The Gospel's beginning on earth   1 : 6

A man called John was sent by God as a witness to the
Light, so that any man who heard his testimony might
believe in the Light. This man was not himself the Light :
he was sent simply as a personal witness to that Light.

That was the true Light which shines upon every man
into the world. He came into the World—the World
He had created—and the World failed to recognise Him. He
came into His own creation, and His own people would not
accept Him. Yet wherever men did accept Him He gave
them the power to become sons of God. These were the men
who truly believed in Him, and their birth depended not on
the course of nature nor on any impulse or plan of man, but
on God.

So the Word of God became a human being and lived
among us. We saw His splendour (the splendour as of a
father's only son), full of grace and truth. And it was about
Him that John stood up and testified, exclaiming : " Here
is the One I was speaking about when I said that although
He would come after me He would always be in front of
me ; for He existed before I was born ! " Indeed, every one
of us has shared in His riches—there is a grace in our lives
because of His grace. For while the Law was given by

Moses, Love and Truth came through Jesus Christ. It is
true that no one has ever seen God at any time. Yet the
divine and only Son, Who lives in the closest intimacy with
the Father, has made Him known.

John's witness   1 : 19

This then is the testimony of John, when the Jews sent
priests and Levites to ask him who he was. He admitted
with complete candour, " I am not Christ."

So they asked him, " Who are you then? Are you
Elijah? "

" No, I am not," he replied.

" Are you the Prophet? "

" No," he replied.

" Well then," they asked again, " who are you? We want
to give an answer to the people who sent us. What would
you call yourself? "

" I am a Voice shouting in the desert. ' *Make straight the
way of the Lord!* ' as Isaiah the prophet said."

Now some of the Pharisees had been sent to John, and
they questioned him, " What is the reason, then, for your
baptizing people if you are not Christ and not Elijah and not
the Prophet? "

To which John returned, " I do baptize—with water. But
somewhere among you stands a Man you do not know. He
comes after me, it is true, but I am not fit to undo His
shoes! " (All this happened in Bethany on the far side of
the Jordan where the baptisms of John took place.)

On the following day, John saw Jesus coming towards
him and said, " Look, there is the Lamb of God Who will
take away the sin of the world! This is the Man I meant
when I said ' A Man comes after me Who is always in front
of me, for He existed before I was born! ' It is true I have
not known Him, yet it was to make Him known to the
people of Israel that I came and baptized people with water."

Then John gave this testimony, " I have seen the Spirit
come down like a dove from Heaven and rest upon Him.
Indeed, it is true that I did not recognise Him by myself, but
He Who sent me to baptize with water told me this : ' The
One on Whom you will see the Spirit coming down and rest-
ing is the Man Who baptizes with the Holy Spirit! ' Now I

have seen this happen and I declare publicly before you all
that *He is the Son of God!*"

Men begin to follow Jesus   1 : 35

On the following day John was again standing with two
of his disciples. He looked straight at Jesus as He walked
along and said, "There is the Lamb of God!" The two
disciples heard what he said and followed Jesus. Then Jesus
turned round and when He saw them following Him, spoke
to them. "What do you want?" He said.

"Master, where are you staying?" they replied.

"Come and see," returned Jesus.

So they went and saw where He was staying and remained
with Him the rest of that day. (It was then about four o'clock
in the afternoon.) One of the two men who had heard what
John said and had followed Jesus was Andrew, Simon Peter's
brother. He went straight off and found his own brother,
Simon, and told him, "We have found the Messiah!"
(meaning, of course, Christ). And he brought him to Jesus.

Jesus looked steadily at him and said, "You are Simon,
the son of John. From now on your name is Cephas"—
(that is, Peter, meaning "a rock").

The following day Jesus decided to go into Galilee. He
found Philip and said to him, "Follow me!" Philip was a
man from Bethsaida, the town that Andrew and Peter came
from. Now Philip found Nathanael and told him, "We have
discovered the Man Whom Moses wrote about in the Law
and about Whom the Prophets wrote too. He is Jesus, the
son of Joseph and comes from Nazareth."

"Can anything good come out of Nazareth?" retorted
Nathanael.

"You come and see," replied Philip.

Jesus saw Nathanael coming towards Him and remarked,
"Now here is a true man of Israel; there is no deceit in
him!"

"How can you know me?" returned Nathanael.

"When you were underneath that fig-tree," replied Jesus,
"before Philip called you, I saw you."

At which Nathanael exclaimed, "Master, You are the Son
of God, You are the King of Israel!"

"Do you believe in Me," replied Jesus, "because I said

I had seen you underneath that fig-tree? You are going to see something greater than that! Believe Me," He added, "I tell you all that you will see Heaven wide open and God's angels ascending and descending around the Son of Man!"

The Son of God and a village wedding   2 : 1

Two days later there was a wedding in the Galilean village of Cana. Jesus' mother was there and He and His disciples were invited to the festivities. Then it happened that the supply of wine gave out, and Jesus' mother told Him, "They have no more wine."

"Is that your concern, or Mine?" replied Jesus. "My time has not come yet."

So His mother said to the servants, "Mind you do whatever He tells you."

In the room six very large stone water-jars stood on the floor (actually for the Jewish ceremonial cleansing), each holding about twenty gallons. Jesus gave instructions for these jars to be filled with water, and the servants filled them to the brim. Then He said to them, "Now draw some out and take it to the Master of Ceremonies," which they did. When this man tasted the water, which had now become wine, without knowing where it came from, (though naturally the servants who had drawn the water knew), he called out to the bridegroom and said to him, "Everybody I know puts his good wine on first and then when men have had plenty to drink, he brings out the poor stuff. But you have kept back your good wine till now!" Jesus gave this, the first of His Signs, at Cana in Galilee. He demonstrated His power and His disciples believed in Him.

Jesus in the Temple   2 : 12

After this incident, Jesus, accompanied by His mother, His brothers and His disciples, went down to Capernaum and stayed there a few days. The Jewish Passover was approaching and Jesus made the journey up to Jerusalem. In the Temple He discovered cattle and sheep dealers and pigeon-sellers, as well as money-changers sitting at their tables. So He made a rough whip out of rope and drove the whole lot of them, sheep and cattle as well, out of the Temple.

He sent the coins of the money-changers flying and turned their tables upside down. Then He said to the pigeon-dealers, " Take those things out of here. Don't you dare turn My Father's house into a market ! " His disciples remembered the Scripture—

The zeal of thine house shall eat me up.

As a result of this, the Jews said to Him, " What sign can you give us to justify what you are doing ? "

" Destroy this temple," Jesus retorted, " and I will rebuild it in three days ! "

To which the Jews replied, " This Temple took forty-six years to build, and are you going to rebuild it in three days ? "

He was, in fact, speaking about the temple of His own body, and when He was raised from the dead the disciples remembered what He had said to them and that made them believe both the Scripture and what Jesus had said.

While He was in Jerusalem at Passover-time, during the festivities many believed in Him as they saw the Signs that He gave. But Jesus, on His side, did not trust Himself to them—for He knew them all. He did not need anyone to tell Him what people were like : He understood human nature.

Jesus and a religious leader   3 : 1

One night Nicodemus, a leading Jew and a Pharisee, came to see Jesus.

" Master," he began, " we realise that you are a teacher who has come from God. Obviously no one could show the Signs that you show unless God were with him."

" Believe Me," returned Jesus, " a man cannot even see the Kingdom of God without being born again."

" And how can a man who's getting old possibly be born ? " replied Nicodemus. " How can he go back into his mother's womb and be born a second time ? "

" I assure you," said Jesus, " that unless a man is born from water and from spirit he cannot enter the Kingdom of God. Flesh gives birth to flesh and spirit gives birth to spirit : you must not be surprised that I told you that all of you must be born again. The wind blows where it likes, you can hear the sound of it but you have no idea where it comes from and where it goes. Nor can you tell how a man is born by the wind of the Spirit."

"How on earth can things like this happen?" replied Nicodemus.

"So you are a teacher of Israel," said Jesus, "and you do not recognise such things? I assure you that we are talking about something we really know and we are witnessing to something we have actually observed, yet men like you will not accept our evidence. Yet if I have spoken to you about things which happen on this earth and you will not believe Me, what chance is there that you will believe Me if I tell you about what happens in Heaven? No one has ever been up to Heaven except the Son of Man Who came down from Heaven. The Son of Man must be lifted above the heads of men—as Moses lifted up that serpent in the desert—so that any man who believes in Him may have eternal life. For God loved the world so much that He gave His only Son, so that everyone who believes in Him should not be lost, but should have eternal life. You must understand that God has not sent His Son into the world to pass sentence upon it, but to save it—through Him. Any man who believes in Him is not judged at all. It is the one who will not believe who stands already condemned, because he will not believe in the character of God's only Son. This *is* the judgment—that light has entered the world and men have preferred darkness to light because their deeds are evil. Anybody who does wrong hates the light and keeps away from it, for fear his deeds may be exposed. But anybody who is living by the truth will come to the light to make it plain that all he has done has been done through God."

Jesus and John again   3 : 22

After this Jesus went into the country of Judaea with His disciples and stayed there with them while the work of baptism was being carried on. John, too, was in Aenon near Salim, baptizing people because there was plenty of water in that district and they were still coming to him for baptism. (John, of course, had not yet been put in prison.)

This led to a question arising between John's disciples and some of the Jews about the whole matter of being cleansed. They approached John and said to him, " Master, look, the man who was with you on the other side of the Jordan, the one you testified to, is now baptizing and everybody is coming to him ! "

" A man can receive nothing at all," replied John, " unless it is given him from Heaven. You yourselves can witness that I said, ' I am not Christ but I have been sent as His forerunner.' It is the bridegroom who possesses the bride, yet the bridegroom's friend who merely stands and listens to him can be overjoyed to hear the bridegroom's voice. That is why my happiness is now complete. He must grow greater and greater and I less and less.

" The One Who comes from above is naturally above everybody. The one who arises from the earth belongs to the earth and speaks from the earth. The One Who comes from Heaven is above all others and He bears witness to what He has seen and heard—yet no one is accepting his testimony. Yet if a man does accept it, he is acknowledging the fact that God is true. For the One Whom God sent speaks the authentic words of God—and there can be no measuring of the Spirit given to *Him* ! The Father loves the Son and has put everything into His hand. The man who believes in the Son has eternal life. The man who refuses to believe in the Son will not see life ; he lives under the anger of God."

Jesus meets a Samaritan woman   4 : 1

Now, when the Lord found that the Pharisees had heard that " Jesus is making and baptizing more disciples than John "—although, in fact, it was not Jesus who did the baptizing but His disciples—He left Judaea and went off again to Galilee, which meant His passing through Samaria. There He came to a little town called Sychar, which is near the historic plot of land that Jacob gave to his son, Joseph, and " Jacob's Spring " was there. Jesus, tired with the journey, sat down beside it, just as He was. The time was about midday. Presently, a Samaritan woman arrived to draw some water.

" Please give Me a drink," Jesus said to her, for His disciples had gone away to the town to buy food. The Samaritan woman said to Him, " How can you, a Jew, ask for a drink from me, a woman of Samaria?" (For Jews have no dealings with Samaritans.)

"If you knew what God can give," Jesus replied, "and if you knew Who it is that said to you, 'Give Me a drink,' I think you would have asked Him, and He would have given you living water!"

"Sir," said the woman, "you have nothing to draw water with and this well is deep—where can you get your living water? Are you a greater man than our ancestor, Jacob, who gave us this well, and drank here himself with his family, and his cattle?"

Jesus said to her, "Everyone who drinks this water will be thirsty again. But whoever drinks the water I will give him will never be thirsty again. For My gift will become a spring in the man himself, welling up into eternal life."

The woman said, "Sir, give me this water, so that I may stop being thirsty—and not have to come here to draw water any more!"

"Go and call your husband and then come back here," said Jesus to her.

"I haven't got a husband!" the woman answered.

"You are quite right in saying, 'I haven't got a husband,'" replied Jesus, "for you have had five husbands and the man you have now is not your husband at all. Yes, you spoke the simple truth when you said that."

"Sir," said the woman again, "I can see that you are a prophet! Now our ancestors worshipped on this hill-side, but you Jews say that Jerusalem is the place where men ought to worship——"

"Believe Me," returned Jesus, "the time is coming when worshipping the Father will not be a matter of 'on this hill-side' or 'in Jerusalem.' Nowadays you are worshipping with your eyes shut. We Jews are worshipping with our eyes open, for the salvation of mankind is to come from our race. Yet the time is coming, yes, and has already come, when true worshippers will worship the Father in spirit and in reality. Indeed, the Father looks for men who will worship Him like that. God is Spirit, and those who worship Him can only worship in spirit and in reality."

"Of course I know that Messiah is coming," returned the

woman, " you know, the One Who is called Christ. When He comes He will make everything plain to us."

" *I am Christ, speaking to you now,*" said Jesus.

At this point His disciples arrived, and were very surprised to find Him talking to a woman, but none of them asked, " What do You want ? " or " What are You talking to her about ? " So the woman left her water-pot behind and went into the town and began to say to the people, " Come out and see the man who told me everything I've ever done ! Can this be ' Christ ' ? " So they left the town and started to come to Jesus.

Meanwhile the disciples were begging Him, " Master, do eat something."

To which Jesus replied, " I have food to eat that you know nothing about."

This, of course, made the disciples ask each other, " Do you think anyone has brought Him any food ? "

Jesus said to them, " My food is doing the Will of Him Who sent Me and finishing the work He has given Me. Don't you say, ' Four months more and then comes the harvest ? ' But I tell you to open your eyes and look at the fields—they are gleaming white all ready for the harvest ! The reaper is already being rewarded and getting in a harvest for eternal life, so that sower and reaper may be glad together. For in this harvest the old saying comes true, ' One man sows and another reaps.' I have sent you to reap a harvest for which you never laboured ; other men have worked hard and you have reaped the result of their labours."

Many of the Samaritans who came out of that town believed in Him through the woman's testimony—" He told me everything I've ever done." And when they arrived they begged Him to stay with them. He did stay there two days and far more believed in Him because of what He Himself said. As they told the woman, " We don't believe any longer now because of what you said. We have heard Him with our own ears. We know now that this must be the Man Who will save the world ! "

Jesus in Cana again, heals in response to faith   4 : 43

After the two days were over, Jesus left and went away to Galilee. (For Jesus Himself testified that a prophet enjoys

no honour in his own country.) And on His arrival the
people received Him with open arms. For they had seen all
that He had done in Jerusalem during the Festival, since
they had themselves been present. So Jesus came again to
Cana in Galilee, the place where He made the water into
wine. At Capernaum there was an official whose son was
very ill. When he heard that Jesus had left Judaea and had
arrived in Galilee, he went off to see Him and begged Him
to come down and heal his son, who was by this time at the
point of death.

Jesus said to him, " I suppose you will never believe
unless you see signs and wonders ! "

" Sir," returned the official, " please come down before
my boy dies ! "

" You can go home," returned Jesus, " your son is alive
and well."

And the man believed what Jesus had said to him and went
on his way.

On the journey back his servants met him with the report :
" Your son is alive and well." So he asked them at what
time he had begun to recover, and they replied : " The fever
left him yesterday at one o'clock in the afternoon." Then
the father knew that this must have happened at the very
moment when Jesus had said to him, " Your son is alive
and well." And he and his whole household believed in
Jesus. This, then, was the second Sign that Jesus gave on
His return from Judaea to Galilee.

Jesus heals in Jerusalem   5 : 1

Some time later came one of the Jewish feast-days and
Jesus went up to Jerusalem. There is in Jerusalem near the
sheep-gate a pool surrounded by five arches, which has the
Hebrew name of Bethzatha. Under these arches a great
many sick people were in the habit of lying ; some of them
were blind, some lame, and some had withered limbs. (They
used to wait there for the " moving of the water," for at
certain times an angel used to come down into the pool and
disturb the water, and then the first person who stepped into
the water after the disturbance would be healed of whatever
he was suffering from.) One particular man had been there
ill for thirty-eight years. When Jesus saw him lying there on

his back—knowing that he had been like that for a long time, He said to him, " Do you want to get well again ? "

" Sir," replied the sick man, " I just haven't got anybody to put me into the pool when the water is all stirred up. While I'm trying to get there somebody else gets down into it first."

" Get up," said Jesus, " pick up your bed and walk ! "

At once the man recovered, picked up his bed and walked.

This happened on a Sabbath day, which made the Jews keep on telling the man who had been healed, " It's the Sabbath, you know ; it's not right for you to carry your bed."

" The man who made me well," he replied, " was the one who told me, ' Pick up your bed and walk.' "

Then they asked him, " And who is the man who told you to do that ? "

But the one who had been healed had no idea who it was, for Jesus had slipped away in the dense crowd. Later Jesus found him in the Temple and said to him, " Look : you are a fit man now. Do not sin again or something worse might happen to you ! "

Then the man went off and informed the Jews that the One Who had made him well was Jesus. It was because Jesus did such things on the Sabbath day that the Jews persecuted Him. But Jesus' answer to them was this, " My Father is still at work and therefore I work as well."

This remark made the Jews all the more determined to kill Him, because not only did He break the Sabbath but He referred to God as His own Father, so putting Himself on equal terms with God.

Jesus makes His tremendous claim   5 : 19

Jesus said to them, " I assure you that the Son can do nothing of His own accord, but only what He sees the Father doing. What the Son does is always modelled on what the Father does, for the Father loves the Son and shows Him everything that He does Himself. Yes, and He will show Him even greater things than these to fill you with wonder. For just as the Father raises the dead and makes them live, so does the Son give life to any man He chooses. The Father is no man's judge : He has put judgment entirely into the Son's hands so that all men may honour the Son equally with the Father. The man who does not honour the Son does not honour the Father Who sent Him. I solemnly assure you that the man who hears what I have to say and believes in the One Who has sent Me has eternal life. He does not have to face judgment; he has already passed from death into life. Yes, I assure you that a time is coming, in fact has already come, when the dead will hear the voice of the Son of God and when they have heard it *they will live*! For just as the Father has Life in Himself, so by the Father's gift, the Son also has Life in Himself. And He has given Him authority to judge because He is Son of Man. No, do not be surprised—the time is coming when all those who are dead and buried will hear His voice and out they will come—those who have done right will rise again to life, but those who have done wrong will rise to face judgment!

"By Myself I can do nothing. As I hear, I judge, and My judgment is true because I do not live to please Myself but to do the Will of the Father Who sent Me. You may say that I am bearing witness about Myself, that therefore what I say about Myself has no value, but I would remind you that there is One Who witnesses about Me and I know that His witness about Me is absolutely true. You sent to John, and he testified to the truth. Not that it is man's testimony that I accept—I only tell you this to help you to be saved. John certainly was a lamp that burned and shone, and for a time you were willing to enjoy the light that he gave. But I have a higher testimony than John's. The work that the Father gave Me to complete, yes, these very actions which I do are My witness that the Father has sent Me. This is how the Father Who sent Me has given His own personal testimony to Me.

"Now you have never at any time heard what He says or seen what He is like. Nor do you really believe His Word in your hearts, for you refuse to believe the Man Whom He has sent. You pore over the Scriptures for you imagine that you will find eternal life in them. And all the time they give their testimony to Me! But you are not willing to come to Me to have real life! Men's approval or disapproval means nothing to Me, but I can tell that you have none of the love of God in your hearts. I have come in the Name of

My Father and you will not accept Me. Yet if another man comes simply in his own name, you will accept him. How on earth can you believe while you are for ever looking for each other's approval and not for the glory that comes from the one God? There is no need for you to think that I have come to accuse you before the Father. You already have an accuser—Moses, in whom you put all your confidence! For if you really believed Moses, you would be bound to believe me; for it was about Me that he wrote. But if you do not believe what he wrote, how can you believe what I say?"

Jesus shows His power over material things   6 : 1,

After this, Jesus crossed the lake of Galilee (or Tiberias) and a great crowd followed Him because they had seen the Signs which He gave in His dealings with the sick. But Jesus went up the hill-side and sat down there with His disciples. The Passover, the Jewish festival, was near. So Jesus, raising His eyes and seeing a great crowd on their way towards Him, said to Philip, " Where can we buy food for these people to eat?" (He said this to test Philip, for He Himself knew what He was going to do.)

" Ten pounds' worth of bread would not be enough for them," Philip replied, " even if they had only a little each."

Then Andrew, Simon Peter's brother, another disciple, put in, " There is a boy here who has five little barley loaves and a couple of fish, but what's the good of that for such a crowd?"

Then Jesus said, " Get the people to sit down."

There was plenty of grass there, and the men, some five thousand of them, sat down. Then Jesus took the loaves, gave thanks for them and distributed them to the people sitting on the grass, and He distributed the fish in the same way, giving them as much as they wanted. When they had eaten enough, Jesus said to His disciples, " Collect the pieces that are left over so that nothing is wasted."

So they did as He suggested and filled twelve baskets with the broken pieces of the five barley loaves which were left over after the people had eaten! When the men saw this Sign of Jesus' power, they kept saying, " This certainly is the Prophet who was to come into the world!"

Then Jesus, realising that they were going to carry Him off and make Him their king, retired once more to the hill-side quite alone.

In the evening His disciples went down to the lake, embarked on the boat and made their way across the lake to Capernaum. Darkness had already fallen and Jesus had not returned to them. A strong wind sprang up and the water grew very rough. When they had rowed about three or four miles, they saw Jesus walking on the water and coming towards the boat, and they were terrified. But He spoke to them, " Don't be afraid : it is I Myself."

So they gladly took Him aboard, and at once the boat reached the shore they were making for.

Jesus teaches about the true bread   6 : 22

The following day, the crowd who had remained on the other side of the lake noticed that only one boat had been there, and that Jesus had not embarked on it with His disciples, but that they had in fact gone off by themselves. Some other small boats from Tiberias had landed quite near the place where they had eaten the food and the Lord had given thanks. When the crowd realised that neither Jesus nor the disciples were there any longer, they themselves got into the boats and went off to Capernaum to look for Jesus. When they had found Him on the other side of the lake, they said to Him, " Master, when did you come here ? "

" Believe Me," replied Jesus, " you are looking for Me now not because you saw My Signs but because you ate that food and had all you wanted. You should not work for the food which does not last but for that food which lasts on into eternal life. This is the food the Son of Man will give you, and He is the One Who bears the stamp of God the Father."

This made them ask Him, " What must we do to carry out the work of God ? "

" The work of God for you," replied Jesus, " is to believe in the One whom He has sent to you."

Then they asked Him, " Then what sign can you give us that will make us believe in you ? What work are you doing ? Our forefathers ate manna in the desert just as the Scripture says :

He gave them bread out of heaven to eat."

To which Jesus replied, "Yes, but what matters is not that Moses *gave you* bread from Heaven but that My Father *is giving you* the true bread from Heaven. For the bread of God which comes down from Heaven gives life to the world."

This made them say to Him, "Lord, please give us this bread, always ! "

Then Jesus said to them, "I Myself am the bread of life. The man who comes to Me will never be hungry and the man who believes in Me will never again be thirsty. Yet I have told you that you have seen Me and do not believe. Everything that My Father gives Me will come to Me and I will never refuse anyone who comes to Me. For I have come down from Heaven, not to do what I want, but to do the Will of Him Who sent Me. The Will of Him Who sent Me is that I should not lose anything of what He has given Me, but should raise it up when the Last Day comes. And this is the Will of the One Who sent Me, that everyone who sees the Son and trusts Him should have eternal life, and I will raise him up when the Last Day comes."

At this, the Jews began grumbling at Him because He said, " I am the bread which came down from Heaven," remarking, " Is not this Jesus, the son of Joseph, whose parents we know ? How can he say that ' I have come down from Heaven ' ? "

So Jesus answered them, " Do not grumble among yourselves. Nobody comes to Me unless he is drawn to Me by the Father Who sent Me, and I will raise him up when the Last Day comes. In the Prophets it is written—

And they shall all be taught of God,

and this means that everybody who has heard the Father's Voice and learned from Him will come to Me. Not that anyone has ever seen the Father except the One Who comes from God—He has seen the Father. I assure you that the man who trusts in Him has eternal life already. I Myself am the bread of life. Your forefathers ate manna in the desert, *and they died*. This is bread that comes down from Heaven, so that a man may eat it and not die. I Myself am the living bread which came down from Heaven, and if anyone eats this bread he will live for ever. The bread which I will give is My body and I shall give it for the life of the world."

This led to a fierce argument among the Jews, some of them saying, " How can this man give us his body to eat ? "

So Jesus said to them, " Unless you do eat the body of the Son of Man and drink His blood, you are not really living at all. The man who eats My flesh and drinks My blood has eternal life and I will raise him up when the Last Day comes. For My body is real food and My blood is real drink. The man who eats My body and drinks My blood shares My life and I share his. Just as the living Father sent Me and I am alive because of the Father, so the man who lives on Me will live because of Me. *This* is the Bread which came down from Heaven ! It is not like the manna which your forefathers used to eat, *and died*. The man who eats this Bread will live for ever."

Jesus said all these things while teaching in the synagogue at Capernaum. Many of His disciples heard Him say these things, and commented, " This is hard teaching indeed ; who could accept that ? "

Then Jesus knowing intuitively that His disciples were complaining about what He had just said went on, " Is this too much for you ? Then what would happen if you were to see the Son of Man going up to the place where He was before ? It is the Spirit which gives life. The flesh will not help you. The things that I have told you are spiritual and are Life. But some of you will not believe Me."

For Jesus knew from the beginning which of His followers did not trust Him and who was the man who would betray Him. Then He added, " This is why I said to you, ' No one can come to Me unless My Father puts it into his heart to come.' "

As a consequence of this, many of His disciples withdrew and no longer followed Him. So Jesus said to the Twelve, " And are you too wanting to go away ? "

" Lord," answered Simon Peter, " who else should we go to ? *Your words have the ring of eternal life !* And we believe and are convinced that You are the Holy One of God."

Jesus replied, " Did I not choose you Twelve—and one of you has the devil in his heart ? "

He was speaking of Judas, the son of Simon Iscariot, one of the Twelve, who was planning to betray Jesus.

Jesus delays His arrival at the Festival   7 : 1

After this, Jesus moved about in Galilee but decided not to do so in Judaea since the Jews were planning to take His life. A Jewish festival, " The Feast of the Tabernacles ", was approaching and his brothers said to Him, " You ought to leave here and go to Judaea so that your disciples can see what you are doing, for nobody works in secret if he wants to be known publicly. If you are going to do things like this, let the world see what you are doing." For not even His brothers had any faith in Him. Jesus replied by saying, " It is not yet the right time for Me, but any time is right for you. You see, it is impossible for you to arouse the world's hatred, but I provoke hatred because I show the world how evil its deeds really are. No, you go up to the Festival ; I shall not go up now, for it is not yet time for Me to go." And after these remarks He remained where He was in Galilee.

Later, after His brothers had gone up to the Festival, He went up later Himself, not openly but as though He did not want to be seen. Consequently, the Jews kept looking for Him at the Festival and asking, " Where is that man ? " And there was an undercurrent of discussion about Him among the crowds. Some would say, " He is a good man," others maintained that he was not, but that he was " misleading the people." Nobody, however, spoke openly about Him for fear of the Jews.

Jesus openly declares His authority   7 : 14

But at the very height of the Festival, Jesus went up to the Temple and began teaching. The Jews were amazed and remarked, " How does this man know all this—he has never been taught ? "

Jesus replied to them, " My teaching is not really Mine but comes from the One Who sent Me. If anyone wants to do God's Will, he will know whether My teaching is from God or whether I merely speak on My own authority.

A man who speaks on his own authority has an eye for his own reputation. But the man who is considering the glory of God Who sent him is a true man. There can be no dishonesty about him.

"Did not Moses give you the Law? Yet not a single one of you obeys the Law. *Why are you trying to kill Me?*"

The crowd answered, "You must be mad! Who is trying to kill you?"

Jesus answered them, "I have done one thing and you are all amazed at it. Moses gave you circumcision (not that it came from Moses originally but from your forefathers), and you will circumcise a man even on the Sabbath. If a man receives the cutting of circumcision on the Sabbath to avoid breaking the Law of Moses, why should you be angry with Me because I have made a man's body perfectly whole on the Sabbath? You must not judge by the appearance of things but by the reality!"

Some of the people of Jerusalem, hearing Him talk like this, were saying, "Isn't this the man that they are trying to kill? It's amazing—he talks quite openly and they haven't a word to say to him. Surely our rulers haven't decided that this really is Christ! But then, we know this man and where he comes from—when Christ comes, no one will know where He comes from."

Jesus makes more unique claims   7 : 28

Then Jesus, in the middle of His teaching, called out in the Temple, "So you know Me and know where I have come from? But I have not come of My own accord; I am sent by One Who is true and you do not know Him! I do know Him, because I come from Him and He has sent Me here."

Then they attempted to arrest Him, but actually no one laid a finger on Him because the right moment had not yet come. Many of the crowd believed in Him and kept on saying, "When Christ comes, is He going to show greater signs than this man?"

The Pharisees heard the crowd whispering these things about him, and they and the Chief Priests sent officers to arrest Him. Then Jesus said, "I shall be with you only a little while longer and then I am going to Him Who sent Me. You will look for Me then but you will never find Me. You cannot come where I shall be."

This made the Jews say to each other, " Where is he going to hide himself so that we cannot find him? Surely he's not going to our refugees among the Greeks to teach Greeks? What does he mean when he says, ' You will look for me and you will never find me ' and ' You cannot come where I shall be ' ? "

Then, on the last day, the climax of the Festival, Jesus stood up and cried out, " If any man is thirsty, he can come to Me and drink! The man who believes in Me, as the Scripture said, will have rivers of living water flowing from his inmost heart." (Here he was speaking about the Spirit which those who believe in Him would receive. The Holy Spirit had not yet been given because Jesus had not yet been glorified.) When they heard these words, some of the people were saying, " This really is the Prophet." Others said, " This is Christ! " But some said, " And does Christ come from Galilee? Don't the Scriptures say that Christ will be descended from David, and will come from Bethlehem, the village where David lived? "

So the people were in two minds about Him—some of them wanted to arrest Him, but so far no one laid hands on Him.

Then the officers returned to the Pharisees and Chief Priests who said to them, " Why haven't you brought him? "

" No man ever spoke like that! " they replied.

" Has he pulled the wool over your eyes too? " retorted the Pharisees. " Have any of the authorities or any of the Pharisees believed in him? But this crowd, who know nothing about the Law, is damned anyway! "

One of their number, Nicodemus, (the one who had previously been to see Jesus), remarked to them, " But surely our Law does not condemn the accused without hearing what he has to say, and finding out what he has done? "

" Are you a Galilean, too? " they answered him. " Look where you will—you won't find that any prophet comes out of Galilee! "

So they broke up their meeting and went home, while Jesus went off to the Mount of Olives.[1]

Jesus deflates the rigorists   8 : 2

Early next morning He returned to the Temple and the entire crowd came to Him. So He sat down and began to teach them. But the Scribes and Pharisees brought in to Him a woman who had been caught in adultery. They made her stand in front, and then said to Him, " Now, Master, this woman has been caught in adultery, in the very act. According to the Law, Moses commanded us to stone such women to death. Now, what do you say about her ? "

They said this to test Him, so that they might have some good grounds for an accusation. But Jesus stooped down and began to write with His finger in the dust on the ground. But as they persisted in their questioning, He straightened Himself up and said to them, " If there is one among you who has not sinned, let him throw the first stone at her." Then he stooped down again and continued writing with His finger. And when they heard what He said, they were convicted by their own consciences and went out, one by one, beginning with the eldest until they had all gone.

Jesus was left alone, with the woman still standing where they had put her. So He stood up and said to her, " Where are they all—did no one condemn you ? "

And she said, " No one, sir."

" Neither do I condemn you," said Jesus to her. " Go home and do not sin again."

Jesus' bold claims—about Himself—and His Father   8 : 12

Later, Jesus spoke to the people again and said, " I am the Light of the world. The man who follows Me will never walk in the dark but will live his life in the light."

This made the Pharisees say to Him, " You are testifying to yourself—your evidence is not valid."

Jesus answered, " Even if I am testifying to Myself, My evidence is valid, for I know where I have come from and I know where I am going. But as for you, you have no idea where I come from or where I am going. You are judging by human standards, but I am not judging anyone. Yet, if

[1] See Appendix, Note 5.

I should judge, My decision would be just, for I am not alone—the Father Who sent Me is with Me. In your Law, it is stated that the witness of two persons is valid. I am one testifying to Myself and the second witness to Me is the Father Who sent Me."

"And where is this father of yours?" they replied.

"You do not know My Father," returned Jesus, "any more than you know Me: if you had known Me, you would have known Him."

Jesus made these statements while He was teaching in the Temple treasury. Yet no one arrested Him, for His time had not yet come.

Later, Jesus spoke to them again and said, "I am going away and you will try to find Me, but you will die in your sins. You cannot come where I am going."

This made the Jews say, "Is he going to kill himself, then? Is *that* why he says, 'You cannot come where I am going'?"

"The difference between us," Jesus said to them, "is that you come from below and I am from above. You belong to this world but I do not. That is why I told you you will die in your sins. For unless you believe that I am Who I am, you will die in your sins."

Then they said, "*Who are you?*"

"I am what I have told you I was from the beginning," replied Jesus. "There is much in you that I could speak about and condemn. But He Who sent Me is true and I am only speaking to this world what I Myself have heard from Him."

They did not realise that He was talking to them about the Father. So Jesus resumed, "When you have lifted up the Son of Man, then you will realise that I am Who I say I am, and that I do nothing on My own authority but speak simply as My Father has taught Me. The One Who sent Me is with Me now: the Father has never left Me alone for I always do what pleases Him." And even while He said these words, many people believed in Him.

Jesus speaks of personal freedom   8 : 31

So Jesus said to the Jews who believed in Him, "If you are faithful to what I have said, you are truly My disciples.

And you will know the truth and the truth will set you free ! "

" But we are descendants of Abraham," they replied, " and we have never in our lives been any man's slaves. How can you say to us ' You will be set free ' ? "

Jesus returned, " Believe Me when I tell you that every man who commits sin is a slave. For a slave is no permanent part of a household, but a son is. If the Son, then, sets you free, you are really free. I know that you are descended from Abraham, but some of you are looking for a way to kill Me because you can't bear My words. I am telling you what I have seen in the presence of My Father, and you are doing what you have seen in the presence of your father."

" Our father is Abraham ! " they retorted.

" If you were the children of Abraham, you would do the sort of things Abraham did. But in fact, at this moment, you are looking for a way to kill Me, simply because I am a man who has told you the truth that I have heard from God. Abraham would never have done that. No, you are doing your father's work."

" We are not illegitimate ! " they retorted. " We have one Father—God."

" If God were really your Father," replied Jesus, " you would have loved Me. For I came from God ; I did not come of My own accord—He sent Me, and I am here. Why do you not understand My words ? It is because you cannot bear to hear what I am really saying. Your father is the devil, and what you are wanting to do is what your father longs to do. He always was a murderer, and has never dealt with the truth, since the truth will have nothing to do with him. Whenever he tells a lie, he speaks in character, for he is a liar and the father of lies. And it is because I speak the truth that you will not believe Me. Which of you can prove Me guilty of sin ? If I am speaking the truth, why is it that you do not believe Me ? The man who is born of God can hear the words of God and the reason why you cannot hear the words of God is simply this, that you are not the sons of God."

" How right we are," retorted the Jews, " in calling you a Samaritan, and mad at that ! "

" No," replied Jesus, " I am not mad. I am honouring

My Father and you are trying to dishonour Me. But I am not concerned with My own glory: there is One Whose concern it is, and He is the true Judge. Believe Me when I tell you that if anybody accepts My words, he will never see death at all."

"Now we know that you're mad," replied the Jews. "Why, Abraham died and the prophets, too, and yet you say, 'If a man accepts my words, he will never experience death!' Are you greater than our father, Abraham? He died, and so did the prophets—who are you making yourself out to be?"

"If I were trying to glorify Myself," returned Jesus, "such glory would be worthless. But it is My Father Who glorifies Me, the very One Whom you say is your God—though you have never known Him. But I know Him, and if I said I did not know Him, I should be as much a liar as you are! But I do know Him and I am faithful to what He says. As for your father, Abraham, his great joy was that he would see My coming. Now he has seen it and he is overjoyed."

"Look," said the Jews to Him, "you are not fifty yet—and has Abraham seen you?"

"I tell you in solemn truth," returned Jesus, "before there was an Abraham, I AM!"

At this, they picked up stones to hurl at Him, but Jesus disappeared and made His way out of the Temple.

Jesus and blindness, physical and spiritual   9 : 1

Later, as Jesus walked along He saw a man who had been blind from birth.

"Master, whose sin caused this man's blindness," asked the disciples, "his own or his parents'?"

"He was not born blind because of his own sin or that of his parents," returned Jesus, "but to show the power of God at work in him. We must carry on the work of Him Who sent Me while the daylight lasts. Night is coming, when no one can work. I am the world's light as long as I am in it."

Having said this, He spat on the ground and made a sort of paste with the saliva. This He applied to the man's eyes and said, "Go and wash in the pool of Siloam." (Siloam means " one who has been sent.") So the man went off and washed and came home with his sight restored.

His neighbours and the people who had often seen him before as a beggar remarked, " Isn't this the man who used to sit and beg ? "

" Yes, that's the one," said some.

Others said, " No, but he's very like him."

But he himself said, " I'm the man all right ! "

" Then how was your blindness cured ? " they asked.

" The man called Jesus made some paste and smeared it on my eyes," he replied, " and then he said, ' Go to Siloam and wash.' So off I went and washed—and that's how I got my sight ! "

" Where is he now ? " they asked.

" I don't know," he returned.

So they brought the man who had once been blind before the Pharisees. (It should be noted that Jesus made the paste and restored his sight on a Sabbath day.) The Pharisees asked the question all over again as to how he had become able to see.

" He put a paste on my eyes; I washed it off; now I can see—that's all," he replied.

Some of the Pharisees commented, " This man cannot be from God since he does not observe the Sabbath."

" But how can a sinner give such wonderful signs as these ? " others demurred. And they were in two minds about Him. Finally, they asked the blind man again, " And what do *you* say about him ? You're the one whose sight was restored."

" I believe he is a prophet," he replied.

The Jews did not really believe that the man had been blind and then had become able to see, until they had summoned his parents and asked them, " Is this your son who you say was born blind ? How does it happen that he can now see ? "

" We know that this is our son, and we know that he was born blind," returned his parents, " but how he can see now, or who made him able to see, we have no idea. Why don't you ask him ? He is a grown-up man; he can speak for himself."

His parents said this because they were afraid of the Jews

who had already agreed that anybody who admitted that
Christ had done this thing should be excommunicated. It
was this fear which made his parents say, " Ask him, he is a
grown-up man."

So, once again they summoned the man who had been
born blind and said to him, " You should give God the glory
for what has happened to you. We know that this man is a
sinner."

" Whether he is a sinner or not, I couldn't tell, but one
thing I am sure of," the man replied, " I used to be blind,
now I can see ! "

" But what did he *do* to you—how did he make you see ? "
they continued.

" I've told you before," he replied. " Weren't you listening ? Why do you want to hear it all over again ? Are you
wanting to be his disciples too ? "

At this, they turned on him furiously.

" You're the one who is his disciple ! We are disciples of
Moses. We know that God spoke to Moses, but as for this
man, we don't even know where he came from."

" Now here's the extraordinary thing," he retorted, " you
don't know where he came from and yet he gave me the
gift of sight. Everybody knows that God does not listen
to sinners. It is the man who has a proper respect for God
and does what God wants him to do—he's the one God
listens to. Why, since the world began, nobody ever heard
of a man who was born blind being given his sight. If this
man did not come from God, he couldn't do such a thing ! "

" You misbegotten wretch ! " they flung back at him.
" Are you trying to teach *us* ? " And they threw him out.

Jesus heard that they had expelled him and when He
had found him, He said, " Do you believe in the Son of
Man ? "

" And who is he, sir ? " the man replied. " Tell me, so
that I can believe in him."

" You have seen Him," replied Jesus. " It is the One
Who is talking to you now."

" Lord, I do believe," he said, and worshipped Him.

Then Jesus said, " My coming into this world is itself a
judgment—those who cannot see have their eyes opened
and those who think they can see become blind."

Some of the Pharisees near Him overheard this and said, "So we're blind, too, are we?"

"If you were blind," returned Jesus, "nobody could blame you, but, as you insist 'We can see,' your guilt remains."

Jesus declares Himself the true shepherd of men   10 : 1

Then Jesus said, "Believe Me when I tell you that anyone who does not enter the sheepfold through the door, but climbs in by some other way, is a thief and a rogue. It is the shepherd of the flock who goes in by the door. It is to him the door-keeper opens the door and it is his voice that the sheep recognise. He calls his own sheep by name and leads them out of the fold, and when he has driven all his own flock outside, he goes in front of them himself, and the sheep follow him because they know his voice. They will never follow a stranger—indeed, they will run away from him, for they do not recognise strange voices."

Jesus gave them this illustration but they did not grasp the point of what He was saying to them. So Jesus said to them once more, "I do assure you that I Myself am the 'door' for the sheep. All who have gone before Me are like thieves and rogues, but the sheep did not listen to them. I am the 'door.' If a man goes in through Me, he will be safe and sound; he can come in and out and find his food. The thief comes with the sole intention of stealing and killing and destroying, but I came to bring them life, and far more than before. I am the good shepherd. The good shepherd will give his life for the sake of his sheep. But the hired man, who is not the shepherd, and does not own the sheep, will see the wolf coming, desert the sheep and run away. And the wolf will attack the flock and send them flying. The hired man runs away because he is only a hired man and has no interest in the sheep. I am the good shepherd, and I know those that are Mine and My sheep know Me, just as the Father knows Me and I know the Father. And I am giving My life for the sake of the sheep.

"And I have other sheep who do not belong to this fold. I must lead these also, and they will hear My voice. So there will be one flock and one Shepherd. This is the reason why the Father loves Me—that I lay down My life, and I lay it

down to take it up again! No one is taking it from Me, but
I lay it down of My own free will. I have the power to lay
it down and I have the power to take it up again. This is
an order that I have received from My Father."

Jesus plainly declares Who He is   10 : 19

Once again, the Jews were in two minds about Him
because of these words, many of them remarking, "The
devil's in him and he's insane. Why do you listen to him?"

But others were saying, "This is not the sort of thing a
devil-possessed man would say! Can a devil make a blind
man see?"

Then came the Dedication Festival at Jerusalem. It was
winter-time and Jesus was walking about inside the Temple
in Solomon's Cloisters. So the Jews closed in on Him and
said, "How much longer are you going to keep us in
suspense? If you really are Christ, tell us so straight out!"

" I have told you," replied Jesus, "and you do not believe
it. What I have done in My Father's Name is sufficient to
prove My claim, but you do not believe because you are not
My sheep. My sheep recognise My voice and I know who
they are. They follow Me and I give them eternal life. They
will never die and no one can snatch them out of My hand.
My Father, Who has given them to Me, is greater than all.
And no one can tear anything out of the Father's hand. I and
the Father are One."

Again the Jews reached for stones to stone Him to death,
but Jesus answered them, "I have shown you many good
things from the Father,—for which of these do you intend
to stone Me?"

"We're not going to stone you for any good things,"
replied the Jews, "but for blasphemy: because you, who
are only a man, are making yourself out to be God."

"Is it not written in your own Law," replied Jesus, "'I
have said ye are gods'? and if he called those men 'gods'
to whom the Word of God came (and the Scripture cannot
be broken), can you say to the One Whom the Father has
consecrated and sent into the world, 'You are blaspheming'
because I said, 'I am the Son of God'? If I fail to do what
My Father does, then do not believe Me. But if I do, even
though you have no faith in Me personally, then believe in

the things that I do. Then you may come to know and realise that the Father is in Me and I am in the Father."

And again they tried to arrest Him, but He moved out of their reach.

Then Jesus went off again across the Jordan to the place where John had first baptized and there He stayed. A great many people came to Him, and said, " John never gave us any sign but all that he said about this man was true."

And in that place many believed in Him.

Jesus shows His power over death   11 : 1

Now there was a man by the name of Lazarus who became seriously ill. He lived in Bethany, the village where Mary and her sister Martha lived. (Lazarus was the brother of the Mary who poured perfume upon the Lord and wiped His feet with her hair.) So the sisters sent word to Jesus : " Lord, Your friend is very ill."

When Jesus received the message, He said, " This illness is not meant to end in death ; it is going to bring glory to God—for it will show the glory of the Son of God."

Now Jesus loved Martha and her sister and Lazarus. So when He heard of Lazarus' illness He stayed where He was two days longer. Only then did He say to the disciples, " Let us go back into Judaea."

" Master ! " returned the disciples, " only a few days ago, the Jews were trying to stone You to death—are You going there again ? "

" There are twelve hours of daylight every day, are there not ? " replied Jesus. " If a man walks in the daytime, he does not stumble, for he has the daylight to see by. But if he walks at night he stumbles because he cannot see where he is going."

Jesus spoke these words ; then after a pause He said to them, " Our friend Lazarus has fallen asleep, but I am going to wake him up."

At this, His disciples said, " Lord, if he has fallen asleep, he will be all right."

Actually Jesus had spoken about his death, but they thought that He was speaking about falling into natural sleep. This made Jesus tell them quite plainly, " Lazarus has died, and I am glad that I was not there—for your sakes, that you may learn to believe. And now, let us go to him."

Thomas (known as the Twin) then said to his fellow disciples, " Come on, then, let us all go and die with Him ! "

When Jesus arrived, He found that Lazarus had already been in the grave four days. Now Bethany is quite near Jerusalem, rather less than two miles away, and a good many of the Jews had come out to see Martha and Mary to offer them sympathy over their brother's death. When Martha heard that Jesus was on His way, she went out and met Him, while Mary stayed in the house.

" If only You had been here, Lord," said Martha, " my brother would never have died. And I know that, even now, God will give You whatever You ask from Him."

" Your brother will rise again," Jesus replied to her.

" I know," said Martha, " that he will rise again in the resurrection at the last day."

" I Myself am the Resurrection and the Life," Jesus told her. " The man who believes in Me will live even though he dies, and anyone who is alive and believes in Me will never die at all. Can you believe that ? "

" Yes, Lord," replied Martha. " I do believe that You are Christ, the Son of God, the One Who was to come into the world." Saying this, she went away and called Mary her sister, whispering, " The Master's here and is asking for you." When Mary heard this she sprang to her feet and went to Him. Now Jesus had not yet arrived at the village itself, but was still where Martha had met Him. So when the Jews who had been condoling with Mary in the house saw her get up quickly and go out, they followed her, imagining that she was going to the grave to weep there.

When Mary met Jesus, she looked at Him and then fell down at His feet. " If only You had been here, Lord," she said, " my brother would never have died."

When Jesus saw Mary weep and noticed the tears of the Jews who came with her, He was deeply moved and visibly distressed.

" Where have you put him ? " He asked.

" Lord, come and see," they replied, and at this Jesus Himself wept.

" Look how much he loved him ! " remarked the Jews, though some of them asked, " Could he not have kept this man from dying if he could open that blind man's eyes ? "

Jesus was again deeply moved at these words, and went on to the grave. It was a cave, and a stone lay in front of it.

" Take away the stone," said Jesus.

" But Lord," said Martha, the dead man's sister, " he has been dead four days. By this time he will be decaying. . . ."

" Did I not tell you," replied Jesus, " that if you believed, you would see the wonder of what God can do ? "

Then they took the stone away and Jesus raised His eyes and said, " Father, I thank You that You have heard Me. I know that You always hear Me, but I have said this for the sake of these people standing here so that they may believe that You have sent Me."

And when He had said this, He called out in a loud voice, " Lazarus, come out ! "

And the dead man came out, his hands and feet bound with grave-clothes, and his face muffled with a handkerchief.

" Now unbind him," Jesus told them, " and let him go home."

Jesus' miracle leads to deadly hostility   11 : 45

After this many of the Jews who had accompanied Mary and observed what Jesus did, believed in Him. But some of them went off to the Pharisees and told them what Jesus had done. Consequently, the Pharisees and Chief Priests summoned the Council and said, " What can we do ? This man obviously shows many remarkable signs. If we let him go on doing this sort of thing we shall have everybody believing in him. Then we shall have the Romans coming and that will be the end of our Holy Place and our very existence as a nation ! "

But one of them, Caiaphas, who was High Priest that year, addressed the meeting : " You plainly don't understand what is involved here. You do not realise that it would be a good thing for us if one man should die for the sake of the people —instead of the whole nation being destroyed." (He did not make this remark on his own initiative but, since he was High Priest that year, he was in fact inspired to say that Jesus was going to die for the nation's sake—and in fact not for that nation only, but to bring together into one family all the children of God scattered throughout the world.) From that day then, they planned to kill Him. As a consequence Jesus made no further public appearance among the Jews but went away to the countryside on the edge of the desert, and stayed with His disciples in a town called Ephraim. The Jewish Passover was approaching and many people went up from the country to Jerusalem before the actual Passover, to go through a ceremonial cleansing. They were looking for Jesus there and kept saying to one another as they stood in the Temple, " What do you think ? Surely he won't come to the Festival ? "

It should be understood that the Chief Priests and the Pharisees had issued an order that anyone who knew of Jesus' whereabouts should tell them, so that they could arrest Him.

An act of love as the end approaches   12 : 1

Six days before the Passover, Jesus came to Bethany, the village of Lazarus whom He had raised from the dead. They gave a supper for Him there, and Martha waited on the party while Lazarus took his place at table with Jesus. Then Mary took a whole pound of very expensive perfume and anointed Jesus' feet and then wiped them with her hair. The entire house was filled with the fragrance of the perfume. But one of His disciples, Judas Iscariot, (the man who was going to betray Jesus) burst out, " Why on earth wasn't this perfume sold ? It's worth thirty pounds, which could have been given to the poor ! "

He said this, not because he cared about the poor, but because he was dishonest, and when he was in charge of the purse used to help himself from the contents.

But Jesus replied to this outburst, " Let her alone, let her keep this for the day of My burial. You have the poor with you always—you will not always have Me ! "

The large crowd of Jews discovered that He was there and came to the scene—not only because of Jesus but to catch sight of Lazarus, the man whom He had raised from the dead. Then the Chief Priests planned to kill Lazarus as well, because he was the reason for many of the Jews' going away and putting their faith in Jesus.

Jesus experiences a temporary triumph   12 : 12

The next day, the great crowd who had come to the Festival heard that Jesus was coming into Jerusalem, and went out to meet Him with palm branches in their hands, shouting, " God save Him ! God bless the man who comes in the Name of the Lord, God bless the King of Israel ! "

For Jesus had found a young ass and was seated upon it, just as the Scripture foretold—

Fear not, daughter of Zion : behold, thy King cometh, sitting on an ass's colt.

(The disciples did not realise the significance of what was happening at the time, but when Jesus was glorified, then they recollected that these things had been written about Him and that they had carried them out for Him.)

The people who had been with Him, when He had summoned Lazarus from the grave and raised him from the dead, were continually talking about Him. This accounts for the crowd who went out to meet Him, for they had heard that He had given this Sign. Seeing all this, the Pharisees remarked to one another, " You see ?—There's nothing one can do ! The whole world is running after him."

Among those who had come up to worship at the Festival were some Greeks. They approached Philip (whose home town was Bethsaida in Galilee) with the request, " Sir, we want to see Jesus."

Philip went and told Andrew, and Andrew went with Philip and told Jesus.

Jesus told them, " The time has come for the Son of Man to be glorified. I tell you truly that unless a grain of wheat falls into the earth and dies, it remains a single grain of wheat ; but if it dies, it brings a good harvest. The man who loves his own life will destroy it, and the man who hates his life in this world will preserve it for eternal Life. If a man wants to enter My service, he must follow My way ; and where I am, My servant will also be. And my Father will honour every man who enters My service.

" Now comes My hour of heart-break, and what can I say, ' Father, save Me from this hour ' ? No, it was for this very purpose that I came to this hour. 'Father, honour Your own Name!'"

At this there came a Voice from Heaven, "I have honoured it and I will honour it again!"

When the crowd of bystanders heard this, they said it thundered, but some of them said, "An angel spoke to him."

Then Jesus said, "That Voice came for your sake, not for Mine. Now is the time for the judgment of this world to begin, and now will the spirit that rules this world be driven out. As for Me, if I am lifted up from the earth, I will draw all men to Myself." (He said this to show the kind of death He was going to die.)

Then the crowd said, "We have heard from the Law that Christ lives for ever. How can you say that the Son of Man must be 'lifted up'? Who is this Son of Man?"

At this, Jesus said to them, "You have the light with you only a little while longer. Go on while the light is good, before the darkness comes down upon you. For the man who walks in the dark has no idea where he is going. You must believe in the light while you have the light, that you may become the sons of Light."

Jesus said all these things, and then went away out of their sight. But though He had given so many Signs, yet they did not believe in Him, so that the prophecy of Isaiah was fulfilled, when he said:

Lord, who hath believed our report?
And to whom hath the arm of the Lord been revealed?

Thus, they could not believe, for Isaiah said again—

He hath blinded their eyes, and he hardened their heart:
Lest they should see with their eyes, and perceive with their heart,
And should turn,
And I should heal them.

Isaiah said these things because he saw the glory of Christ, and spoke about Him. Nevertheless, many even of the authorities did believe in Him. But they would not admit it for fear of the Pharisees, in case they should be excommunicated. They were more concerned to have the approval of men than to have the approval of God.

But later, Jesus cried aloud, " Every man who believes in Me, is believing in the One Who sent Me : and every man who sees Me is seeing the One Who sent Me. I have come into the world as Light, so that no one who believes in Me need remain in the dark. Yet, if anyone hears My sayings and does not keep them, I do not judge him—for I did not come to judge the world but to save it. Every man who rejects Me and will not accept My sayings has a judge—at the Last Day, the very words that I have spoken will be his judge. For I have not spoken on My own authority : the Father Who sent Me has commanded Me what to say and what to speak. And I know that what He commands means eternal life. All that I say I speak only in accordance with what the Father has told Me."

Jesus teaches His disciples humility   13 : 1

Before the Festival of the Passover began, Jesus realised that the time had come for Him to leave this world and return to the Father. He had loved those who were His own in this world and He loved them to the end. By suppertime, the devil had already put the thought of betraying Jesus into the mind of Judas Iscariot, Simon's son. Jesus, with the full knowledge that the Father had put everything into His hands and that He had come from God and was going to God, rose from the supper-table, took off His outer clothes, picked up a towel and fastened it round His waist. Then He poured water into a basin and began to wash the disciples' feet and to dry them with the towel around His waist.

So He came to Simon Peter, who said to Him, " Lord, are You going to wash my feet ? "

" You do not realise now what I am doing," replied Jesus, " but later on you will understand."

Then Peter said to Him, " You must never wash my feet ! "

" Unless you let Me wash you, Peter," replied Jesus, " you cannot share My lot."

" Then," returned Simon Peter, " please—not just my feet but my hands and my face as well ! "

" The man who has bathed," returned Jesus, " only needs

to wash his feet to be clean all over. And you are clean—though not all of you."

(For Jesus knew His betrayer and that is why He said, "though not all of you.".)

When Jesus had washed their feet and put on His clothes, He sat down again and spoke to them, "Do you realise what I have just done to you? You call Me 'Teacher' and 'Lord' and you are quite right, for I am your Teacher and your Lord. But if I, your Teacher and Lord, have washed your feet, you must be ready to wash one another's feet. I have given you this as an example so that you may do as I have done. Believe Me, the servant is not greater than his master and the messenger is not greater than the man who sent him. Once you have realised these things, you will find your happiness in doing them.

Jesus foretells His betrayal   13 : 18

"I am not speaking about all of you—I know the men I have chosen. But let this Scripture be fulfilled—

He that eateth my bread lifted up his heel against me.

From now onwards, I shall tell you about things before they happen, so that when they do happen, you may believe that I am the One I claim to be. I tell you truly that anyone who accepts My messenger will be accepting Me, and anyone who accepts Me will be accepting the One Who sent Me."

After Jesus had said this, He was clearly in anguish of soul and he added solemnly :

"I tell you plainly, one of you is going to betray Me."

At this the disciples stared at each other, completely mystified as to whom He could mean. And it happened that one of them, whom Jesus loved, was sitting very close to Him. So Simon Peter nodded to this man and said, "Tell us who He means."

He simply leaned forward on Jesus' shoulder and asked, "Lord, who is it?"

And Jesus answered, "It is the one I am going to give this piece of bread to, after I have dipped it in the dish."

Then He took a piece of bread, dipped it in the dish and gave it to Simon's son, Judas Iscariot. After he had taken the piece of bread, Satan entered his heart. Then Jesus said to him, " Be quick about your business ! "

No one else at the table knew what He meant in telling him this. Indeed, some of them thought that, since Judas had charge of the purse, Jesus was telling him to buy what they needed for the Festival, or that he should give something to the poor. So Judas took the piece of bread and went out quickly into the night.

When he had gone, Jesus spoke, " Now comes the glory of the Son of Man, and the glory of God in Him ! If God is glorified through Him, then God will glorify the Son of Man—and that without delay. Oh, My children, I am with you such a short time ! You will look for Me and I have to tell you as I told the Jews, ' Where I am going, you cannot follow.' Now I am giving you a new command—love one another. Just as I have loved you, so you must love one another. This is how all men will know that you are My disciples, because you have such love for one another."

Simon Peter said to Him, " Lord, where are You going ? "

" I am going," replied Jesus, " where you cannot follow Me now, though you will follow Me later."

" Lord, why can't I follow You now ? " said Peter. " I would lay down my life for You ! "

" Would you lay down your life for Me ? " replied Jesus. " Believe Me, you will disown Me three times before the cock crows !

Jesus reveals spiritual truths   14 : 1

" You must not let yourselves be distressed—you must hold on to your faith in God and to your faith in Me. There are many rooms[1] in My Father's House. If there were not, should I have told you that I am going away to prepare a place for you ? It is true that I am going away to prepare a place for you, but it is just as true that I am coming again to welcome you into My own home, so that you may be where I am. You know where I am going and you know the road I am going to take."

" Lord," Thomas remonstrated, " we do not know where You're going, and how can we know what road You're going to take ? "

[1] See Appendix, Note 6.

"I Myself am the Road," replied Jesus, "and the Truth and the Life. No one approaches the Father except through Me. If you had known Who I am, you would have known My Father. From now on, you do know Him and you have seen Him."

Jesus explains His relationship with the Father   14 : 8

Then Philip said to Him, "Show us the Father, Lord, and we shall be satisfied."

"Have I been such a long time with you," returned Jesus, "without your really knowing me, Philip? The man who has seen Me has seen the Father. How can you say, 'Show us the Father'? Do you not believe that I am in the Father and the Father is in Me? The very words I say to you are not My own. It is the Father Who lives in Me Who carries out His work through Me. Do you believe Me when I say that I am in the Father and the Father is in Me? But if you cannot, then believe Me because of what you see Me do. I assure you that the man who believes in Me will do the same things that I have done, yes, and he will do even greater things than these, for I am going away to the Father. Whatever you ask the Father in My name, I will do—that the Son may bring glory to the Father. And if you ask Me anything in My name, I will grant it.

Jesus promises the Spirit   14 : 15

"If you really love Me, you will keep the commandments I have given you and I shall ask the Father to give you Someone else to stand by you, to be with you always. I mean the Spirit of Truth, Whom the world cannot accept, for it can neither see nor recognise that Spirit. But you recognise Him, for He is with you now and will be in your hearts. I am not going to leave you alone in the world—I am coming to you. In a very little while, the world will see Me no more but you will see Me, because I am really alive and you will be alive, too. When that day comes, you will realise that I am in My Father, that you are in Me, and I am in you.

"Every man who knows My commandments and obeys them is the man who really loves Me, and every man who really loves Me will himself be loved by My Father, and I too will love him and make Myself known to him."

Then Judas (not Iscariot) said, "Lord, how is it that You are going to make Yourself known to us but not to the world?"

And to this Jesus replied, "When a man loves Me, he follows My teaching. Then My Father will love him, and We will come to that man and make Our home within him. The man who does not really love Me will not follow My teaching. Indeed, what you are hearing from Me now is not really My saying, but comes from the Father Who sent Me.

"I have said all this while I am still with you. But the One Who is coming to stand by you, the Holy Spirit Whom the Father will send in My name, will be your teacher and will bring to your minds all that I have said to you.

"I leave behind with you—peace; I give you My own peace and My gift is nothing like the peace of this world. You must not be distressed and you must not be daunted. You have heard Me say, 'I am going away and I am coming back to you.' If you really loved Me, you would be glad because I am going to My Father, for My Father is greater than I. And I have told you of it now, before it happens, so that when it does happen, your faith in Me will not be shaken. I shall not be able to talk much longer to you, for the spirit that rules this world is coming very close. He has no hold over Me, but I go on My way to show the world that I love the Father and do what He sent Me to do. . . . Get up now! Let us leave this place.

Jesus teaches union with Himself   15 : 1

"I am the real vine, My Father is the vine-dresser. He removes any of My branches which are not bearing fruit and He prunes every branch that does bear fruit to increase its yield. Now, you have already been pruned by My words. You must go on growing in Me and I will grow in you. For just as the branch cannot bear any fruit unless it shares the life of the vine, so you can produce nothing unless you go on growing in Me. I am the vine itself, you are the branches. It is the man who shares My life and whose life I share who proves fruitful. For the plain fact is that apart from Me you can do nothing at all. The man who does not share My life is like a branch that is broken off and withers

away. He becomes just like the dry sticks that men pick up
and use for firewood. But if you live your life in Me, and My
words live in your hearts, you can ask for whatever you like
and it will come true for you. This is how My Father will
be glorified—in your becoming fruitful and being My
disciples.

"I have loved you just as the Father has loved Me. You
must go on living in My love. If you keep My commandments you will live in My love just as I have kept My Father's
commandments and live in His love. I have told you this
so that you can share My joy, and that your happiness may
be complete. This is My Commandment: that you love
each other as I have loved you. There is no greater love
than this—that a man should lay down his life for his friends.
You are My friends if you do what I tell you to do. I shall
not call you servants any longer, for a servant does not share
his master's confidence. No, I call you friends, now, because
I have told you everything that I have heard from the Father.

"It is not that you have chosen Me; but it is I Who have
chosen you. I have appointed you to go and bear fruit that
will be lasting; so that whatever you ask the Father in My
name, He will give it to you.

Jesus speaks of the world's hatred   15 : 17
"This I command you, love one another! If the world
hates you, you know that it hated Me first. If you belonged
to the world, the world would love its own. But because
you do not belong to the world and I have chosen you out
of it, the world will hate you. Do you remember what I
said to you, 'The servant is not greater than his master'? If
they have persecuted Me, they will persecute you as well,
but if they have followed My teaching, they will also follow
yours. They will do all these things to you as My disciples
because they do not know the One Who sent Me. If I had
not come and spoken to them, they would not have been
guilty of sin, but now they have no excuse for their sin.
The man who hates Me, hates My Father as well. If I had
not done among them things that no other man has ever
done, they would not have been guilty of sin, but as it is
they have seen and they have hated both Me and My Father.
Yet this only fulfils what is written in their Law—

They hated me without a cause.

But when the Helper, that is, the Spirit of Truth, Who comes from the Father and Whom I Myself will send to you from the Father, comes, He will speak plainly about Me. And you yourselves will also speak plainly about Me for you have been with Me from the first.

Jesus speaks of the future without His bodily presence   16 : 1

" I am telling you this now so that your faith in Me may not be shaken. They will excommunicate you from their synagogues. Yes, the time is coming when a man who kills you will think he is thereby serving God ! They will act like this because they have never had any true knowledge of the Father or of Me, but I have told you all this so that when the time comes for it to happen you may remember that I told you about it. I have not spoken like this to you before, because I have been with you ; but now the time has come for Me to go away to the One Who sent Me. None of you asks Me, ' Where are you going ? ' That is because you are so distressed at what I have told you. Yet I am telling you the simple truth when I assure you that it is a good thing for you that I should go away. For if I did not go away, the Divine Helper would not come to you. But if I go, then I will send Him to you. When He comes, He will convince the world of the meaning of sin, of true goodness and of judgment. He will expose their sin because they do not believe in Me ; He will reveal true goodness for I am going away to the Father and you will see Me no longer ; and He will show them the meaning of judgment, for the spirit which rules this world will have been judged.

" I have much more to tell you but you cannot bear it now. Yet when that One I have spoken to you about comes —the Spirit of Truth—He will guide you into everything that is true. For He will not be speaking of His own accord but exactly as He hears, and He will inform you about what is to come. He will bring glory to Me for He will draw on My Truth and reveal it to you. Whatever the Father possesses is also Mine ; that is why I tell you that He will draw on My Truth and will show it to you.

The disciples are puzzled : Jesus explains   16 : 16

"In a little while you will not see Me any longer, and again, in a little while you will see Me."

At this some of His disciples remarked to each other, "What is this that He tells us now, 'A little while and you will not see Me, and again, in a little while you will see Me' and 'for I am going away to the Father'? What is this 'little while' that He talks about?" they were saying. "We simply do not know what He means!"

Jesus knew that they wanted to ask Him what He meant, so He said to them, "Are you trying to find out from each other what I meant when I said, 'In a little while you will not see Me, and again, in a little while you will see Me'? I tell you truly that you are going to be both sad and sorry while the world is glad. Yes, you will be deeply distressed, but your pain will turn into joy. When a woman gives birth to a child, she certainly knows pain when her time comes. Yet as soon as she has given birth to the child, she no longer remembers her agony for joy that a man has been born into the world. Now you are going through pain, but I shall see you again and your hearts will thrill with joy—the joy that no one can take away from you—and on that day you will not ask Me any questions.

"I assure you that whatever you ask the Father He will give you in My name. Up to now you have asked nothing in My name; ask now, and you will receive, that your joy may be overflowing.

Jesus speaks further of the future   16 : 25

"I have been speaking to you in parables—but the time is coming to give up parables and tell you plainly about the Father. When that time comes, you will make your requests to Him in My name, for I need make no promise to plead to the Father for you, for the Father Himself loves you, because you have loved Me and have believed that I came from God. Yes, I did come from the Father and I came into the world. Now I leave the world behind and return to the Father."

"Now You are speaking plainly," cried the disciples, "and are not using parables. Now we know that everything is known to You—no more questions are needed. This makes us sure that You did come from God."

"So you believe in Me now?" replied Jesus. "The time is coming, indeed, it has already come, when you will be scattered, every one of you going home and leaving Me alone. Yet I am not really alone, for the Father is with Me. I have told you all this so that you may find your peace in Me. You will find trouble in the world—but, never lose heart, I have conquered the world!"

Jesus' prayer for His disciples—present and future   17 : 1

When Jesus had said these words, He raised His eyes to Heaven and said, "Father, the hour has come. Glorify Your Son now so that He may bring glory to You, for You have given Him authority over all men to give eternal life to all that You have given to Him. And this is eternal life, to know You, the only true God, and Him Whom You have sent— Jesus Christ.

"I have brought You honour upon earth, I have completed the task which You gave Me to do. Now, Father, honour Me in Your own Presence with the glory that I knew with You before the world was made. I have shown Your Self to the men whom You gave Me from the world. They were Your men and You gave them to Me, and they have accepted Your word. Now they realise that all that You have given Me comes from You—and that every message that You gave Me I have given them. They have accepted it all and have come to know in their hearts that I did come from You—they are convinced that You sent Me.

"I am praying to You for them : I am not praying for the world but for the men whom You gave Me, for they are Yours—everything that is Mine is Yours and Yours Mine— and they have done Me honour. Now I am no longer in the world, but they are in the world and I am returning to You. Holy Father, keep the men You gave Me by Your power that they may be one, as We are One. As long as I was with them, I kept them by the power that You gave Me ; I guarded them, and not one of them was destroyed, except the son of destruction—that the Scripture might come true.

"And now I come to You and I say these things in the world that these men may find My joy completed in themselves. I have given them Your word, and the world has hated them, for they are no more sons of the world than I am. I am not praying that You will take them out of the world but that You will keep them from the evil one. They are no more the sons of the world than I am—make them holy by the Truth; for Your word is the Truth. I have sent them to the world just as You sent Me to the world and I consecrate Myself for their sakes that they may be made holy by the Truth.

"I am not praying only for these men but for all those who will believe in Me through their message, that they may all be one. Just as You, Father, live in Me and I live in You, I am asking that they may live in Us, that the world may believe that You did send Me. I have given them the honour that You gave Me, that they may be one, as We are One—I in them and You in Me, that they may grow complete into one, so that the world may realise that You sent Me and have loved them as You loved Me. Father, I want those whom You have given Me to be with Me where I am; I want them to see that glory which You have made Mine—for You loved Me before the world began. Father of Goodness and Truth, the world has not known You, but I have known You and these men now know that You have sent Me. I have made Your Self known to them and I will continue to do so that the love which You have had for Me may be in their hearts—and that I may be there also."

Jesus is arrested in the Garden   18 : 1

When Jesus had spoken these words, He went out with His disciples across the Cedron valley to a place where there was a garden, and they went into it together. Judas who betrayed Him knew the place, for Jesus often met His disciples there. So Judas fetched the guard and its officers which the Chief Priests and Pharisees had provided for him, and came to the places with torches and lanterns and weapons. Jesus fully realising all that was going to happen to Him, went forward and said to them, "Who are you looking for?"

"Jesus of Nazareth," they answered.

"I am the man," said Jesus. (Judas who was betraying Him was standing there with the others.)

When He said to them, "I am the man," they retreated and fell to the ground. So Jesus asked them again, "Who are you looking for?"

And again they said, "Jesus of Nazareth."

"I have told you that I am the man," replied Jesus. "If I am the man you are looking for, let these others go." (Thus fulfilling his previous words, "I have not lost one of those whom You gave Me.")

At this, Simon Peter, who had a sword, drew it and slashed at the High Priest's servant, cutting off his right ear. (The servant's name was Malchus.) But Jesus said to Peter, "Put your sword back into its sheath. Am I not to drink the cup the Father has given Me?"

Peter follows Jesus, only to deny Him   18 : 12

Then the guard, with its captain and the Jewish officers took hold of Jesus and tied His hands together, and led Him off to Annas first, for he was father-in-law to Caiaphas, who was High Priest that year. Caiaphas was the man who advised the Jews, "that it would be a good thing that one man should die for the sake of the people." Behind Jesus followed Simon Peter, and one other disciple who was known personally to the High Priest. He went in with Jesus into the High Priest's courtyard, but Peter was left standing at the door outside. So this other disciple, who was acquainted with the High Priest, went out and spoke to the door-keeper, and brought Peter inside. The young woman at the door remarked to Peter, "Are you one of this man's disciples, too?"

"No, I am not," retorted Peter.

In the courtyard, the servants and officers stood around a charcoal fire which they had made, for it was cold. They were warming themselves, and Peter stood there with them, keeping himself warm.

Meanwhile the High Priest interrogated Jesus about His disciples and about His own teaching.

"I have always spoken quite openly to the world," replied Jesus. "I have always taught in the synagogue or in the Temple where all Jews meet together, and I have said nothing in secret. Why do you question me? Why not question those who have heard Me about what I said to them ? Obviously, they are the ones who know what I actually said."

As He said this, one of those present, an officer, slapped Jesus with his open hand, remarking, " Is that the way for you to answer the High Priest ? "

" If I have said anything wrong," Jesus said to him, " you must give evidence about it, but if what I said was true, why do you strike Me ? "

Then Annas sent Him, with His hands still tied, to Caiaphas the High Priest.

Peter's denial   18 : 25

In the meantime Simon Peter was still standing, keeping himself warm. Some of them said to him, " Surely you too are one of his disciples, aren't you ? "

And he denied it and said, " No, I am not."

Then one of the High Priest's servants, a relation of the man whose ear Peter had cut off, remarked, " Didn't I see you in the garden with him ? "

And again Peter denied it. And immediately the cock crew.

Jesus is taken before the Roman authority   18 : 28

Then they led Jesus from Caiaphas' presence into the Palace. It was now early morning and the Jews themselves did not go into the Palace, for fear that they would be contaminated and would not be able to eat the Passover. So Pilate walked out to them and said, " What is the charge that you are bringing against this man ? "

" If he were not an evil-doer, we should not have handed him over to you," they replied.

To which Pilate retorted, " Then take him yourselves and judge him according to your law."

" We are not allowed to put a man to death," replied the Jews, (thus fulfilling Christ's prophecy of the method of His own death).

So Pilate went back into the Palace and called Jesus to him. " Are you the king of the Jews ? " he asked.

" Are you asking this of your own accord," replied Jesus, " or have other people spoken to you about Me ? "

" Do you think *I* am a Jew ? " replied Pilate. " It's your

race and your Chief Priests who handed you over to me. What have you done, anyway?"

"My Kingdom is not founded in this world—if it were, My servants would have fought to prevent My being handed over to the Jews. But in fact My Kingdom is not founded on all this!"

"So you are a king, are you?" returned Pilate.

"Indeed I am a King," Jesus replied; "the reason for My birth and the reason for My coming into the world is to witness to the Truth. Every man who loves truth recognises My voice."

To which Pilate retorted, "What is 'truth'?" and went straight out again to the Jews and said:

"I find nothing criminal about him at all. But I have an arrangement with you to set one prisoner free at Passover time. Do you wish me then to set free for you the 'King of the Jews'?"

At this, they shouted out again, "No, not this man, but Barabbas!"

Barabbas was a bandit.

Pilate's vain efforts to save Jesus   19 : 1

Then Pilate took Jesus and had Him flogged, and the soldiers twisted thorn-twigs into a crown and put it on His head, threw a purple robe about Him and kept coming into His presence, saying, "Hail, king of the Jews!" And then they slapped Him with their open hands.

Then Pilate went outside again and said to them, "Look, I bring him out before you here, to show that I find nothing criminal about him at all."

And at this Jesus came outside too, wearing the thorn crown and the purple robe.

"Look," said Pilate, "here's the man!"

The sight of Him made the Chief Priests and Jewish officials shout at the top of their voices, "Crucify! Crucify!"

"You take him and crucify him," retorted Pilate. "He's no criminal as far as I can see!"

The Jews answered him, "We have a Law, and according to that Law, he must die, for he made himself out to be Son of God!"

When Pilate heard them say this, he became much more

uneasy, and returned to the Palace again and spoke to Jesus,
" Where *do* you come from ? "

But Jesus gave him no reply. So Pilate said to Him,
" Won't you speak to me ? Don't you realise that I have
the power to set you free, and I have the power to have you
crucified ? "

" You have no power at all against Me," replied Jesus,
" except what was given to you from above. And for that
reason the one who handed Me over to you is even more
guilty than you are."

From that moment, Pilate tried hard to set Him free but
the Jews were shouting, " If you set this man free, you are
no friend of Caesar ! Anyone who makes himself out to be
a king is anti-Caesar ! "

When Pilate heard this, he led Jesus outside and sat down
upon the Judgment-seat in the place called The Pavement
(in Hebrew, Gabbatha). It was the Preparation Day of the
Passover and it was now getting on towards midday. Pilate
now said to the Jews, " Look, here's your king ! "

At which they yelled, " Take him away, take him away,
crucify him ! "

" Am I to crucify your king ? " Pilate asked them.

" Caesar is our king and no one else," replied the Chief
Priests. And at this Pilate handed Jesus over to them for
crucifixion.

The Crucifixion   19 : 17
So they took Jesus and He went out carrying the cross
Himself, to a place called Skull Hill (in Hebrew Golgotha).
There they crucified Him, and two others, one on each side
of Him with Jesus in the middle. Pilate had a placard written
out and put on the cross, reading, " JESUS OF NAZARETH,
THE KING OF THE JEWS." This placard was read by many of
the Jews because the place where Jesus was crucified was
quite near Jerusalem, and it was written in Hebrew as well
as in Latin and Greek. So the Chief Priests said to Pilate,
" You should not write ' The King of the Jews,' but you
ought to put, ' This man said, I am King of the Jews.' "

To which Pilate retorted, " Indeed ? What I have written,
I have written."

When the soldiers had crucified Jesus, they divided His

clothes between them, taking a quarter-share each. There remained His shirt, which was seamless—woven in one piece from the top to the bottom. So they said to each other, " Don't let us tear it ; let's draw lots and see who gets it."

This happened to fulfil the Scripture which says—

They parted my garments among them,
And upon my vesture did they cast lots.

Jesus provides for His mother, from the Cross 19 : 25
While the soldiers were doing this, Jesus' mother was standing near the cross with her sister, and with them Mary, the wife of Clopas, and Mary of Magdala. Jesus saw His mother and the disciple whom He loved standing by her side, and said to her, " Look, there is your son ! " And then He said to the disciple, " And there is your mother ! "

And from that time the disciple took Mary into his own home.

After this, Jesus, realising that everything was now completed, said (fulfilling the saying of Scripture), " I am thirsty."

There was a bowl of sour wine standing there. So they soaked a sponge in the wine, put it on a spear, and pushed it up towards His mouth. When Jesus had taken it, He cried, " It is finished ! " His head fell forward, and He died.

The body of Jesus is removed 19 : 31
As it was the Day of Preparation for the Passover, the Jews wanted to avoid the bodies being left on the crosses over the Sabbath (for that was a particularly important Sabbath), and they requested Pilate to have the men's legs broken and the bodies removed. So the soldiers went and broke the legs of the first man and of the other who was crucified with Jesus. But when they came to Him, they saw that He was dead already and they did not break His legs. But one of the soldiers pierced His side with a spear, and at once there was an outrush of blood and water. And the man who saw this is our witness : his evidence is true. (He is certain that he is speaking the truth, so that you may believe as well.) For this happened to fulfil the Scripture :

A bone of him shall not be broken.

And again another Scripture says—

They shall look on him whom they pierced.

After it was all over, Joseph (who came from Arimathaea and was a disciple of Jesus, though secretly for fear of the Jews) requested Pilate that he might take away Jesus' body, and Pilate gave him permission. So he came and took His body down. Nicodemus also, the man who had come to Him at the beginning by night, arrived bringing a mixture of myrrh and aloes, weighing about a hundred pounds. So they took His body and wound it round with linen strips with the spices, according to the Jewish custom of preparing a body for burial. In the place where He was crucified, there was a garden containing a new tomb in which nobody had yet been laid. Because it was the Preparation Day and because the tomb was conveniently near, they laid Jesus in this tomb.

The First Day of the week : the risen Lord   20 : 1

But on the first day of the week, Mary of Magdala arrived at the tomb, very early in the morning, while it was still dark, and noticed that the stone had been taken away from the tomb. At this she ran, found Simon Peter and the other disciple whom Jesus loved, and told them, " They have taken the Lord out of the tomb and we don't know where they have put Him."

Peter and the other disciple set off at once for the tomb, the two of them running together. The other disciple ran faster than Peter and was the first to arrive at the tomb. He stooped and looked inside and noticed the linen cloths lying there but did not go in himself. Hard on his heels came Simon Peter and went straight into the tomb. He noticed that the linen cloths were lying there, and that the handkerchief, which had been round Jesus' head, was not lying with the linen cloths but was rolled up by itself, a little way apart. Then the other disciple, who was the first to arrive at the tomb, came inside as well, saw what had happened and believed. (They did not yet understand the Scripture which said that He must rise from the dead.) So the disciples went back again to their homes.

But Mary stood just outside the tomb, and she was crying. And as she cried, she looked into the tomb and saw two angels in white who sat, one at the head and the other at the foot of the place where the body of Jesus had lain.

The angels spoke to her, "Why are you crying?" they asked.

"Because they have taken away my Lord, and I don't know where they have put Him!" she said.

Then she turned and noticed Jesus standing there, without realising that it was Jesus.

"Why are you crying?" said Jesus to her. "Who are you looking for?"

She, supposing that He was the gardener, said, "Oh, sir, if you have carried Him away, please tell me where you have put Him and I will take Him away."

Jesus said to her, "Mary!"

At this she turned right round and said to Him, in Hebrew, "Master!"

"No!" said Jesus, "do not hold Me now. I have not yet gone up to the Father. Go and tell My brothers that I am going up to My Father and your Father, to My God and your God."

And Mary of Magdala went off to the disciples, with the news, "I have seen the Lord!" and told them what He had said to her.

In the evening of that first day of the week, the disciples had met together with the doors locked for fear of the Jews. Jesus came and stood right in the middle of them and said, "Peace be with you!"

Then He showed them His hands and His side, and when they saw the Lord the disciples were overjoyed.

Jesus said to them again, "Yes, Peace be with you! Just as the Father sent Me, so I am now going to send you."

And then He breathed upon them and said, "Receive holy spirit.[1] If you forgive any men's sins, they are forgiven, and if you hold them unforgiven, they are unforgiven."

[1] Lit.: "receive holy spirit"—see Appendix, Note 3.

The risen Jesus and Thomas   20 : 24

But one of the Twelve, Thomas (called the Twin), was not with them when Jesus came. The other disciples kept on telling him, " We have seen the Lord," but he replied, " Unless I see in His own hands the mark of the nails, and put my finger where the nails were and put my hand into His side, I will never believe ! "

Just over a week later, the disciples were indoors again and Thomas with them. The doors were shut, but Jesus came and stood in the middle of them and said, " Peace be with you ! "

Then He said to Thomas, " Put your finger here—look, here are My hands. Take your hand and put it in My side. You must not doubt, but believe."

" My Lord and my God ! " cried Thomas.

" Is it because you have seen me that you believe ? " Jesus said to him. " Happy are those who have never seen Me and yet have believed ! "

Jesus gave a great many other Signs in the presence of His disciples which are not recorded in this book. But these have been written so that you may believe that Jesus is Christ, the Son of God, and that in that faith you may have Life as His disciples.

The risen Jesus and Peter   21 : 1

Later on, Jesus showed Himself again to His disciples on the shore of Lake Tiberias, and He did it this way. Simon Peter, Thomas (called the Twin), Nathanael from Cana of Galilee, the sons of Zebedee and two other disciples were together, when Simon Peter said :

" I'm going fishing."

" All right," they replied, " we'll go with you."

So they went out and got into the boat and during the night caught nothing at all. But just as dawn began to break, Jesus stood there on the beach, although the disciples had no idea that it was Jesus.

" Have you caught anything, lads ? " Jesus called out to them.

" No," they replied.

" Throw the net on the right side of the boat," said Jesus, " and you'll have a catch."

So they threw out the net and found that they were now not strong enough to pull it in because it was so full of fish! At this, the disciple that Jesus loved said to Peter, "*It is the Lord!*"

Hearing this, Peter slipped on his clothes, for he had been naked, and plunged into the sea. The other disciples followed in the boat, for they were only about a hundred yards from the shore, dragging in the net full of fish. When they had landed, they saw that a charcoal fire was burning, with a fish placed on it and some bread. Jesus said to them, "Bring Me some of the fish you've just caught."

So Simon Peter got into the boat and hauled the net ashore full of large fish, one hundred and fifty-three altogether. But in spite of the large number the net was not torn.

Then Jesus said to them, "Come and have your breakfast."

None of the disciples dared to ask Him Who He was; they knew it was the Lord.

Jesus went and took the bread and gave it to them and gave them all fish as well. This is already the third time that Jesus showed Himself to His disciples after His resurrection from the dead.

When they had finished breakfast Jesus said to Simon Peter, "Simon, son of John, do you love Me more than these others?"

"Yes, Lord," he replied, "You know that I am Your friend."

"Then feed My lambs," returned Jesus. He said for the second time:

"Simon, son of John, do you love Me?"

"Yes, Lord," returned Peter, "You know that I am Your friend."

"Then care for My sheep," replied Jesus. Then for the third time, Jesus spoke to him and said:

"Simon, son of John, *are* you My friend?"

Peter was deeply hurt because Jesus' third question to him was "Are you My friend?" and he said, "Lord, You know everything. You know that I am Your friend!"

"Then feed My sheep," Jesus said to him. "I tell you truly, Peter, that when you were younger, you used to dress yourself and go where you liked, but when you are an old man, you are going to stretch out your hands and someone else will dress you and take you where you do not want to go."

(He said this to show the kind of death by which Peter was going to honour God.)

Then Jesus said to him, "You must follow Me."

Then Peter turned round and noticed the disciple whom Jesus loved following behind them. (He was the one who had his head on Jesus' shoulder at supper and had asked, "Lord, who is the one who is going to betray You?") So he said, "Yes, Lord, but what about him?"

"If it is My wish," returned Jesus, "for him to stay until I come, is that your business, Peter? You must follow Me."

This gave rise to the saying among the brothers that this disciple would not die. Yet, of course, Jesus did not say, "He will not die," but simply, "If it is My wish for him to stay until I come, is that your business?"

All the above was written by an eye-witness   21 : 24

Now it is this same disciple who is hereby giving his testimony to these things and has written them down. We know that his witness is reliable. Of course, there are many other things which Jesus did, and I suppose that if each one were written down in detail, there would not be room in the whole world for all the books that would have to be written.

APPENDIX

Note 1

" Scribes."

There is no modern English word by which " Scribes " can be fairly translated. It is therefore necessary to explain that the " Scribes " of the Gospels were the interpreters of the Divine Law (or Torah), for the people of Israel. The Torah was a kind of text-book for both the religious and civil functions of the community. Since in process of time this had become a highly complex matter, the Scribes had to be expert both in knowledge, interpretation and administration. Consequently their position was one of considerable authority and, though there were doubtless noble exceptions, they tended to become both legalist and theological in outlook, and were therefore unprepared to accept the revolutionary teaching of Jesus.

" Pharisees."

The Pharisees were a class of zealous Jews whose chief characteristic lay in their separation from the heathen and from all that they considered evil. They were the Puritans of their day, and emphasised the spiritual rather than the nationalistic side of Judaism. We might fairly say that they were Churchmen rather than statesmen. And, again, though there were good men among them, they tended to concentrate upon rigid outward observances, to the exclusion of human sympathy and understanding. It was this tendency, and the conviction that they alone were right, which brought them into conflict with Jesus.

" Sadducees."

The Sadducees represented the aristocratic conservative element in the Jewish priesthood. Their conservatism, with its desire to maintain things as they were, led them to compromise politically with the Roman occupying power, and thus their moral authority became weakened. Moreover, in clinging to the tenets of the past, they failed to develop in their religion and did not, for example, believe, as the Pharisees did, in the coming Kingdom of God, and only in a very shadowy way did they believe in the immortality of the human soul.

Note 2

Matthew 5, 22—Raca.

"Raca" means a fool or empty-headed fellow, but the Greek word used in the previous sentence means much the same thing. If however it is, as some suggest, a transliteration of the Hebrew "morēh," then we have a further stage of uncharitable condemnation, for this word means "a persistent rebel against God," and thus makes much better sense.

Note 3

Matthew 16: 19 and 18 : 18—"forbidding" and "permitting."

There is a very curious Greek construction here, viz. a simple future followed by the perfect participle passive. If Jesus had meant to say quite simply, "Whatever you forbid on earth will be forbidden in Heaven," can anyone explain why the simple future passive is not used? It seems to me that if the words of Jesus are accurately reported here, and I have no reason to doubt it, then the force of these sayings is that Jesus' true disciples will be so led by the Spirit that they will be following the Heavenly pattern. In other words what they "forbid" or "permit" on earth will be consonant with the Divine rules.

If a simple future passive had been used it would mean an automatic Heavenly endorsement of the Church's actions, which to me, at least is a very different thing.

In the pertinent verses of John's Gospel (chapter 20 : 22, 23), it is quite plain that "holy spirit," of which Christ is giving His disciples a first breath, so to speak, (for the Holy Spirit in person was not given until Pentecost), would be the factor by which alone human beings could perform the Divine function of forgiving or not forgiving sins. There is again no ground for supposing that celestial endorsement automatically follows human action, however exalted.

Note 4

Luke 16, 1-13—The Parable of the Unjust Steward.

This story recorded by St. Luke is well-known for its difficulty of interpretation. Most commentators suggest that the lesson to be learned is that the follower of Christ should be as shrewd about his spiritual future as the rascally steward was about his own immediate security. Personally, I do not feel satisfied with this view as it introduces a note of careful calculation for the future which is quite at variance with Christ's teaching elsewhere. Moreover, the passage in question goes on to state categorically that dishonesty in earthly things is bound to mean dishonesty in the greater, or spiritual, things, and this seems a very odd conclusion to be drawn from the parable !

I am myself somewhat attracted by the suggestion of Professor C. C. Torrey, who is a specialist in Semitic Languages at Yale University, that the original words of Jesus were spoken in Aramaic, and suffered some alterations when written down in Greek. Professor Torrey, in his own translation, makes the two difficult remarks in verses 8 and 9 into questions, viz. " Did the lord of the estate praise his faithless manager . . . ? and do *I* say to *you* . . . ? "

If the above interpretation is true, then the parable is one of faithfulness, illustrating the fact that since even in worldly matters men cannot " get away with it "—how much more essential is faithfulness in spiritual matters. My translation then would read :

" Now did the employer praise this rascally agent because he had been so careful for his own future ? For the children of this world are considerably more shrewd in dealing with the people they live with than the children of light. And do you think I am recommending you to use the false means of money to make friends for yourselves, so that when it fails you, they could welcome you to houses fit for eternity ? No, the man who is faithful in the little things will be faithful in the big things, and the man who cheats in the little things will cheat in the big things too. If you are not trustworthy with the tainted wealth of this world, how can you be trusted with the true riches ? And if you have not been honest with other people's property, who will entrust you with some of your own ? No servant can serve two masters. He is bound to hate one and love the other, or give his loyalty to one and despise the other. You cannot serve God and the power of money at the same time."

But to be fair to the Greek that we possess, one cannot translate the statements by questions, and I have therefore tried to make the best of it by suggesting that our Lord says, in effect, that the Christian must " outsmart " the " smart " by turning money, which has so many potentialities for evil, into a spiritual opportunity. But this still leaves the following verses about faithfulness rather " in the air."

Note 5

John 7, 53-8, 11—The Woman taken in Adultery.

This passage has no place in the oldest manuscripts of John, and is considered by most scholars to be an interpolation from some other source. Almost all scholars would agree that, although the story is out of place here, it is part of a genuine apostolic tradition.

Note 6

John 14, 1—Many rooms.

I am of course well aware that the word translated " mansions " in the A.V. is a word frequently used to mean " resting places," commonly applied to stations on a journey affording accommodation for the night. Commentators make much of this, but it appears to me that they forget that our Lord is stating that such places exist within the Father's *House*. To bring out the sense of resting places on a journey as existing inside a house seems to me to raise a confused picture to the mind. I have therefore translated the word " rooms," which can certainly be used for rest and refreshment, and are normal parts of a house.

THE END